Teaching in Christian Weekday Early Education

Pamela K. Boucher, compiler

PRODUCTION TEAM

Pamela K. Boucher, Compiler
Beth Cole, Special Contributor

Linda W. Grammer, Assistant Editor/Designer
Norma J. Goldman, Editor

Ann Parnell, Church Weekday Education Consultant
Pat Brown, Product Team Leader
Glen L. Schultz, Manager

ISBN 0-7673-9079-2

Dewey Decimal Classification: 372
Subject Heading: WEEKDAY EDUCATION

Printed in the United States of America

Scripture quotations marked (NIV) are from
The Holy Bible, *New International Version*,
copyright © 1973, 1978, 1984 by International Bible Society.
Used by permission of Zondervan Bible Publishers.

All unmarked Scripture quotations are from
The Holy Bible, *King James Version*.

Christian School Resources
LifeWay Christian Resources
127 Ninth Avenue, North
Nashville, TN 37234

ABOUT THE AUTHORS

 Pamela Boucher holds a B.S. degree from Dallas Baptist College and the M.R.E. degree from Southwestern Baptist Theological Seminary, Ft. Worth, TX. She led the writing team in defining concept and content for this exciting new resource. Pamela has served churches in Texas and Missouri as minister of childhood education and was director of the Preschool/Ministries Department for the California Southern Baptist Convention. She continues her ministry at LifeWay as church consultant to preschool/children's ministers in the areas of education, children and worship, and bus ministries.

 Beth Cole served the Baptist Sunday School Board (now LifeWay) for more than 14 years. During that time she served as editor, design editor, and manager in children's curriculum and later in preschool biblical studies. In 1998, Beth's pastor husband was called to a new field in Chattanooga, TN, and she continues her ministry to preschoolers through writing. She holds a B.A. degree from Union University, Jackson, TN, and a Master of Divinity degree from Southern Baptist Theological Seminary, Louisville, KY.

 Kimberly Drake is a graduate of Southwestern Baptist Theological Seminary, Ft. Worth, TX, and now ministers to preschoolers and children in Riverside, California. Kimberly is also an adjunct professor in the area of child development at California Baptist University.

 Lois Gamble was instrumental in forming the Texas Baptist Church Weekday Education Association, and she served as its first president. Her love for weekday programs is evidenced by her rich background of writing both curriculum and articles on early childhood and her teaching experiences at Austin College. She directed Hyde Park Baptist Child Development Center for more than 19 years and continues to minister there with her family.

 Dianne Glasgow holds the B.A. and Master of Science degrees from Louisiana Tech University. For the past ten years she has served as minister to children at the Willow Point Baptist Church in Shreveport, LA. She frequently ministers to a wide audience as a conference leader and writer at both state and denominational levels.

ABOUT THE AUTHORS *continued...*

 Gayle Haywood is a graduate of Coker College, Hartsville, SC, B.A., and Southeastern Seminary, Wake Forest, NC, M.R.E. For the past 17 years, she has served as minister to preschoolers and children at Brentwood Baptist Church, Brentwood, TN. Gayle's love for children is evidenced by a lifetime of commitment to religious childhood education.

 Kay Henry co-authored the original edition of *Teaching in Church Weekday Education*. Over the past 25 years, Kay has served as director of preschool ministries in several churches and has directed weekday programs. Today she ministers as assistant vice president for development at Oklahoma Baptist University in Shawnee, OK.

 Jewell Nelson characterizes herself as a continuing advocate for children and their families. She holds an M.R.E. degree from Southern Baptist Theological Seminary, Louisville, KY, and earned an Associate of Arts degree from Southwest Baptist University, Bolivar, MO. She has taught in public, private, and church-related schools for more than 40 years, writing throughout that time.

 Glen Schultz continues his life passion of educating young people through his work as manager of Christian School Resources at LifeWay. A graduate of Roberts Wesleyan College, Rochester, NY (B.A.) and the University of Virginia (M.Ed. School Administration, and Ed.D., Educational Leadership and Policy Studies), Glen is a frequently sought after conference leader and speaker. His published works include *Kingdom Education*, *A Parent's Greatest Joy*, and *The ABCs of Selecting a School for Your Child*.

contents

section 1:

The Biblical Foundation for Weekday Early Education

Teaching in Christian Weekday Early Education

"O God, you are my God, earnestly I seek you"
(Ps. 63:1, NIV).

Chapter 1

The Eternal Perspective: Knowing God

Teaching in a Christian weekday education program is a high calling from God. The work that you will be doing is extremely vital to laying a foundation by which a young child can come to know God in a personal way. Too often, little importance is placed on the role that weekday preschool program teachers play.

I was recently invited to speak at a church in Alabama. The church had a weekday preschool program and planned to add a few elementary grades the following year. I was asked to speak to the congregation on the importance of Christian education. Before I spoke, someone sang a song that I had never heard. As I listened to the words, I was moved by their meaning. The words clearly present the role you will play as you teach in a weekday program.

The song, entitled "We're Building Temples," was written by Kathie Hill. Carefully consider the words to this amazing song.

We're Building Temples

This child fast asleep, looks so content as I watch over her bed.
But I need to think back on the day we have spent, to all I did and said.
Did she feel safe and know that I care? Did I say the things that made her feel loved?
For my life and my words form the image of the person she someday will become.

Chorus:
We're building temples for Jesus to live in;
Rooms warm and welcome where He'll reside.
These children are our own
But someday when they're grown we pray they'll be the temples where Jesus will abide.

Lord, help us to build a foundation of trust knowing that we love them so.
With walls of pure faith that will stand against the winds of doubt that blow.
Let your love be the roof that covers their lives and protects them from the rains of defeat.
Help mold in their hearts open windows where the light of Your salvation will stream.

Chorus:

We're building temples for Jesus to live in; rooms warm and welcome where He'll reside.
These children are our own but someday when they're grown
we pray they will be the temples where Jesus will abide.[1]

Every weekday education teacher must realize she is a part of the process of building a temple where Jesus can reside. What an amazing thought and what an amazing role you will play in this life-changing process called teaching!

Proverbs 22:6 instructs, "Train up a child in the way he should go: and when he is old, he will not depart from it." In this one small verse, there is tremendous insight into God's way of training a child. The words *train up* literally mean to create within the child a desire to learn. Everything you do as a weekday teacher should have the goal of helping children develop a thirst for learning. Your role is not to merely create a desire in the child to learn a lot of facts. Rather, a Christian weekday teacher must help each child find joy in learning and provide a foundation for trust.

We refer to God's plan of education as *kingdom education.* Kingdom education has specific principles that guide the entire educational process for a child. It is defined as *the life-long, Bible-based, Christ-centered process of . . .*

. . . leading a child to Christ,
. . . building the child up in Christ,
. . . and equipping the child to serve Christ.

Let's look at a story in the Old Testament that will give us an analogy of our roles in weekday early education. Recall the words of Kathie Hill's song, *"We're building temples for Jesus to live in."* First Kings, chapter 6, provides an account of Solomon building the first temple.

It was a magnificent edifice, made from strong timbers, precious metals, and beautiful fabrics. When completed, it was ready for occupancy. Scripture tells us how a cloud filled the temple, and God, Himself, took up residence there.

When the nation of Israel passed by the temple which Solomon built, imagine some of the conversations that might have been overheard. There were probably comments such as: "Look how beautiful the temple is." "What magnificent detail work is in the wood!" "Have you ever seen something more splendid than the metal work?"

There was part of the temple, however, that never received any public recognition once the temple was completed. First Kings 5:15-18 reveals one of the most significant aspects of the entire building project. In these verses we read about those who cut the rocks from the quarry, brought them to the building site, and laid these huge pieces of granite as the temple's foundation.

When you study this portion of God's Word, you discover there were literally thousands of unsung heroes, simply referred to as *stone hewers and burden bearers.* However, if these individuals had not performed their tasks properly, the temple would never have been completed. Once the foundation was in place, it was covered up, never to receive its due credit. The attention was directed to the visible building, not on its essential foundation.

This is the role that you, the Christian weekday education teacher, play in the building of God's temples. You are one of the stone hewers or burden bearers. The work is extremely hard and tedious. It begins anew every day. Your work helps to lay a foundation on which others will come along and do the finishing work. Unfortunately, like the burden bearers and stone hewers of the Old Testament, the work of the Christian weekday teacher sometimes goes unnoticed, and many do not place proper importance on this crucial task.

But God takes note and He strengthens all those engaged in this work. As stone hewers and burden bearers, you are taking the rough pieces of stone and helping parents start to shape each life so it can be built into a beautiful temple where Jesus will reside. Three basic tools you will use in the task are:

1. Your hands
2. Your lips
3. Your heart

This resource will give you valuable information to assist in knowing what you should do with your hands, what you should say with your lips and what you should show from your heart to be a successful Christian weekday education teacher.

As you study each aspect presented in the pages that follow, remember these very important facts. Every child who enters your classroom has three fundamental needs. You will play a significant role in helping meet these needs, which are:

1. Unconditional Christ-like **love**
2. Spirit-guided **direction**
3. Biblically-based **correction**.

It is our prayer that you will become an expert stone hewer and burden bearer. As you become more and more skilled in your role as a teacher, God will use you to develop that foundation in a child's life so that one day he or she will become a beautiful temple where Jesus will abide.

*"Do not forget the things your
eyes have seen or let them
slip from your heart as long
as you live. Teach them to
your children and to their
children after them" (Deut.
4:9, NIV).*

Chapter 2

The Home Environment: A Model for Learning

Picture a young husband and wife eagerly anticipating the birth of their baby, welcoming the baby into their home and hearts, taking their baby to church for the first time and watching as the caring community at church warmly enfolds the baby. One day the parents encourage and rejoice when their child takes her first tottering steps. As the days and months continue, the father and mother and the caring community at church help the child grow and learn in many ways.

In the early chapters of Genesis, we learn about God's plan for families. God created Adam and Eve. Children were born to Adam and Eve. From the beginning, God planned for families to help children grow and learn in ways that would be pleasing to Him.

God also planned for an earthly home and family for His Son Jesus. Throughout Jesus' boyhood, Mary and Joseph helped Jesus grow and become strong, wise, and pleasing to God and other people.

Parents are the most important influence in a child's life. God has an ideal plan for the home and family. Paul also taught that husbands and wives are to submit to one another out of reverence and love for Christ (Eph. 5:21-25). While children are to honor and obey their parents, fathers are admonished not to exasperate their children but to bring them up in the instruction of the Lord (Eph. 6:1-4). These are the ideal standards presented in God's Word. These are the ideals we should strive with God's help to model in our personal lives and to teach to children in our care and to their families.

But in the Bible we also learn about children who grew up in less than ideal circumstances.

- Jacob and Esau took sibling rivalry to the extreme (Gen. 25—27).

- Joseph, who grew up in a blended family, was hated by his brothers because of his father's favoritism (Gen. 35, 37-47).

- Moses was adopted by the Pharaoh's daughter and grew up in a culture different than that of his birth family. (Ex. 2).

- A boy was raised by a single mother who had limited material resources (1 Kings 17).

- Timothy grew up in a multigenerational family where he was taught the Scriptures by his Christian mother and grandmother even though his father was not a Christian (Acts 16:1-3; 2 Tim. 1:5, 3:15).

Personal Learning Activity

Think about the boys and girls you teach. How are the circumstances of the children similar to the examples of the families from the Bible? How can you support God's ideal for the family while being sensitive and demonstrating God's love to all children?

Essential Factors in Strong Families

Even though the Bible provides examples of many types of families — some less than ideal — the Bible also offers some essential factors for strong families.

TRUST

Trust in the Home

Anticipation of the birth of a child may be accompanied by feelings of anxiety and apprehension. Inexperienced parents may wonder whether they have enough knowledge, understanding, and patience to be responsible for the new life that is soon to come.

The writer of Proverbs advises, "Trust in the Lord with all your heart and lean not on your own understanding; in all your ways

acknowledge him, and he will make your paths straight" (Prov. 3:5-6, NIV). Parents can begin by — trusting that God loves them and their baby, trusting that God will give them understanding, and trusting that God will guide them and their baby in the paths He wants them to go.

The Bible gives great help in understanding what it means to obey and to be faithful to teach about God in the ordinary, day-to-day activities with their children.

A beautiful example of this kind of teaching occurred recently at a public aquarium. A young child exclaimed, "Oooh, look!" as he and his mother moved close to a large tank of shimmering, iridescent jellyfish. His mother bent close to the child and asked, "Who made the beautiful jellyfish?" The child smiled and answered, "God." The mother responded, "Yes, God made the jellyfish."

Psalm 78:1-8 lifts up the importance of telling the next generation of God's goodness. Parents can share stories of God's goodness from the Bible and from their own families. A father says, as he shows his son a picture of his grandmother, "This is a picture of your grandmother. She taught me that God loves me, and she taught many other children at church that God loves them." Then as the father proudly holds a baby picture of his son, he exclaims: "I'm so glad God sent you to be a part of our family. I'm glad you are learning that God loves you, too."

Parents can begin when their child is an infant to communicate the faith through simple Bible phrases such as **"God made us"** (Ps. 100:3) and **"God loves us"** (Ps. 107:1). Parents help the child understand these simple Bible phrases while repeating them during daily times together. For example, as Daddy feeds his daughter, he says, "God loves you. God gives you good applesauce to eat." As the child grows, parents help her understand and live out the meaning of other Bible phrases. As her daughter helps set the table, a mother says: "Thank you for helping. The Bible says to **help one another**" (Gal. 5:13). Through gentle, daily teaching, parents are learning and helping their child learn what it means to obey and be faithful to God.

As parents are faithful and obedient to God, they are also building an environment of trust for their child. As parents meet their child's needs by responding with a dry diaper, good food, a safe and appropriate toy, a snuggle, and a gentle word, the child is learning that she can trust her parents to meet her needs. If a child learns during her early years to trust the people who are important to her, she is more likely one day to trust God to meet her most important need — the need for salvation from sin and a new life with Jesus Christ.

Parents can also learn to trust others who assist in caring for and teaching their children. A mother may have ambivalent feelings as she returns to work and entrusts her baby to a caregiver. A parent may even feel some sense of displacement as a little boy comes home talking constantly about Mrs. Betty and how Mrs. Betty says things should be done. Hopefully, parents will understand that their lives and the life of their child are enriched as they trust others to help teach their child about God's love and how God wants the child to grow.

Trust in the Weekday Early Education Setting

Trust is also important in the weekday early education setting as it is in the home. The first step for teachers is to trust God.

Have you experienced God's amazing love for you? This love is so great that God sent His only Son Jesus into the world to save you. Have you trusted Jesus to save you from your sin and to give you new life, eternal life? If not, you can do nothing more important than to prayerfully read John 3:16 and place your own name in the blanks below:

God loved _____ so much that He gave His only Son so that if _____ believed in Him, _____ would not perish, but _____ would have everlasting life.

As a Christian teacher, you can trust God to help you obey Him and be faithful to Him. God will provide many teachable moments so that you can help boys and girls learn about God and His love. As you and the children explore the wonders of God's world, you can help them know, through your words and actions, that God made flowers and trees, water and food, animals and people, and that God loves them very much.

You will have many opportunities to use the Bible in your teaching. Let children touch, hold, and look at the Bible as they learn that the Bible is a special book. Use Bible phrases:

- As children play together — "The Bible says to **be kind**. You are being kind when you take turns with the doll."

- As children talk about their families — "The Bible says, **'God is good to us.'** God gave you a mommy and a daddy to take care of you."

- As children prepare to eat — "**God gives food to us**. Thank You, God, for good food."

- When a child is afraid — "**God is with us always**. He helps us when we are afraid." Open the Bible and tell Bible stories that relate to children's activities and understanding:

  - The story of Rachel caring for the sheep as someone brings an animal to visit the classroom or as children talk about helping care for a pet at home

  - The story of Ruth gathering grain as you and the children make and bake bread

  - The story of Jesus at church as you visit the church's worship center

  - The story of four men who helped their friend who could not walk as you invite the children to think of ways they can help someone who is sick

  - The story of Jesus and the children to help children know that Jesus loves them.

You will also help children learn to trust others as you meet their needs as promptly as possible. It is important that children feel loved and secure in the weekday early education setting. Through meeting the needs of young children, you are laying a foundation on which their trust of other people and their trust of God can be built.

Personal Learning Activity

In what ways can you develop the trust of parents in the following areas:

- Teaching the child about God through daily activities

  _____

  _____

  _____

- Sharing stories of God's goodness

  _____

  _____

  _____

- Relating Bible phrases and stories to the child's activities

  _____

  _____

  _____

- Meeting the child's needs

  _____

  _____

  _____

COMMITMENT TO EFFECTIVE COMMUNICATION

Effective Communication in the Home

Effective communication is at the heart of good parenting. The Bible helps us understand that communication is a two-way process of receiving and sending messages. Communication is both listening to understand and speaking to be understood.

Listening must come first. "He who answers before listening — that is his folly and his shame" (Prov. 18:13, NIV). "Everyone should be quick to listen, slow to speak and slow to become angry" (Jas. 1:19, NIV). Think of the many ways a parent can listen to a child. The most obvious is listening with the ears. Isn't it interesting that a parent can distinguish between an infant's cries of pain, hunger, tiredness, and the need to be picked up and cuddled? As the child grows, a parent delights in and understands the child's earliest attempts at words. The parent later listens with interest as the child describes an event with amazing detail or asks the same question repeatedly. Listening with the ears is a skill that parents can develop.

Listening with the eyes is also an important skill. A child's body language may communicate more than his words. Facial expressions may show joy, surprise, fear, anger, uncertainty, or boredom. Listening with both the ears and the eyes enhances understanding.

Perhaps most important is listening with the heart. The heart listens for feelings and meanings. The heart listens with empathy as the parent attempts to see and feel things from the child's point of view. Empathetic listening enables the parent to understand and accept the child and her needs.

Parents learn early that they speak with much more than the mouth. A mother shares a simple game with her young daughter. The mother looks into her daughter's eyes and gently strokes her face. Before long, the little girl looks into Mommy's eyes and pats her face. What powerful love mother and child communicate through this simple game.

The Book of Proverbs speaks often of the power of our words, "A gentle answer turns away wrath, but a harsh word stirs up anger" (Prov. 15:1, NIV).

A good test for communication is:

- Are my words true?

- Are my words spoken in love?

- Will my words help build up the other person?

- Do my words consider the needs of the other person?

- Are my words kind and compassionate?

- Are my words pleasing to Christ?

Effective Communication in the Weekday Early Education Setting

Effective communication begins each day as the first child arrives. Through both your verbal and your nonverbal greeting, you communicate to the child, "I am glad you are here today." Let your eyes, your smile, your hands, your posture, and your words communicate a warm welcome.

Teachers also receive verbal and nonverbal messages from the child as he arrives. Do his eyes communicate eager anticipation, reluctance, or a lack of adequate rest? Does the child skip into the room with arms open wide and ready to choose an interesting activity? Or does his clinging to Mommy indicate a need for the teacher to quietly soothe him with a gentle back rub or by reading a favorite book? The child's words may convey excitement, contentment, anger, sadness, or other emotions. Effective teachers listen with their eyes, ears, and heart during these first important moments of the day.

Throughout the day teachers and children continue to receive and send messages. As you meet the children's needs for food, toileting, rest, and meaningful activities, you communicate love and care. Watch and listen to ensure that the learning activities you provide allow opportunities for success and interesting challenges. As you provide appropriate choices of activities, you communicate: "You are important. You can choose to learn the way that suits you best." Seize teachable moments as children play and work to share important truths. In all of your communication with children you have the privilege of speaking the truth in love and building them up so they can hear and know God's love through you.

Effective communication with the parents of children you teach is also important. Listen carefully for verbal and nonverbal messages parents convey. Be sure that your communication is positive and helpful to the parents as well as to their child.

Personal Learning Activity

The next time a child starts to tell you something, try listening with your ears, your eyes, and your heart. What is the result?

_____
_____
_____
_____

Then when you start to speak to a child, test your words using the list from Paul's advice to the Ephesians (4:15, 29, 32). What is the result?

_____
_____
_____
_____

MUTUAL RESPECT

Mutual Respect in the Home

Effective communication grows out of and enhances mutual respect in the family.

Mutual respect is a result of understanding that each person is made and loved by God. Every person has worth and deserves respect because God created him or her in His image. The apostle Peter wrote, "Show proper respect to everyone" (1 Pet. 2:17, NIV). Paul wrote about the need for mutual submission and respect in the family in Ephesians 5 and 6.

Perhaps some parents have focused so much on the needs and rights of their children that they have disregarded their own needs, while other parents have been so determined to assert their own rights and needs that they have neglected their children's needs. Mutual respect provides the balance for seeking to meet the needs of each person in the family.

When parents model mutual respect in the home, children are more likely to show respect for persons outside the home. They learn to show respect for teachers and other adults. Children also learn to show respect for other children through listening, taking turns, and being kind and helpful. Children learn to show respect for those who are different from them because they are learning that each person has differing strengths and weaknesses.

Because of God's love for us and our love for God, we love others, and we love ourselves. Mutual respect can be an important key for teaching, learning, and living together in harmony in the family.

Mutual Respect in the Weekday Early Education Setting

Perhaps you remember a teacher from your childhood for whom you had great respect. What qualities did this teacher have that called forth your respect? List three:

1. _____
_____
_____

2. _____
_____
_____

3. _____
_____
_____

If these qualities are present in your teaching and your relationships, more than likely children and parents have respect for you. How do you communicate your respect for children and their parents?

- Call the person by name.

- Look at the person as you talk with her.

- Encourage with smiles, words, and appropriate touching.

- Sit or stand on the level of the person with whom you are talking.

- Listen carefully without interruption.

- Focus on the person and his interests.

The classroom setting offers many opportunities to model and teach respect for others. The Homeliving Center is often a favorite with children. As girls and boys play and work in this Center they can:

- Connect home and school experiences
- Try out various roles
- Talk about what they are doing
- Be creative
- Plan and organize
- Solve problems
- Take turns and share
- Practice social skills

Personal Learning Activity

Look at the Learning Centers in your weekday early education setting. How can each Center become a laboratory where children learn respect for themselves and for one another?

GENUINE LOVE

Genuine Love in the Home

Self-giving love is the key ingredient in all relationships. Jesus and Paul also emphasized that this kind of love is modeled after God's unconditional love for us (Mark 12:30-31; Eph. 5:21-33).

First Corinthians 13 can help us look for practical examples of love at work in the home:

- **"Love is patient."** Because of love, parents accept the child as a child, not expecting him to think and act like a miniature adult.

- **"Love is not self-seeking."** Loving parents respond to the genuine needs and interests of their child rather than trying to live out their own desires and ambitions through their child.

- **"Love is not easily angered."** Because parents understand that words spoken hastily in anger can cause scars that may last throughout life, they practice self-control.

- **"Love keeps no record of wrongs."** Instead of bearing grudges and repeatedly bringing up wrongs of the past, parents focus on the strengths of the child and encourage her growth.

- **"Love rejoices with the truth."** Through day-to-day teaching by word and example, parents help children learn to discern and rejoice in God's truth.

- **"Love always trusts."** Parents trust God's good plan for their child and seek to help the child grow in that plan.

- **"Love always hopes and perseveres."** Loving parents never give up. They say and mean, "Nothing you could ever do will cause me to stop loving you, my child."

Genuine Love in the Weekday Early Education Setting

First Corinthians 13 also suggests practical ways to offer unconditional love in the weekday early education setting:

- Love is patient when a teacher encourages a child to practice an emerging skill rather than doing the task for the child.

- Love seeks the good of the child rather than the adult when teachers see each child as an individual and seek to meet individual needs.

- Love is self-control when teachers stay calm and set reasonable limits even when children lose control.

- Love keeps records of rights instead of wrongs when teachers begin conversations with parents by focusing on the positive.

- Love rejoices in the truth when teachers patiently teach Bible truths through activities appropriate for each child.

- Love always trusts when teachers trust God to help them understand and teach each child in the way best for her.

- Love always hopes and perseveres when teachers appreciate children as they are today and look forward to the possibilities for the future.

Unconditional love is the best gift a teacher can give a child. Love enables a child to accept himself and others and to experience God's love.

Personal Learning Activity

As you review the examples of love from 1 Corinthians 13, list ways you can demonstrate each characteristic of love with the children you teach.

_____
_____
_____
_____
_____
_____
_____
_____
_____
_____
_____
_____
_____
_____

"Jesus grew in wisdom and stature, and in favor with God and men" (Luke 2:52, NIV).

Chapter 3

The Child: God's Unique Creation

WONDERFULLY MADE

*"Special, special, you are very special,
God made you that way.
Special, special, you are very special,
God made you!"*[1]

The psalmist captured some of the awe and wonder we feel as we hold a new baby or young child: "For you created my inmost being; you knit me together in my mother's womb. I praise you because I am fearfully and wonderfully made" (Ps. 139:13-14, NIV).

What a miracle that God, who created the majestic mountains, the powerful oceans, and the splendid stars, sun, and moon, is intimately involved in the creation of every child. Each child is created in the image of God and is therefore special.

As we think about the children we teach, it is important to begin by understanding that each child is created and loved by God, that each child is a gift from God.

Scientific research now confirms what the Bible and caring parents, grandparents, and teachers have long acknowledged — that children are wonderfully made. Many sources — television documentaries, news magazines, local newspapers, parenting magazines, the Internet, and even the backs of cereal boxes — provide information about brain development research that confirms the marvelous nature of the human infant and his vast potential to learn from the earliest days. Note the following evidence from recent research:

• Even before they are born, babies can recognize their parents' voices.[2]

• Soon after she is born, a baby can also recognize her mother's distinctive aroma.[3]

- An infant's brain contains 100 billion neurons, nerve cells. This is as many nerve cells as there are stars in the Milky Way! Even before birth, electrical impulses cause rhythmic firing of these neurons, and this firing actually changes the physical structure of the brain.[4]

- Most of the wiring that forms the critical connections which determine emotional, social, and intellectual makeup occurs between birth and three years of age.[5]

- When a baby is four days old, she can distinguish one language from another. By 12 months of age the child probably starts connecting words to meanings. By 18 months she acquires one new word every two hours and she can start combining these words.[6]

- Premature infants who were massaged for at least 15 minutes three times a day gained weight 47% faster than those premature infants who received only minimal touch.[7]

- "Babies come equipped with the 'need to know'; our job is to give them love, acceptance, and the raw material of appropriate stimulation at each level of development."[8]

- There seem to be certain critical periods or windows of opportunity for developing various areas of the brain and consequent abilities.[9]

Brain research increasingly points out the critical nature of the preschool years and especially the first three years of life. Persons who have studied and taught young children through the years have long realized the importance of what the child learns during these early years. We speak of these years as foundational.

Consider the importance of the foundation of a building. It is necessary to think first about the desired final product. The foundation will have a different shape depending on whether a 3-bedroom house for a family or a 20-story office building is planned. Yet in both buildings, the foundation is extremely important.

Before laying the foundation in a child's life, parents and teachers need to consider the desired result. Our ultimate desire for our children is that they may know and experience the love of Christ and have faith in Him so that they will be obedient to God and His good plan for them. What sort of foundation needs to be laid in a child's life if she is to grow to reach her full potential?

Children by their very nature are dependent on others. They depend on parents to meet their needs for food, clothing, shelter, security, guidance, and love. When children learn that they can trust loving adults to meet these needs, the foundation is being laid to trust and depend on God.

A teacher might say, "Thank you for telling me that you spilled the paint. The Bible says to tell the truth. You told me the truth. Now we can use this sponge to clean up the paint." Through gentle teaching as children go about their activities, you are helping them to learn by your example.

Through both example and word, teachers can teach young children how to get along with others. Children are aware of how teachers relate to other teachers and to children. Teachers can model forgiveness even as they set reasonable limits for children. As they greet children warmly, listen to them, and meet their needs with patience and concern, teachers show genuine love.

Brain development research reminds us that "what a child experiences in the first few years of life largely determines how his brain will develop and how he will interact with the world throughout his life."[10] Therefore, it is important that children have the opportunity not only to hear these foundational teachings but also to put them into practice.

Personal Learning Activity

Identify Bible stories, verses, songs, and activities you can use to teach preschoolers.

GROWING IN A BALANCED WAY

Perhaps your kitchen wall has several horizontal marks where you measured the growth of your child. You probably remember the child's excitement as he pointed out how much taller the most recent marking of his height was than the previous mark. Marks on a kitchen wall are one sign of growth. Physical growth may be the most obvious growth to observe, but children are developing in other ways at the same time.

The Bible tells us that "Jesus grew in wisdom and stature, and in favor with God and men" (Luke 2:52, NIV). The children you teach are developing in the same ways Jesus grew: mentally (in wisdom), physically (in stature), spiritually (in favor with God), and socially (in favor with people).

Each kind of growth is important. One kind of growth helps every other kind of growth. If even one kind of growth does not occur, the whole person suffers. Each kind of growth should be cultivated and honored.

Let's see how biblical teachings inform us about each kind of growth.

Growing Mentally: Jesus grew in wisdom (Luke 2:52). The Bible records an account about Jesus' early mental growth.

We have already learned that brain development research demonstrates how much the infant and young child is developing mentally. Important neural connections are being made which enable the young child to learn today and into the future. This research shows that many different types of activities nurture the healthy development of the young child's brain. Talking with the infant, naming objects and what he is doing with the objects, reading books to him, playing simple games together, and sharing his excitement are all ways that teachers and parents can foster the child's mental development. Research suggests that music also plays a role in the development of the child's brain. As parents and teachers speak rhythmically, sing songs, and provide music for listening and moving, they are helping to strengthen the children's cognitive skills. However, this so-called "Mozart Effect" does not only increase brain power. Music can also help children find their identity, soothe their emotions, relax, explore body movements, and enhance creativity.[11] Isn't it exciting that something so enjoyable for both children and adults — music — can have such positive effects?

Researchers have also discovered that exercise makes it easier for children to learn. Children need opportunities to be physically active. Many children retain knowledge better when they can link purposeful movement to the subject matter to be learned.[12] Once again we see how the various types of learning are interrelated.

Growing Physically: Jesus grew in stature (Luke 2:52). He grew physically and had physical needs as other persons do.

As we focus on physical growth, we understand that it cannot really be separated from the other types of human development. Yet how can teachers aid in the physical growth of children?

The first step is understanding basic principles of development. While children will go through the same stages of development, the rate of development will be as different as individual children. Even though

developmental charts are helpful to understand the range when various behaviors may be anticipated, children progress at their own rate. Parents often compare their child to other children around them. Remember that each child is progressing in his or her own way. Each stage of growth is built on the previous stage. Celebrate every stage of growth and the particular pleasures and challenges it brings.

Prepare to meet physical needs in ways appropriate at each stage of growth. Just as you would not feed an infant carrot sticks, you would not confine a five-year-old's diet to milk. In the same way, you will plan appropriate physical activities based on the developmental stage of the child. Motor-skill development moves from large muscles (those involved in rolling a ball, etc.) to small muscles (those involved in drawing, etc.) At each stage the child needs appropriate opportunities to explore safely.

Growing Spiritually: Jesus grew in favor with God (Luke 2:52).

Young children today are also developing spiritually, and this spiritual development is related to all other areas of growth. The young child learns about spiritual matters the same way she learns about other things — through relationships with caring persons, through her senses, through concrete experiences, through play, through curiosity, and through satisfaction. Through all of these avenues of learning, the child learns the following concepts and more:

- God made me.
- God gave me a family.
- God loves me.
- God made things I can enjoy.
- I can love and help other people.
- Church is a place where I can learn.

As the child grows, he builds on these concepts and continues to develop spiritually.

Growing Socially: Jesus grew in favor with men (Luke 2:52).

How can we help young children grow in relationship to others? Lilian Katz and Diane McClellan in *Fostering Children's Social Competence: The Teacher's Role* suggest the following strategies for fostering social development.

- Respect children's feelings.
- State expectations simply, clearly, and politely.

- Think and speak of children in positive terms.
- Encourage self-control.
- Value individual differences.
- Encourage children to seek solutions when confrontations arise.
- Appeal to children's good sense.
- Help children cope with problems.
- Communicate openly with families.[13]

Growing as God Planned: Dr. Stanley I. Greenspan in *The Child with Special Needs* identified six fundamental developmental skills or milestones for learning and development in all children. These milestones illustrate again how a child grows in several different ways and how these areas of development work together.

- The ability to process the sights, sounds, and tactile delights around her and to use these experiences to calm herself.
- The ability to relate in positive ways with others.
- The ability to communicate by hearing and responding with gestures and speech.
- The ability to combine a series of actions to solve problems.
- The ability to form ideas.
- The ability to express ideas in words and in actions.[14]

unique and special to god

Each child is unique and special. Just as no two sets of finger prints are identical, no two children are exactly alike. Even identical twins have differences in personalities, interests, and abilities.

Celebrate the uniqueness of each child as you sing or read the words of this song:

"Look all the world over,
*   there's no one like me,*
*   no one like me, no one like me.*
Look all the world over,
*   there's no one like me,*
*   There's no one exactly like me."*[15]

Howard Gardner has challenged us to recognize that there is more than one way to be intelligent. Gardner has identified at least eight ways of being smart.[16] As we think about each category of intelligence, we will list the strengths of persons with that intelligence, the way Jesus used that intelligence in His teaching, and one or more Bible persons who exhibit that intelligence.

Verbal/Linguistic (Word Smart) — The person with this kind of intelligence has strengths using words, talking, reading, and writing. Jesus taught through stories (Matt. 13:3). Peter exhibited this intelligence. He was always eager to jump in with an answer, such as when Jesus asked "Who do you say I am?" (Matt. 16:15-16). Paul used his "word smarts" to write letters to many churches.

Logical/Mathematical (Number or Logic Smart) — This person has problem-solving skills, asks questions, and can figure out cause and effect. Jesus asked questions to challenge the attitude of His hearers (Matt. 7:3). The story of the four men who figured out how to get their friend who could not walk to Jesus is an example of using problem-solving skills. Because of the crowd surrounding Jesus, they lowered their friend through the roof to Jesus. Because of their faith, Jesus healed their friend (Mark 2:1-12).

Visual/Spatial (Picture Smart) — The person with this kind of intelligence uses his imagination, sees what something could be as easily as what it is, and can find his way around. Jesus used visuals to help people remember important truths. Jesus asked the crowd to look at a child as one having the qualities necessary to enter the kingdom of heaven (Matt. 18:2-4). Joseph, Jacob's son, had dreams of his own and interpreted the dreams of others to help people in need (Gen. 41:14-57). John had visions and wrote about them to give believers hope and courage (Revelation).

Bodily/Kinesthetic (Body Smart) — This kind of intelligence enables a person to have coordination and control over her body, the ability to make things with her hands and to use the ability to solve problems. This person may learn best while moving. Jesus used active learning, such as when He told His disciples, "Throw your net on the right side of the boat and you will find some [fish]" (John 21:6, NIV). Noah built the ark just as God had instructed so that he and his family would be safe (Gen. 6:9-21). Zacchaeus climbed a tree to see Jesus over the crowd (Luke 19:1-10).

Musical/Rhythmic (Music Smart) — A "music smart" person may recognize and produce simple songs, play a musical instrument, and be sensitive to the emotional power of music. Jesus and His disciples sang a hymn following their supper together (Matt. 26:30). Miriam sang and played the tambourine to praise God for delivering the Hebrews from the Egyptians (Ex. 15:19-21). David played his harp to calm King Saul (1 Sam. 16:14-23).

Naturalist/Scientific (Nature Smart) — This person enjoys the beauty of God's creation and taking care of plants and animals. Jesus said: "Look at the birds of the air; they do not sow or reap or store away in barns, and yet your heavenly Father feeds them . . . See how the lilies of the field grow" (Matt. 6:26,28, NIV). Rachel took care of her family's sheep (Gen. 29:1-10). David wrote psalms about the beauty of God's creation and God's care of people (Ps. 8; 104).

Interpersonal (People Smart) — The person with interpersonal intelligence understands other people, has leadership skills, and shows concern for others. Jesus saw the value of small groups of people working together. "He appointed twelve — designating them apostles — that they might be with him and that he might send them out to preach" (Mark 3:14, NIV). Deborah was a leader and a judge who settled the people's disputes (Judg. 4:4-5). Barnabas introduced Paul to the Christians in Jerusalem (Acts 9:26-28).

Intrapersonal (Self Smart) — The person who is self smart understands himself, has a realistic sense of his strengths, is aware of his own feelings and values, and may enjoy working and being alone. Even though Jesus spent a great deal of time with people, He sought solitude and quiet reflection at other times (Mark 6:46-47). Solomon prayed that God would give him wisdom (1 Kings 3:3-15). Paul understood that he was saved by God's grace and that He was called by God to preach to others (Gal. 1:1-24).

As you read about these categories of intelligence, were you able to identify your own ways of being smart? Each person has several different intelligences which can be used in combination. For example, David could illustrate almost all of the listed ways of being smart.

The child's personality, learning styles, and types of intelligence will determine whether she learns best through words, music, movement, or through working with others. A combination of all these methods will work best for some children. A conference leader asked, "Why do we try to teach all children the same way when each one is so different?" When we honor the individual differences of each child, all children will have better opportunities to learn foundational truths so that they will not turn from them as they grow.

Personal Learning Activity

Read again about each of the intelligences. List each child in your class. Identify each child's kind of smart. Think about how you can capitalize on these strengths and interests as you teach, so that each child can learn foundational truths in his or her own way.

_____

_____

_____

_____

_____

_____

_____

_____

_____

_____

_____

_____

A MODEL FOR ADULTS

As adults we consider teaching children a great privilege and responsibility. However, it is also our privilege and responsibility to learn from the children we teach.

We often talk about our responsibility to teach children because they are the "leaders of tomorrow." And that it is important because the examples and the teaching we provide for children today will determine the type of leaders they will be in the future. However, it is also important to remember who children are *today*. Children are loved by God for who they are right now as well as for the persons they will become in the future.

Even as we enjoy the responsibility of teaching children, may we also benefit from the privilege of learning from them.

Personal Learning Activity

Write in the space below something you have learned from a child.

_____

_____

_____

_____

_____

_____

_____

_____

"You are the light of the world. A city on a hill cannot be hidden. Neither do people light a lamp and put it under a bowl. Instead they put it on its stand, and it gives light to everyone in the house. In the same way, let your light shine before men, that they may see your good deeds and praise your Father in heaven" (Matt. 5:14-16, NIV).

Chapter 4

The Teacher: A Partner in God's Plan

Apainted wooden apple in a crafts booth displayed these words, "Teachers bring light to the darkness." Do you wonder about the story behind that wooden apple? Some teacher must have gently touched the maker of that wooden apple in a very special, life-changing way.

You may be unaware of the difference you make in the lives of the children in your classroom. The time they spend with you may be the only time when someone really listens to what they say, looks at what they are wearing, or takes time to understand their feelings. Many children are starving for basic attention. Your being a part of their lives brings "light to their darkness."

What difference will it make for you as a teacher and for the children you teach when you think of yourself as a bringer of light into the darkness and one who helps sustain the life and spirit of a child? How does being a bringer of light make you a partner in God's plan?

A Teacher Joins God at Work in the World

Reading the morning newspaper or watching the evening news may cause us to feel pessimistic about the world. We may see mainly the "bad news." Can we train our eyes to also see the good news as we seek to bring light into the darkness?

Experiencing God, a popular study that many Christians find helpful, states that "God is always at work around you," and that "God invites you to become involved with Him in His work."[1]

Our ability to see God at work around us increases as we grow in our trust of God. Through trust in God we experience God's love for us in a new and dynamic way, and we want to return His love. Then God "opens our eyes" to His activity around us.

Where do you see God at work around you?

- Do you see God in loving parents and teachers who nurtured you when you were a child?

- Do you see God at work in friends and family members who encourage you today?

- Do you see God at work in the possibilities in your weekday situation?

- Do you see God at work in the lives of other teachers?

- Do you see God at work in the lives of girls and boys who are eager to learn about God and His world?

- Do you see God at work in parents who want to be Christian role models for their children?

- Do you see God at work in the worship and ministry of your church?

A weekday teacher tells of praying that God would show her where He was at work and where she could join Him in that work. One morning, the mother of a little girl in her class was obviously upset as she and her daughter arrived. The teacher breathed a silent prayer and then asked the mother: "Would you like to talk? How can I pray for you?" When the mother responded that she would like to talk, the teacher asked an aide to watch her class. The teacher and mother moved to a vacant room down the hall. The mother said: "My husband is packing up his truck. He is planning to leave us today. I have been praying that someone could help

me change his mind." The teacher and the mother then went to talk with the pastor, who drove to the home with the mother. Indeed, the father was packing the truck, but he was willing to talk with the pastor. He confessed his confusion, his feelings of inadequacy, and his impression that the family might be better off without him. The pastor gently shared with this father the good news of God's love and God's power to change lives and heal broken relationships. The father trusted Jesus as His Savior and unpacked his truck. The entire family now is growing in God's love and in their love for one another because *one teacher* was able to see where God was at work and to join Him there. Jesus promised: "Whoever has my commands and obeys them, he is the one who loves me. He who loves me will be loved by my Father, and I too will love him and show myself to him" (John 14:21, NIV).

Personal Learning Activities

Where do you see God at work around you?

_____

_____

_____

_____

_____

_____

_____

_____

Will you pray about what God is doing there and that He would reveal to you how you can join Him in His work?

A Teacher Follows Jesus' Example

Jesus is our best example as a teacher and bringer of light into the darkness. Jesus said: "I am the light of the world. Whoever follows me will never walk in darkness, but will have the light of life" (John 8:12). J. M. Price in *Jesus the Teacher* lists these principles that Jesus followed as He related to persons:

• **Jesus took the long view.** Jesus looked beyond the present weaknesses of persons to future possible strengths. Many saw Simon as a rough fisherman, but Jesus saw his possibilities as a disciple. He changed Simon's name to Peter and called Peter and his brother Andrew to be His followers (Mark 1:16-18). Peter was often the first of the disciples to venture either a question or a response. Peter was the disciple who recognized Jesus as the Christ, the promised Messiah (Mark 8:27-29). However, becoming Jesus' follower did not immediately erase all of Peter's flaws. Jesus recognized that it takes time to develop the kind of character that God desires. Even after promising to stay with Jesus no matter what the consequences (Mark 14: 29-31), Peter denied knowing Jesus (Mark 14:66-72). Later after Jesus' death and resurrection, Jesus offered Peter forgiveness, restoration, and the call to continued ministry (John 21:15-19). Peter fulfilled Jesus' belief in him when on the day of Pentecost Peter preached, and about three thousand people were saved (Acts 2:14-41).

Teachers have the opportunity to take the long view with boys and girls as they focus on strengths rather than weaknesses. Teachers also understand that it takes time for children to develop character, attitudes, behaviors, and habits that are pleasing to God.

• **Jesus spent time with individuals.** Admittedly, Jesus spent time teaching the crowds that gathered around Him. However, He spent much of His time relating to individuals or His small group of disciples. Often, when He saw a person in need, Jesus drew that person away from the crowd and responded to this individual's needs. Zacchaeus climbed a sycamore tree so that He could see Jesus over the crowd that had gathered in Jericho. Jesus looked up into the tree and called for Zacchaeus to come down so that He could stay at Zacchaeus' house. Even though the crowd complained because Zacchaeus was a hated tax collector, Jesus went home with Zacchaeus. Because of Jesus' reaching out in friendship, Zacchaeus promised to give half of all he owned to the poor and pay back four times anything he might have taken wrongly. Jesus responded, "Today salvation has come to this house" (Luke 19:1-10, NIV).

How can a busy teacher focus on one child when several children may be clamoring for her attention? A teacher can sit or bend down to the child's level, look into the child's eyes, perhaps place a gentle hand on her shoulder, and listen to what she has to say. The teacher may involve the child in helping her or another child do something, such as stacking the blocks on the shelf or folding the doll clothes. The teacher can then turn to the next child who needs her attention.

- **Jesus started where people were.** Jesus always started with the other person's interests and needs rather than starting with a prepared speech. Jesus understood where people were and was willing to begin with them there, hoping to lead them eventually where He wanted them to go. Jesus approached the woman at the well who had come to draw water by asking her to give Him a drink of water. Jesus' request led to a conversation about living water — a natural extension of the setting and the interest of the woman. Shunned by the townspeople because of her multiple marriages and divorces, the woman hurried back to her village and invited the people to come out and meet Jesus. Many of these people believed in Jesus because of her witness (John 4:1-42).

A caring teacher starts where children are by understanding the developmental characteristics and needs of children. The teacher does not try to teach a four-year-old as she would an adult. The teacher also understands the different interests and abilities of each child and matches her methods accordingly.

- **Jesus focused on what was important.** Jesus did not allow Himself to be drawn into peripheral issues. He focused on truths that could make a life-changing dif-

ference for persons. Nicodemus, a Pharisee and religious leader, came to Jesus at night. He began by complimenting Jesus on the miracles He performed. Jesus moved to the heart of the matter and proclaimed that one must be born again to enter the Kingdom of God. When Nicodemus questioned how such a physical rebirth was possible, Jesus taught how a person can experience salvation and eternal life (John 3:1-21). Jesus focused on issues that had eternal significance.

Teachers have the opportunity to focus on the truly important as they help children learn to depend on God, to obey and love God, and to relate to other people with respect and love. This kind of teaching can occur in the natural, day-to-day activities of a weekday setting when teachers follow Jesus' example.

- **Jesus drew out people's best possibilities.** Because Jesus saw the future possibilities of people, He could inspire them to reach for their best. When John came to Jesus, he was known as a "Son of Thunder" (Mark 3:17). This characteristic did not leave John immediately. When Samaritan villagers refused to welcome Jesus and His disciples, John and James asked Jesus whether He wanted them to call down fire from heaven. But because Jesus continued to teach and to encourage him, John came to be known as the beloved disciple. From the cross, Jesus entrusted His mother's care to this disciple (John 19:26-27). After Jesus' death and resurrection, John and Peter were arrested for teaching about

Jesus. When the religious leaders demanded that they stop preaching, John and Peter replied, "We cannot help speaking about what we have seen and heard" (Acts 4:1-20). John is assumed by many to be the writer of the Gospel of John, the Epistles of John, and Revelation. John lived up to the best that Jesus saw in him!

We have often heard that children live up to their teachers' expectations of them. If a teacher labels a child as lazy and uncooperative, the child is more likely to exhibit these characteristics. If a teacher expects a child to be cooperative, he will probably try hard to live up to these expectations. Teachers today can draw out the best for children as they accept them where they are now and expect the best from them.

• **Jesus knew that people learn best by doing.** Jesus gave His followers opportunities to practice what He was teaching them. Jesus sent out His disciples to teach, preach, and heal those who were sick. As they went, the twelve also learned lessons about depending on God (Luke 9:1-6).

Studies have shown that children learn best when they are actively involved in their learning. Children learn Bible truths as they thank God, pray for God's help, do kind things, and practice doing what is right.

Personal Learning Activities

Review each of the examples of the way Jesus related to persons. List two examples you will seek to follow as you teach preschoolers:

1. _____
   _____
   _____
   _____

2. _____
   _____
   _____
   _____

A Teacher Studies the Bible

The psalmist used the image of light when he spoke of the influence of God's Word, "Your word is a lamp to my feet and a light for my path" (Ps. 119:105, NIV). Therefore the Bible can be our guide as we seek to be bringers of light into the darkness.

Regular Bible study will enhance your personal growth as a Christian, and the overflow of your study will enrich your teaching. Examine several methods of Bible study and choose the one that best suits your interests and needs.

Individual Passages — Examine a passage of Scripture in detail by asking questions, finding cross-references, and looking up words in a Bible dictionary or encyclopedia. Consider how the Bible passage applies to your own life situation and the needs of the children you teach.

You might choose a passage based on a Bible story you will be telling the children. Information you learn about the setting of the story can help the children picture the story. For example, understanding that most of the houses of Jesus' day had a flat roof and stairs on the outside of the house leading up to the roof would help children better understand the story of the four friends who cut a hole in the roof to let their friend down to Jesus (Mark 2:1-12). You may even find in a Bible dictionary a picture of a typical house from biblical times that you can show to the children. Contrast this new insight with the visual image children may have of the men climbing up and cutting a hole through the typical pitched roof that we see on houses today.

Biographies — Research all the verses about a Bible person in order to study his or her life and characteristics. Make notes on attitudes, strengths, weaknesses, and how God worked in the person's life. Consider how you are like and unlike the person you have studied. What has God shown you about your life through the study of this person?

You could choose to do further study of a person who is the main character in one of the Bible stories you plan to tell. For example, if you will tell the story of Paul's teaching Lydia and her friends about Jesus (Acts 16:11-15), you could read other references to Paul (Saul). You could learn what Paul's life was like before he became a Christian, about Christians who encouraged him, and the dangers Paul faced as a missionary.

Personal Qualities — Choose a personal quality suggested in a Bible passage and study what the Bible says about that quality. You may do a word study, use cross-references, or study a Bible person who demonstrated that quality. Ask God to help you develop this quality and find ways to practice it.

You might choose the quality of *encouragement,* since being an encourager is one way to bring light into the darkness. A concordance will list references about God's encouragement of persons and the need for believers to be encouragers to others. Barnabas is an excellent biblical example of an encourager (Acts 4:36-37; 9:26-27; 11:19-30; 15:1-21).

Words and Phrases — Use Bible dictionaries, concordances, and commentaries to dig out and explain the meanings of key words and phrases.

We have used the word *trust* often in talking about the need for children to learn to trust and our need to trust God. Therefore *trust* could be a good word to study.

Themes and Topics — Choose a scriptural theme or topic. Use a concordance to collect and compare all the verses you can find on the topic. Make notes on how this theme applies to your life.

You might choose a topic that arises out of a Bible story you will teach, or you might choose another topic of interest to you. For example, you might choose to study the theme of *teaching*. You will find many references to various forms of the word *teach*. An in-depth study of this biblical theme can enrich your own teaching ministry.

Read the Bible Through — Some teachers may choose to read the Bible through in a specific period of time, such as a year. You can find various plans or Bibles to assist you in this method. It may be helpful to choose a plan that guides you to read from both the Old and New Testaments on a daily or weekly basis rather than reading all the Old Testament before beginning to read the New Testament.

You may note some overlap in the methods suggested above. For example a biographical study of Barnabas could lead to studying the personal quality of *encouragement* or studying individual passages about his missionary journeys. Any of these methods will enrich your study of the Bible, your personal journey of faith, and your teaching.

Personal Learning Activities

Use this guide to record your insights as you use one of the Bible study methods.

● **The Bible Passage as a Whole:**

Read the Bible passage as if you had never read it before. List questions or impressions from your reading.

Questions/Impressions:

_____

_____

_____

_____

_____

_____

_____

● **God's Message for That Day:**

Historical Setting: When was this passage written, and what was God revealing about Himself, His purposes, or His ways?

_____

_____

_____

_____

● **God's Message for Today:**

What is God revealing to you through this passage about Himself, His purposes, and His ways?

_____

_____

_____

_____

What is God revealing to you today through this passage about how He would like for you to join Him at work in His world?

_____

_____

_____

_____

A Teacher Prepares

The teacher who would be a "bringer of light" prepares. Jesus told a parable of ten virgins who took their lamps and went out to meet the bridegroom. Five of them were wise; in addition to their lamps they took flasks containing extra oil for their lamps. Five were foolish; they took no extra oil. For some reason the bridegroom did not arrive at the marriage feast when expected. When the announcement came at midnight that the bridegroom was about to arrive, the women woke up and trimmed the burned wicks from their lamps and lighted them.

Much to the dismay of the five foolish women, their lamps began to go out because they were out of oil. While they hurried out to buy more oil, the bridegroom arrived, the festivities began without the foolish women, and the door was shut. Because of their lack of preparation, the foolish women did not get to join the celebration. Paul wrote to Timothy, "Be prepared in season and out of season" (2 Tim. 4:2, NIV). In what ways can we prepare?

Prepare by Understanding the Purpose

The Bible includes some of the following purposes or aims of teaching.

- **Wisdom** — "Blessed is the man who finds wisdom, the man who gains understanding (Prov. 3:13, NIV). Wisdom is much more than knowledge of facts; it is understanding that enables one to relate well to God, to self, and to other people.

- **Guidance for Living** — The psalmist prayed: "Guide me in your truth and teach me, for you are God my Savior" (Ps. 25:5, NIV) and "How can a young man keep his way pure? By living according to your word. I seek you with all my heart; do not let me stray from your commands. I have hidden your word in my heart" (Ps. 119:9-11, NIV).

- **Correction** — "All Scripture is God-breathed and is useful for teaching, rebuking, correcting and training in righteousness" (2 Tim. 3:16, NIV).

- **Spiritual Renewal** — Paul wrote to the Romans: "Do not conform any longer to the pattern of this world, but be transformed by the renewing of your mind. Then you will be able to test and approve what God's will is — his good, pleasing, and perfect will" (Rom. 12:2, NIV) and "Never be lacking in zeal, but keep your spiritual fervor, serving the Lord. Be joyful in hope, patient in affliction, faithful in prayer" (Rom. 12:11-12, NIV).

- **Effective Witnessing** — Jesus commissioned His followers, "You will receive power when the Holy Spirit comes on you; and you will be my witnesses" (Acts 1:8, NIV). Peter wrote: "Always be prepared to give an answer to everyone who asks you to give the reason for the hope that you have. But do this with gentleness and respect, keeping a clear conscience" (1 Pet. 3:15-16, NIV).

Prepare Through Training

Just as athletes train for a race or other athletic event so they can do their best, it is vital that teachers train to do their best. Paul wrote to Timothy: "Do your best to present yourself to God as one approved, a workman who does not need to be ashamed and who correctly handles the word of truth" (2 Tim. 2:15, NIV) and "So that the man [teacher] of God may be thoroughly equipped for every good work" (2 Tim. 3:17, NIV). Opportunities for training and equipping yourself as a teacher are varied and can be chosen to suit your own interests, needs, and time.

- **Training Events** — No doubt, various training events will be offered in your area, and you may be encouraged to go to maintain certification. These training events not only provide excellent speakers and workshops, but they also offer opportunities to exchange ideas and solutions to problems with other teachers.

- **Books and Other Printed Materials** — Books such as the one you are reading offer training. Keep this guide handy and refer to it as needs and questions arise. Perhaps you and other teachers in your weekday setting could exchange books and meet occasionally to discuss what you are learning. You will also find helpful articles about early childhood education in journals, magazines, newspapers, and on the Internet. Keeping a file of these articles will make them more readily accessible.

- **Multimedia** — Video and audiotapes and CD ROMs allow you to benefit from training at a time that suits your schedule. Television documentaries may offer current information about young children.

- **Observation** — Ongoing training occurs as you learn from observing children. As you observe, make notes about how your observations relate to what you are learning from books, articles, workshops, and multimedia. You may observe an experienced and respected teacher in your own program or observe a teacher in another weekday program in your community.

Talk with the director of your weekday program about training needs and creative ways those needs might be met.

A Teacher Prepares Through the Curriculum

The *WEE Learn Curriculum Guides* provide a wide range of age-appropriate activities to help you lay a solid foundation with young children. This curriculum will enable you to follow a balanced and comprehensive plan that will meet the developmental needs of boys and girls. As you review the suggested activities, choose the methods that best suit the boys and girls you teach.

A Teacher Makes Personal Preparation

The personal preparation you make increases the probability of positive learning experiences for boys and girls.

Prayer is an important part of personal preparation. "Pray in the Spirit on all occasions with all kinds of prayers and requests. With this in mind, be alert and always keep on praying" (Eph. 6:18, NIV). As you wake in the morning, commit the day and yourself to God. Ask God to guide you throughout the day that you might join Him at work in the world. Pray with the boys and girls you teach, thanking God for the beauty of the world, for good food, for the children by name. Pray silently for patience and guidance when difficulties arise during the day. Before you sleep, pray as you review the day. Thank God for opportunities you had to share His love. Ask God's forgiveness for missed opportunities. Pray for children and families who have special needs. As you pray throughout the day, you can be assured that God hears and cares.

Plan Ahead: Before a new week begins, think ahead to your plans for the week. Make a list of supplies you may need to request or secure. At the end of a teaching day, it will be helpful if you can begin preparations for the next day. Make sure unneeded items are put away and that supplies you need for the next day are available. Arrive in your classroom early to finalize preparations for the day. Arriving early gives you time to make the room ready before welcoming the children. It takes time to greet them with genuine interest.

Preparation, which is another word for planning, is one of the keys to effective teaching. The writer of Proverbs promised, "Those who plan what is good find love and faithfulness" (Prov. 14:22, NIV). Our prayer for you, the weekday teacher, echoes the prayer of the psalmist, "May he give you the desire of your heart and make all your plans succeed" (Ps. 20:4, NIV).

A Teacher is Accountable

What does the fact that you are accountable mean to you? Paul wrote, "Each of us will give an account of himself to God" (Rom. 14:12, NIV). We sometimes think of being held accountable as a scary prospect, but that does not have to be the case. For those who have trusted Jesus as Savior, there need be no fear about one's salvation. Paul assured the Romans, "If you confess with your mouth, 'Jesus is Lord,' and believe in your heart that God raised him from the dead, you will be saved. . . . As the Scripture says, 'Anyone who trusts in him will never be put to shame.'" (Rom. 10:9,11, NIV).

Let's look further at the meaning of *accountability*. It comes from the root word *account*. One of the meanings of the word *account* is value or importance. So we could rephrase the statement "I am accountable" to say "I count. What I do has value. My life is important. I can make a difference." All of this is true because God made you in His own image (Gen. 1:27). God loved you so much that He sent His only Son, Jesus, to die for you so that you might have eternal life.

You may not realize that you make a difference in the lives of your children — in their confidence, their self-image, and their feelings of well-being. Yes, your teaching accounts for something. Paul wrote, "God, who said, 'Let light shine out of darkness,' made his light shine in our hearts to give us the light of the knowledge of the glory of God in the face of Christ" (2 Cor. 4:6, NIV). Teachers have the marvelous opportunity to share the light of Christ with children and their families. So then, "Live as children of light (for the fruit of the light consists in all goodness, righteousness and truth) and find out what pleases the Lord" (Eph. 5:8-10, NIV).

Jesus' words about light challenge us and help us understand the true purpose of being bringers of light: "You are the light of the world . . . Neither do people light a lamp and put it under a bowl. Instead they put it on its stand, and it gives light to everyone in the house. In the same way, let your light shine before men, that they may see your good deeds and praise your Father in heaven" (Matt. 5:14-16, NIV). Our purpose as bringers of light is that boys and girls might experience the love of God fully expressed in Jesus, the Light of the world.

As you consider your accountability, take heart from Paul's words: "It is God who works in you to will and to act according to his good purpose . . . shine like stars in the universe as you hold out the word of life" (Phil. 2:13,15, NIV).

PERSONAL LEARNING ACTIVITY

Look around you. Where can you bring light into the darkness? Pray the following or your own prayer:

"God, thank You for creating the light of the sun, the moon, and the stars. Thank You for sending Your Son as the Light of the world. Help me to be Your light for the boys and girls I teach so that they may know Your love. Amen."

Section 2:

The Preschooler You Teach

Teaching in Christian Weekday Early Education

"I praise you because I am fearfully and wonderfully made; your works are wonderful, I know that full well" *(Psalm 139:14, NIV).*

Chapter 5

Wonderfully Made

I will make a child, God must have thought; and when I do, I will take from the best, put it together in exactness, touch it with softness, and give it to Woman and Man for them to love and nourish.

And so God began early in the morning and captured the dampness of dewdrops, the pinks of the dawn, and the softness of river's fog. God borrowed the songs of birds and from the mule a bit of determination. He gathered the wispiness of the clouds and the sparkle of sunlight. God saw mystery in the wind and chuckles in the bubbling brook — He needed those.

With the wisdom of Deity and the art of creation a child is born.[1]

Ah, isn't she sweet? She has eyes like her daddy, a mouth like her mommy, and a disposition like her Aunt Fran. But how can it be — one child of so many, yet, so much "her own self"? There is not another being exactly like Sarah. She is wonderfully made, individually made, and she is not yet finished. Each age, each stage will be wonderfully made in her individual mold.

You have probably said some of the same words Sarah's observers said. You recognized characteristics and behavior in children that are seen in their close relatives. The gene pool gives the child physical traits, emotional temperament, and intellectual potential. Her environment, relationships, and experiences help determine what the child will do with her heredity.

You, dear teacher, are a key element in the process of the growing of Sarah. Consider yourself the "parent away from parent." For a time, each child is yours to nurture, love, guide, and protect. What an awesome responsibility you have! How significant and important you are in the lives of children.

As you plan and teach, consider the individuality of each child. Consider the child's ethnic background, home environment, abilities, limitations, personality, giftedness, and qualities that may be his or hers alone. Keep in mind how wonderfully children are made and how you can enhance their unique characteristics. Personalize Psalm 139:13-14. It could read: "God created my inmost being, He put me together in my mother's womb . . . and I am fearfully and wonderfully made; God's works are wonderful!" Value that wonderfulness in yourself and in each child. The environment, experiences, and the relationship you provide must nurture the nature of each child.

CHILDREN KNOW WHY THEY ARE WONDERFULLY MADE — ASK THEM

WHY DID GOD MAKE EYES?

"To look and see."
"To blink."
"So we can see every-
     body."
"I can wink with my
     eyes."
"To shut my eyes."
"So we can sleep with
     our eyes."

Changes in eye growth cannot be as easily measured or observed as a child's weight or height. Eyes and vision do change with the child's growing body. Baby's eyes need interesting things to see in order to develop well. The young child enjoys seeing a mobile with contrasting colors.

Pictures and books with easily-defined illustrations are good for the eyes of the young preschooler. As baby grows, she will move her head and her body to follow a picture or an object of interest.

Hold the Musical Mirror so David can see himself. Sing "The Mirror" (p. 72, 'Specially Special Songs). Prop a teaching picture (backed with cardboard and covered with clear adhesive) in Eric's bed. Place Eric on his stomach so he can lift his head and see the picture. Point to people in the picture. Talk about what you see.

Gain Carly's interest as you point to her eyes, or point to the eyes of a baby in a picture. Say: "Eyes — Carly has pretty brown eyes. Thank You, God, for Carly's pretty brown eyes."

A child's range of vision increases with maturation. Vision change may bring changes in how a child acts. According to Ames and Ilg, "There is a fluidity, flexibility, and looseness in the visual patterns of the typical Four-year-old. He is definitely more stable visually than he was at Three, and definitely more outgoing in his visual response. His attention is to the horizon, and he often goes far afield in his pursuit of that horizon."[2]

In planning activities for fours and fives, eye-hand coordination must be considered. Five-year-olds, and older, are still having visual changes within their eyes. Misbehavior, whining, and even illness can occur when a child is asked to do close work that his eyes literally cannot take into focus.

The age of technology has made the computer screen a common visual for even the very young child. Some preschoolers will have access to a "mouse" at home. Do them a favor and provide good manipulative toys when they are in the weekday program. Good eye-hand coordination needs large-muscle movement that is limited by a mouse. Consider the flux and flow of eye growth when you ask a child to use a computer or do any other close eye-involvement activities.

Various sized boxes, blocks, manipulative toys, large crayons, and large brushes give boys and girls opportunities to "grow all over." These items provide an extended visual range and stimulate overall muscular movements. Less frustration will be evident when children are encouraged to do only what maturation enables them to do.

The "eyes" have it — so give them focus as you plan and teach. Share the book *Look at Me* with Toddlers. At a teachable moment with one or more children, sing "God Gave Me Eyes" or "Thank You for My Eyes" (pp. 23 and 67, *'Specially Special Songs*).

Why are eyes closed during prayer time? Explain to older preschoolers that they can listen better with closed eyes. They can concentrate on what is said in the prayer, instead of looking at something distracting.

Take boys and girls on a "seeing walk." As they walk, you can expect twos and threes to happily talk about what they see. You might want to ask older preschoolers to keep their lips closed and observe while they walk. After a walk, give each child a turn to talk about one or two things she saw as she walked.

Children learn through all their senses. Some learn best by seeing. Too much to see can be over-stimulating and can cause the visual learner to become hyperactive. Or, too much to take in visually can cause the visual learner to "turn off" and do nothing.

Color can affect feelings and behavior. Shades of warm colors — such as yellow, red, and orange — are stimulating. Cool colors of soft shades of blues and greens are calming. The visually sensitive child is especially affected by color. An uncluttered room with walls in a soft, cool color is good for all — not just the visual/spatial learner.

Bring bright colors into the room in teaching items. Sing "Colors, Shapes, and Numbers" (p.18, *'Specially Special Songs*) as boys and girls point to a vivid color, a shape, and a number.

Easel paints need to be definite colors, not murky. Red, yellow, green, and blue paints, used one at a time, are easiest for beginning painters to identify. For a visual experiment, older preschoolers can mix two primary colors to create another color. Yellow with a bit of red makes orange. Blue mixed with red becomes purple.

Harsh lighting can "hyper" the visual learner, as well as other children and teachers! Natural lighting is calming, if it is not too bright. Children need to face away from windows during group time.

Any time you affirm, direct, or redirect a child, get on the child's eye level. Preschoolers, especially the visual learners, need to "see" what you are saying as well as hear what you are saying.

WHY DID GOD MAKE EARS?

"To hear."
"To hold Bo's hearer" (hearing aid).
"To hold glasses on."
"So we can listen."
"For earrings!"
"So my daddy says, 'Come here, now!'"

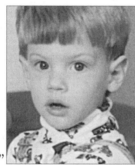

Your voice pleasantly speaking a child's name is one of the best sounds for a child's ears. As you rock Angie, softly say, "God made Angie special." Sing "You're A Special Child" (p. 88, *Specially Special Songs*). Say: "In the Bible we read, 'God made us.' He gave us ears to hear."

When a young child is fussy, cries easily, or rubs her ear, you might suspect an earache. Professional medical attention may be needed. Allergies often affect the ears, and a child's behavior can be affected by allergies.

When you observe a child behaving in a positive way, speak words of affirmation into that child's listening ears. When you affirm a child, use his name, "Thank you, Chad, for putting the puzzle away." Associating affirmation with his name is good for the child's memory bank. Affirmation for good behavior brings better results than scolding for bad behavior.

The child who is an auditory learner (acute hearing awareness) needs less noise and clear, distinct directions. A hearing learner may be distracted from a story you are reading by an outside noise. Whereas, a seeing learner may concentrate on the book and never notice a noise beyond the room.

Children enjoy the words and rhythm as you read to them. An award-winning book that has more than good words and rhythm is *Bein' with You This Way*. The book is large, well-illustrated, pleasantly colorful, with a cast of multi-cultures. Preschoolers will enjoy the story and rhythm of the words. They will also learn what fun it is to have friends of many cultures.

Select books and pictures with a purpose. Remember Bo with the ear hearer? *I Have a Sister — My Sister Is Deaf* is a book to help preschoolers become sensitive to others who have a hearing loss. Take advantage of libraries for a vast resource of wonderful listening experiences through cassette tapes, CDs, and books. Set up regular story times in a library. Arrange for children to check out chosen books as they leave.

Preschoolers like to hear stories that include the sounds that animals or machines make. Baby's first book is usually a book about animals. His first words may be repeating what the animals say.

How to calm the noise: exaggerate your mouth movements, but speak quietly. You may even whisper. Children must listen to hear what you say. If you try to "out noise" children, they may raise their level of sound.

Play a quiet game. Ask children to stand and keep their feet still. Ask if they can move their heads, shoulders, bodies, arms, and hands — without making a sound.

Take a "listening walk," as you did the seeing walk. This time girls and boys are to close their mouths and walk quietly. They must use their ears to discover sounds. After the walk, talk about specific sounds they heard.

A listening time in the room is a pleasant way to get children to settle for resting. Ask preschoolers to lie quietly and listen for sounds outside the room. Or, listen to quiet music playing in the room.

Print a list as fours or fives tell you names of animals and things that are very quiet. Another day you might ask the children to help you list names of things that are very noisy. During group time, girls and boys may enjoy dictating a story, using a noisy or a quiet list for story ideas.

Place a noisy or quiet list near the art area. Read from the list as a child paints or uses crayons. The list may trigger ideas for a child's creativity.

Noisy List
Dog
Lion
Elephant
Fire Truck
Airplane
Drum
Television

Play the cassette *Adventures in Sound* or *Quiet Time* near the art area. As children paint, or create with other art materials, observe how, or if, they listen and react to the music. The child most responsive to the music may be an auditory learner or a child of musical talent.

Preschoolers enjoy the song "Bells Make Music" (p.14, *'Specially Special Songs*). Middle and older preschoolers like to use bells, sticks, or drums during the song. Toddlers like to hear the Corn Popper make pop-pop-poppity sounds. Babies enjoy hearing the Rolling Bells toy.

Think about this: Do you need to talk less, use your ears more, and listen to children? Sometimes a nod of the head, a smile or frown, a shaking of your head, or touching a child can replace words. Give children's ears a rest!

Use your ears when there are disagreements. Wait before you interfere. Children can often solve their own problems. Separate gently, to prevent physical contact. Your soft voice may calm the conflict. Speak clearly and in words the children understand. Tell older preschoolers to talk and listen, instead of using their hands, when they are angry. Listen to both sides of a conflict. Ask children to listen to each other. Then, ask each child to tell how the disagreement might be solved. Thank each child when you hear an agreeable resolution.

Children are wonderfully made. Your calm verbal guidance enhances their wonderfulness.

Personal Learning Activities

1. In order to evaluate my verbal communication in the classroom, I should speak clearly and distinctly so preschoolers can hear and understand me. I will _____
_____.

2. When I maintain a low-volume voice, children respond by _____
_____.

3. One thing I will do next week to be more "sound sensitive" is _____
_____.

WHY DID GOD MAKE NOSES?

"To smell, and to smell flowers."

"To blow our nose."

"It can hold your glasses up."

"We breathe with noses."

"It is to wipe when it itches."

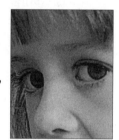

"We can sneeze with our nose."

From magazines, cut several pictures of animals and people with obviously-interesting noses. Cover these pictures with clear adhesive. Place the covered pictures on the floor in the Learning Centers, or you might choose to put them at the diaper-changing station. Say, "God made noses." Paste a large, easily-defined face on a piece of cardboard. Cover with clear contact plastic. Encourage a young preschooler to pat and touch the picture as you talk about the face. Point to the eyes, ears, nose, and mouth as you describe the features.

When Tiffany sees her reflection in a Musical Mirror, point to, and say, "nose, ears, eyes, mouth." Sing "You're A Special Child" (p. 88, *Specially Special Songs*).

Hold baby Andy on your lap. Let him touch and pat the Bible. Say: "Bible. This is the Bible. In the Bible I read that God made you. He made your eyes, your ears, and your nose." (Point to Andy's eyes, ears, and nose.)

At the Art Center or Writing Center, older preschoolers may choose to make collages or nose books from pictures of noses cut from magazines. Print information, a poem, or story a child makes up to go with his or her nose book. Help older boys and girls think of words that rhyme with nose. They may be able to create a poem. Alfred did, "A nose blows!"

Provide a tissue for each child to include in his or her nose book. Talk about the importance of using tissues, and explain that they need to be used to prevent germs from spreading to others.

A child may not "sniff" until he is two years old, or older. Sniffing a few safe fragrances can be an interesting experience for middle and older preschoolers. The item to sniff should not be powdery. For example, cinnamon stick is preferable to powdered cinnamon for sniffing. A soap wrapper is safer than a soap bar. A flower must be free of insects before it is sniffed. As a child enjoys smelling a flower, say: "Thank you, God, for a nose. Thank you for the fragrant flower (soap, cinnamon)."

Place short strands of yarn in a Bible at the following Bible phrases: "God made us" (Ps. 100:3); "I am wonderfully made" (Ps. 139:14); "God gave us ears to hear and eyes to see (nose to smell)" (Prov. 20: 12). Sit on the floor with the Bible on your lap during activity time or group time. Help a child open the Bible to a marker. Point to the Bible verse. Say the Bible phrase from the verse. Talk about it. The child may be able to say the Bible phrase.

Rest and relaxation comes easier for older preschoolers as they learn proper breathing. Ask them to sit up straight with their arms at their sides. Say: "Close your lips. Breathe in v-e-r-y slowly through your nose. Now, open your lips and breathe out v-e-r-y slowly through your mouth." Repeat the instructions until the children get the idea of the exercise.

This relaxing exercise (game) is calming when preschoolers are lying on their backs with their arms to their sides and their legs straight. Try the exercise when children become restless or rowdy. Do not make it a punishment, but say, "Boys and girls, let's play our relaxing game."

Personal Learning Activities

1. The breathing exercise suggested for preschoolers helped me face a tense situation last week when _____

_____

_____ .

Deep breathing can help you when you face a tense situation during the day. It can help you turn off the daily activities at night.

2. A Louisville pediatrician has a bulletin board displaying items he has taken out of small noses. Be nosey: carefully check the room and storage spaces for items that could get into small noses. Discard, or box and label the items with: "Warning! These are items young children might put into their noses or mouths." Items I discarded included:

_____

_____

_____

_____ .

WHY DID GOD MAKE MOUTHS?

"To hold our teeth from falling out!"
"And to hold our tongue."
"To smile."
"To kiss and to whistle."
"To make our voice come out."
"A mouth is to open."

Infants respond to your facial expressions. Smile. Use your mouth to make exaggerated lip movements and sounds. Demonstrate the correct way to make words come out of their mouths. Speak softly and enunciate your words clearly.

A child puts things into his mouth to feel, to explore, or because of teething. When a toddler bites another child, do not assume it is mean-spirited. Biting is probably to soothe toddlers' teething gums, to explore with his mouth, or to "taste" the other child. Give the biting child a clean, safe teether. Say: "You cannot bite Heather. You may bite this." Redirect the biting child to something else of interest — a book, puzzle, doll, waterplay, etc.

Thumb-sucking is a part of mouthing. It also represents security, comfort, and an escape from boredom for a child. Do not call attention to thumb-sucking. Do provide choices of a few age-appropriate, interesting books and manipulative toys. Stack 'm Up Cups, Wobbly Fun Ball, or the book *Let's Play* can get the toddler's attention.

Toys, or anything children might put their mouths on or around, must be clean and safe. Any item that can pass through a toilet tissue tube can also go into the throat and choke a child. Supervise small, "swallowable" items well, or keep them out of preschoolers' reach.

The mouth can indicate feelings. Pictures of smiling children, pouting children, or angry children can be used as you teach about feelings. Say, "Is this child happy or sad?" Or, say: "Point to a smiling face. Point to a sad face." Ask children to make their mouths show happy, sad, and mad feelings.

Food tasting is an appropriate experience to use when you are talking about the importance of the mouth. As you plan food-tasting experiences with middle or older preschoolers, be sure there are no food allergies. Use only one food for a tasting experience. The food needs to be nutritious and safe from choking. Puzzles "Easy Fruit" or "Vegetables" give opportunities to talk about healthy foods with young preschoolers.

Reading the book *The Lunch Box Surprise* is a delightful way to introduce a session about food.

Older fives may be stressed about teeth loss. Make these losses pluses. Teach healthy care of teeth. Each middle and older preschooler needs a toothbrush. Direct brushing teeth after eating, especially if the child is in a weekday program all day.

Take children outdoors and suggest they watch each other use their lips to blow soap bubbles. After they blow bubbles, mouths usually turn into smiles. Mingle the floating bubbles with "The Bubble Song" (p. 70, *'Specially Special Songs*).

Girls and boys enjoy using their mouths to make soft and loud sounds, sing, whisper, or whistle. After demonstrations by those who choose to make sounds, sing, whisper, or whistle, remind children how wonderfully God has made each one of them. Ask children to put their hands on their laps, close their eyes, and listen. Then, thank God for making each person special.

Personal Learning Activities

1. Read at least one article in a current publication on children and biting. The main points of the article are _____
_____
_____
_____
_____
_____
_____.

2. Work with all leaders from other church programs, such as Mission Friends, music, Sunday School, and make the room "mouthing" clean and safe. I met with _____, on _____, and we decided to _____ _____ _____.

WHY DID GOD MAKE HANDS?

"To clap and wave."
"Hands are to pat people."
"Hands are for holding onto so you won't fall off."
"Hands are so you can paint and stuff."
"You can fix puzzles with your hands."
"See, I can hold my hands up high!"

Catch moments when a child is using her hands in a positive way. Commend the child, "Thank you, Leah, for using your hands to put away the blocks." "Thank you, Cameron, for using your hands to help Zach pick up the crayons."

The hands-on (bodily/kinesthetic) learner requires creative activities, so hands and body, as well as eyes and ears, are used. Sitting and listening is not easy, especially for the learner who likes to move and work with his hands. God encourages using the hands. "Make it your ambition to work with your hands" (I Thes. 4:11, NIV).

Learning Centers (for twos through fives) must provide for the hands-on children (and most are) to touch, feel, handle, push, pull, clap, pound, make, and build. Results: fewer behavioral problems, much more learning. Refer to chapters 7 and 17 for more information about Learning Centers.

Older preschoolers can have a good experience in manners as you teach them introductions with a handshake. Say, "Hello, my name is (Ms. Margie)" and extend your hand. Guide girls and boys in introducing a friend and encourage the friend to extend her hand. Say, "Hands are for shaking and meeting new friends."

A toddler may begin to show a right or left-hand preference according to her brain design. She will, however, use both hands more than one alone. Share the book *I Touch* with toddlers.

Play a game to help older preschoolers with left and right awareness. Form a circle and hold hands.

Give a gentle squeeze to the hand at your right as you say, "Right." That child passes on the squeeze with his right hand. Each child squeezes until the squeeze comes back to your left hand. Then, squeeze the hand to your left as you say, "Left." The child to your left passes on the squeeze.

Learn these hand songs: "Clapping" and "I Love to Clap My hands" (pp. 17 and 37, *'Specially Special Songs*).

With older preschoolers, sing a familiar song such as "Mary Had a Little Lamb." Sing it again and replace a word with a clap. Continue as children are able to follow the idea of substituting a clap for a word.

Finger games increase hand dexterity. Involve older preschoolers in singing "Ten Little Children" to the tune of "Ten Little Indians." Ask girls and boys to hold out both hands with fingers extended. Begin with a thumb, and as each number is sung, that number thumb or finger is brought into the palm of the hand.

One little, two little, three little children,
Four little, five little, six little children,
Seven little, eight little, nine little children,
Ten little children in bed.

Sing it again, and as each number is sung, that number finger straightens. The last line is "Ten lift up their heads."

"Two Little Blackbirds" and "Where Is Thumbkin?" (pp. 78 and 85, *'Specially Special Songs*) are good songs to sing with any-aged preschooler.

Ask children to tell, or show, good ways to use hands. Remind them that touching should be gentle and easy.

Show preschoolers the proper way to wash their hands: Soap well, scrub, rinse well, dry, and place paper towel in the trash. Hands need to be washed after using the restroom and before eating. Ask for the children to tell you other times that hands may need to be washed.

Ways preschoolers strengthen their hand and finger muscles include: handling and manipulating toys, working puzzles, building with blocks, creating with play dough, using finger paints, and using large brushes and large crayons on large paper.

Turning pages in a book requires hand-and-finger dexterity. Teach children at an early age to turn the pages in books and the Bible very gently. Say: "This is the Bible. We use our hands to turn the pages very carefully." Say, "Thank you for turning the pages carefully," when you see a child doing so as he looks at a book.

Personal Learning Activities

1. Use your hands to make a book. For each "page," cut the front of a cereal box into a rectangle or square, defining the picture on the box. Cut each rectangle or square the same size. Stack the cardboard pages like a book. Punch two holes at the binding side of the pages. Run short pieces of yarn or twine through the matching holes and tie the pages together.

2 Preschoolers enjoyed the cereal-box book when they _____

_____.

3 A teacher should wash her hands when

_____

_____.

WHY DID GOD MAKE FEET?

"To run very fast."
"To walk and run."
"Also, to hop and
    jump."
"To wear shoes."

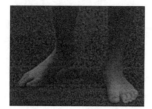

"Feet are where your toes are."
"Feet tickle."

An infant's feet are often free of shoes and socks. Discovering his feet is a major milestone for baby. Opening his mouth and inserting his toe is dually satisfying. It gives pleasure. It occupies time. Gently touch the baby's feet and talk about feet. Say: "In the Bible we read 'God made us.' God made Billy. God made Billy's feet." Say, "Feet are for walking, and one day Billy will walk!"

Applaud the young child who is just learning to stand on her feet. What an accomplishment! The floor needs to be safe from obstacles, and very clean, when young children are crawling and standing in pursuit of walking.

Give as much space as possible to the toddling child. Child-sized tables, chairs, or other chin-high obstacles can be more of a detriment than a joy for a toddler. A child with the new skill of walking may follow her feet without noticing where she is going. Become the eyes for the child in her newly-expanded mobility.

Provide safe textures for small bare feet to touch. A square of velvet or satin, sand, or shallow water in a plastic pan feels good to the touch. Sit on the floor. Hold Marta on your lap and let her feet touch the different textures, the water, or the sand. Sing "I Am Very Special" (p. 34, *Specially Special Songs*). Say: "God made you special. He made your feet. You are wonderfully made."

Say, "Thank you for walking in the room," to those who do. Commending the walking child will encourage other children to walk, rather than run in the room. "We *walk* in the room," is often needed.

Feet have to learn to hop, skip, and jump — according to each child's individual growth. Four-year-old Julie was hopping on her right foot. Her teacher asked her if she could hop on her other foot. Julie replied: "No. It's too heavy." As Julie's body grows, her other foot will not be "too heavy."

For healthy growth, physical activity must be a big part of the preschoolers' day. During outdoor play suggest (according to age and ability), "Let's run, (jump, skip, hop) to the fence." Involve older preschoolers in "Keeping the Steady Beat" or "All Fall Down" (pp. 8 and 49, *Specially Special Songs*). For a calming effect, sit in the shade and show the books *Busy Feet* and *Shoes* as you read them.

During outdoor play or group time, ask girls and boys to pretend they are walking barefoot on a hot sidewalk, or through grass, or in mud or sand. They might pretend they are walking barefoot in snow.

As in eye development and hearing, a child's motor skills mature according to his or her God-given blueprint. According to Ames and Ilg of the Gesell Institute, a growth spurt (disequilibrium) can interfere with the mobile steadiness the child had just a few months earlier, and he can become temporarily clumsy and awkward again.

Rejoice in their feelings of freedom as preschoolers (steadily or unsteadily) express their many ways of mobility. Make way for boys and girls to put their wonderfully-made feet into action, and their whole bodies will benefit.

After outdoor play, ask preschoolers to tell ways they used their eyes, ears, nose, mouth, hands, or feet as they played. Remind the children that God made their eyes to see, ears to hear, nose to smell, mouth to eat, hands to clap, and feet to run.

Personal Learning Activities

1. Read 1 Corinthians 12:14-26. The body is more than one member. Consider God's special design for our physical bodies. Which sense or physical ability do you enjoy most and how? (Example: listening to music, walking in a garden, talking with a friend)

   _____
   _____
   _____
   _____
   _____
   _____.

2. How well are you caring for your eyes, ears, nose, mouth, hands, and feet? I plan

to take care of my body by _____

   _____
   _____
   _____
   _____
   _____.

WONDERFULLY-MADE CHILDREN WITH SPECIAL NEEDS

The book *The Lunch Box Surprise* tells two stories. One story is in words. The other story is in the depicting of a variety of children: Dan has red hair and freckles; brown-toned Jan has black, curly hair; Pam is in a wheelchair; Asian Kim has black hair but no curls; ditto for Max. Max, Kim, Jan, Dan, and Pam all help their good friend Sam. Pam's wheelchair is no more significant to these friends than are freckles, brown-tone skin, or curly or straight hair.

How wise you are to help preschoolers know that all children are wonderfully made, no matter how they are shaped, what color they are, how they are mobile, or how they communicate.

Certainly some children have greater challenges than do others. With great challenges children often adapt and become "more" than some who are not as challenged.

• At age five, Nick had a leg amputated because of bone cancer. As an adult, he is an avid skier.

- As a child, Olivia had a speech impediment. As an adult, Olivia delivers the nightly news on TV.
- Warren was born deaf. As an adult, he completed graduate school and is now doing research for a chemical company.
- A child who was known to be hyperactive before hyper was medicated, is now a well-known minister.
- Steve, Caroline, Josh, and others were "gold medal" winners in this year's Special Olympics.

Never give up on a child! Meeting special needs may require:

1. getting someone to be with the challenged child for individual guidance
2. finding out all you can about a specific disease, handicap, or giftedness
3. working closely with the child's family
4. early intervention

"Scientists are discovering just how dramatically the rapidly-growing brain of a small child is influenced by his environment. In the case of children who are injured or born with a disability, doctors are learning more daily about how starting treatment early — often in infancy — can have a huge impact."[3]

Give each child respect, acknowledgment of his importance, and opportunities to be successful (even in small ways). Each child truly is wonderfully made.

The active child is not always ADD. When a group of adults are asked to describe preschoolers with only one word, that word is usually active or busy. Why? Because active best describes how preschoolers are designed. God intended little bodies to move so they would develop into bigger bodies.

ADD (Attention Deficit Disorder) and AD/HD (Attention Deficit/Hyperactivity Disorder) are words familiar to parents and teachers. Some children are labeled ADD or AD/HD (and medicated), and sometimes without proper diagnosis.

Certainly there are children who need medication for hyperactivity. But, parents, teachers, and doctors may be mistaking too many wonderfully-made, "nature-ly" active preschoolers as hyper.

"Children as young as one year old are being diagnosed with attention deficit/hyperactivity disorder, and doctors are treating supposedly hyperactive toddlers with drugs including Ritalin, Clonidine, and Prozac, a Michigan researcher has found."[4]

Here are some characteristics of children who can be "hyper" without being ADD or AD/HD:

- the curious child who is too young to reason or understand, and who goes about in her new-found joyous mobility
- the child who is given too many "Nos" and not enough positive choices
- the gifted child who is expected to conform to adult's art or music concept and not allowed to create from within

- the highly-intelligent child who is not challenged to his or her capacity
- the bored child who needs more choices
- the immature child who may be the age of his peers but who has not emotionally or mentally caught up — but will, if given time and not "labeled" slow
- the child with a personality that conflicts with the adult in control
- the child whose learning style is not taken into consideration
- the child whose family is dysfunctional or temporarily disrupted
- and, yes, even pinworms can cause hyperactivity!

If all the above factors are considered, and none relates to the child, a child development medical expert in hyperactivity may need to be consulted.

Being prepared to teach the hyperactive child will benefit all children:[5]

- Arrive early and be prepared before the first child arrives.
- Establish good eye contact with the child when giving instructions.
- Provide consistent routine and structure.
- Get to know the child; find his strengths and build on them.
- Be flexible but do not get into "negotiating" with the child.
- Be consistent with classroom rules.
- Give positive feedback to help build the child's self-esteem.
- Stay calm even when the child is emotional or disruptive.

- Tell the child what to do rather than what not to do.
- Spend time alone with the child when possible.
- Plan active learning as well as quiet activities.
- Share positive experiences with parents.
- Commend the child's good behavior immediately and enthusiastically by being specific with your affirmation.

Meeting needs of the gifted child can benefit all children. It means children will have choices!

The younger, gifted preschooler needs choices of toys, books, Blockbusters, and the choice to move about safely as his curiosity and abilities allow. The older, gifted preschooler will be able to express her level of artistic abilities if the Art Center is properly equipped with materials for creative expression. Access to musical instruments (such as an Autoharp) allows all children to enjoy, create, and compose as talents dictate.

The older preschooler will appreciate a Writing Center with markers; large, easy-grip pencils; and large paper. The gifted, as well as the less-gifted child, will have a choice to manipulate writing tools at his level. A computer in the Writing Center may attract some gifted children, but not all. Interest and development determine computer savvy.

Meeting needs of the mentally-challenged child can benefit all children. The mentally-challenged child enjoys Learning Centers, too. An assigned adult may need to assist the child in use of hands and materials. Encourage other children, especially the mentally gifted, or the take-charge personality, to assist the child who needs help. Helping the mentally challenged to care for a doll, or showing her a book, becomes a learning experience for both children.

Meeting the needs of the physically-challenged child can benefit all children. State regulations benefit the physically-challenged child by making public buildings accessible. The room where you teach must also be easy for the physically-challenged (mentally and visually) child to move around. Keep clear paths and open spaces for all children to move about easily.

Meeting needs of the older, visually-challenged preschooler, or the older preschooler with immature finger dexterity, can benefit all children. Provide loop, left-handed, or double-ring scissors. Glue sticks are easier to use than glue bottles. Large crayons and brushes are needed when finer finger muscles are underdeveloped.

The visually-limited child needs more stimulation through her senses of hearing and touching. Tape-recorded books and music are valuable for the visually-impaired — and other children. The gifted child, the auditory learner, or the take-charge personality may want to help with the tape player. Cooperation benefits both children.

The visually-impaired may need guidance in a touching tour of the room. Ask a visual learner to help the visually-impaired child become familiar with the room. Do not change the arrangement of the room during the year unless necessary. If it does become necessary, advise the visually impaired with a touching tour.

Children begin to learn non-discrimination and appreciation for others now. Teach children to be aware of their own abilities. Teach them to see the accomplishments (great or small) of other children.

"For you created my inmost being; you knit me together in my mother's womb. I praise you because I am fearfully and wonderfully made; your works are wonderful, I know that full well" (Ps. 139: 13-14, NIV).

Personal Learning Activities

1. List the names of children you teach. By each child's name write two positive attributes of that child. Add more as the year progresses.

   _____
   _____
   _____
   _____
   _____
   _____
   _____
   _____
   _____
   _____

2. Get the book *Love, Laughter and Learning*[6] for more information about the special needs child.

"When I was a child, I talked like a child, I thought like a child, I reasoned like a child . . . ." (1 Corinthians 13:11, NIV).

Chapter 6

Characteristics and Needs

God designed each child so uniquely that no child fits squarely in the middle of any set of characteristics during any age or stage. No one can predict a child's personality, his or her abilities, or the speed at which each child will travel toward maturity. However, educators, psychologists, and parents have observed and studied children as they grow. There is a consensus that children develop through each age or stage, demonstrating similar characteristics.

The child enters a stage in development and reacts physically, mentally, and emotionally according to her God-given nature, the people she encounters, her experiences, and her environment.

Each child's growth-pattern will rise and level off, but it usually stays somewhere within the normal range of growth.

Researchers in the Gesell Institute of Child Development[1] call the rise and leveling of a child's growth pattern "disequilibrium and equilibrium."

Disequilibrium (a state of unrest and growth) occurs at approximately 18 months, two and one-half years, three and one-half years, and four and one-half years.

Equilibrium (a state of balance and slowing of growth) occurs at approximately two years, three years, four years, and five years.

Within the realm of disequilibrium, the child's actions tend to be erratic. The intensity of this state will depend on the individual's nature (personality). During equilibrium the child is more at peace with himself.

Florence Littauer illustrates personality characteristics in her book *Raising Christians — Not Just Children*.[2] She describes four basic personalities: the Popular, the Powerful, the Perfectionist, and the Peaceful. Children often begin to show specific personality traits even as preschoolers.

Each personality is wonderful! All are happier when teachers and parents recognize each child's personality and "train up" the child in the way *his* or *her* personality should go.

All children have basic needs. Those needs include:

- LOVE: "God is love" (1 John 4: 16b, NIV). As you love a child, you build trust in adults which lays a foundation for a child to accept Christ later, through faith. Read 1 Corinthians 13:4-8a for a true meaning of love.

- ACCEPTANCE: Accept each child as she is — in size, actions, personality, and characteristics. In acceptance you can help guide each child to become his or her own best self.

- SECURITY: Children are so vulnerable and so trusting. They expect, and rightly so, that adults will take care of them. Every precaution must be taken so the environment, personnel, and safety guidelines benefit each child at all times.

- DISCIPLINE: Discipline means to "disciple." Your example of kind speech, gentle actions, and positive guidance is the best method for disciplining children. Children can learn self-control from age-appropriate activities and an environment with consistent positive guidelines.

Personal Learning Activities

1. List the basic needs of children:
   _____,
   _____,
   _____, and
   _____.

2. I express love to children in the following ways:

   _____
   _____
   _____
   _____
   _____
   _____
   _____
   _____

3. Three ways I guide preschoolers positively are:
   (1) _____
   _____
   (2) _____
   _____
   (3) _____
   _____

YOUNG INFANTS NEED COMFORT[3]

A comfortable child is a happy child. The need for comfort is physical, mental, and emotional.

Physical Characteristics of Young Infants

A child develops from the head (brain) down the spinal column and outward. The mouth (sucking), the eyes (looking at you), and head (moving side to side) develop the earliest. Control of arms, legs, hands, and fingers follow.

Longer waking hours display the rapid development of a young child. By three months she smiles and moves what she can in response to familiar voices and faces. Her eyes can steadily follow a close object or a person of interest. Large motor skills are evident as a baby makes deliberate movements of her arms, hands, legs, and feet. Soon she enjoys playing with her hands and fingers and reaches for toys, indicating the developing of finer motor skills.

By six to eight months, rolling over is easy. When she is on her stomach, "turtle" movements begin mobility. Sitting should be steady.

Meet physical needs by providing a safe, comfortable environment. Supply tender touches, cozy snuggling, rocking, and soft sounds of music. Help a new baby adjust to his expanded environment outside his mother's womb.

A child's up-to-date schedule, taped to the end of his bed, enables teachers to meet his needs more efficiently.

Mental Characteristics of Young Infants

Technology has literally opened a window into the brain. Television news hour and the computer allow the world to peek into that window. Researchers can look directly into the brain and see a child's thinking in motion without harm to the child. Studies show that an infant's brain is far more formidable than anyone had imagined. What you *do* and *say* can "imprint" the brain!

"Baby's brain doubles in weight in the first year due not only to the growth in the number of brain cells but to the connections between them. These connections begin to form only when the baby has to 'think' about something."[4]

Meet mental (cognitive) needs by giving baby something to "think" about. Sing, talk, and show pictures and colorful toys to a baby. Place a colorful mobile over his bed. Brain stimulation is essential from birth onward.

Emotional and Social Characteristics of Young Infants

The very young express anger, excitement, distress, or the need for attention through crying. They express joy and satisfaction more obviously as they grow older. At two months, a baby may smile spontaneously; by three months he will be smiling deliberately at others. His social life has begun!

At four months a baby becomes more communicative and expressive with his face and body. He soon begins using two-syllable, babbling sounds in his effort to communicate. Responsive sounds of coos, chuckles, gurgles, and laughs are evidence of his feelings about his comfort with life. He enjoys the play of peek-a-boo and pat-a-cake and may cry when the playing stops.

Meet emotional and social needs by cuddling a child when he needs it and sometimes when he does not. How you react to a baby's emotional and social needs can help determine the child's development. Positive reactions encourage a baby to respond easily. Negative reaction, or no reactions, can cause him to become less responsive.

Socialize with a baby when you are near him, and as you care for physical needs. Sing quietly to him. Turn your face into happy and funny expressions for him. Watch him respond.

Spiritual Characteristics of Young Infants

Spiritual development only comes as a foundation is built. View the spiritual characteristic of a baby as her ability to feel the comfort and love that surrounds her.

Meet the spiritual needs of babies by showing they can trust you to meet their physical and emotional needs. Begin to build a spiritual foundation by singing and talking about God, Jesus, the Bible, and church.

Personal Learning Activities

1. Describe six (or more) characteristics of the young infant.

   _____

   _____

   _____

   _____

   _____

   _____

2. List three reasons for keeping each baby's schedule up-to-date.

   _____

   _____

   _____

   _____

   _____

   _____

OLDER INFANTS NEED CONSISTENCY

Consistency in schedule, caregivers, and guidance will help make life pleasant and secure for the older infant.

Physical Characteristics of Older Infants

Large motor skills begin developing the infant into a scooting, crawling, then toddling investigator, usually within the eight to fourteen-month span. The child's horizons are broadening. He is like a butterfly out of a cocoon, darting from one sweet experience to another. His new mobility knows no bounds. Normal, natural activity is expanding rapidly!

The activity of pushing and pulling, and putting things into and taking them out of a container, reflects a baby's growing physical ability. His finer motor skills have progressed to the use of both hands together in accomplishing a task. Grasping with his fingers, eating finger foods, and drinking from a cup are milestones for this age.

Standing and climbing show that the young child's gross motor skills are developing as God intended at the months around year one.

Meet physical needs by reducing the number of toys and obstacles in the child's mobility space. Encourage crawling. Crawling helps develop eye-hand coordination in readiness for reading! A few durable manipulative toys aid in the development of a baby's hands, arms, and body.

Play music, sing, and clap for the joy of the newly-mobile child. He may respond with giggles and body movements. Pat-a-cake and peek-a-boo are still favorite games, but now the child may try to imitate the actions.

Mental Characteristics of Older Infants

Michael was shown flowers in hanging pots on the porch many times during the months before he was verbal. In the autumn the hanging pots of flowers were taken down. It was not until the next spring that pots of flowers were hung on the porch again. Toddling Michael, now verbal, saw the flowers and said, "The flowers are back!"

The experience with Michael indicates that the non-verbal child understands what he sees before he can talk about it. Before he can speak, the young child can follow directions like, "Bring me the book." He knows a comb goes with his hair and a toothbrush into his mouth. He can look at, or put his hand on, the correct picture or object when it is named.

The one-year-old can say a few words. He can name some objects. One word can mean a full sentence. "Blankey," may mean: "I see my blanket." "Where is my blanket?" or "I want my blanket!"

Meet mental needs by providing an environment that says, "Come and explore." Mobility is a priority. So, make floor space

more available than "stuff." Access to a few books, a Bible, a teaching picture, and a big-piece puzzle gives opportunities for mental stimulation. A few, durable toys provide physical joy without cluttering floor space. Spend time sitting on the floor with the child. Occasionally capture the moving child with interest in a book, the Bible, or a picture. Sing and talk to the older infant. Imprint his growing brain with good information.

Emotional and Social Characteristics of Older Infants

The older infant can show fear, anger, joy, and affection. Fear of separation and strangers may occur around the eight to fourteen-month span. These fears may surface because of the child's increasing awareness of other people and his broadening environment.

A child's personality can play a part in his ability to accept separation and people he does not know. There are children who, by nature, like people and new experiences. There are also individuals that seem, from early life, to be wary of new faces and new places.

Meet emotional and social needs by suggesting that a parent allow the child experiencing separation syndrome to bring a "security" blanket or toy from home.

Do not let the parent slip away from a crying child. Ask Daddy to say a happy: "Bye-bye. I will be back." and leave! You say, "Daddy will be back." Talk or sing soothingly to the child as you get him involved with a favorite book or toy.

Your calm, easy manner will enable a child to feel better emotionally. An interesting, age-appropriate room will help the young child adjust to separation and his expanding environment.

Spiritual Characteristics of Older Infants

Older infants like sameness. Seeing the same teachers in his room at the weekday program, and at his church, is very important. A new face (stranger) can create anxiety and fear. The young child needs to build trust. When a child learns to trust his teachers to be in his room when he arrives, his spiritual foundation is strengthened.

Meet spiritual needs by being prompt, prepared, present, and prayerful as you care for infants.

Personal Learning Activities

1. Six characteristics of the older infant are:

   _____

   _____

   _____

   _____

   _____

   _____

2. Why is it important for you to be at the same height of the child as you speak to him?

TODDLERS SEEK COMPETENCE

It is not easy being a toddler. Competency seems to be her goal, but getting there is strewn with bumps, falls, limitations, and frustrations.

Physical Characteristics of Toddlers

The ages fourteen to twenty-four months are usually the toddling time for preschoolers. Some little bodies and minds take longer meeting the "average" abilities than others. Judge each child by his or her own God-given blueprint of development.

The child new at toddling holds her hands out from her sides for balance. Holding, dropping, and throwing toys and other objects show a toddler's improved motor skills. Climbing up stairs is great fun for toddlers; getting down is not!

A toddler is ready to indulge in the essence of life as she goes from unsteady toddling to running, jumping, and climbing.

Meet physical needs by protecting toddlers from doors and drawers that might close on fingers and from "stuff" that may cause a fall. Provide safe indoor and outdoor places for toddling, walking, running, jumping, and climbing.

Because of a toddler's desire to keep on the move, a schedule alternating between activities and quiet times is needed. It may mean sitting with one or more children and sharing books or listening to quiet music.

Mental Characteristics of Toddlers

Remember Michael and the hanging pots of flowers? He was taking more into his mind as a non-verbal child than he could send out. The children you are teaching have learned much more than they can tell. They will continue to mentally build on what you teach.

Curiosity is essential for mind growth. It is a reason a toddler "gets into everything." The more curious child may be the more intelligent child. Toddlers' tools of exploration are sight, sound, smell, taste, and touch. Their world is rapidly expanding and changing. They are hurrying to keep up and to make sense through their senses.

Meet mental needs by affirming and helping toddlers put their thoughts into words. When they attempt to verbalize, listen. Say words to them in clear enunciation.

Regularly say the names of teachers and other friends for toddlers. They will be able to put a name to a face before they can speak the name. Help them name objects, body parts, and pictures of animals. Help toddlers "read" books, work puzzles, and explore the outdoors.

Emotional and Social Characteristics of Toddlers

Toddlerhood has the first disequilibrium jolt. There are times of sweetness and calm among the screams and demands of this self-centered, amazing creature.

Emotionally, toddlers can be very negative. "No" is a favorite word. Perhaps it is because the word gets so much attention. Disequilibrium may be the reason. Negativism may stem from a toddler's "want to" (mental ability) getting ahead of her "can do" (physical ability). This is often the reason for tantrums. Or, she is unable to verbalize what she wants, and a tantrum occurs.

A toddler's social life is still mostly poking, pulling, and pushing her peers. "Mine" is becoming more meaningful to the toddler. "Yours" is not. At times a toddler will mimic other children and sway, turn, and tumble as they do. This age child still enjoys socializing with adults who play with her and make her the center of attention. Physical affection is shown in response to the affection of others.

Meet emotional and social needs through patience and redirection. Because of a very short attention span, toddlers' periods of negativism can be short. Wait. It may be over soon. Calling attention to a child's negative behavior often increases the negative behavior. Toddlers cannot reason. Redirecting their attention to something they enjoy can ease a negative situation or tantrum.

"Me do it" is a toddler's step toward independence. Give him time. Then, give help if needed.

"No" can be reduced considerably if adults do not ask questions that can be answered with "No," unless "No" is an acceptable choice.

Spiritual Characteristics of Toddlers

A toddler is developing an attitude toward church. She may be happy going into her room at church. Or, she may show separation frustration. Teachers *are* "church" to the young child. Teachers who bond well with toddlers make "church" better for them.

Toddlers are beginning to recognize the Bible as a special book. Jesus and God may be familiar words to them. Toddlers may touch a picture of Jesus when you talk about Jesus.

Meet spiritual needs by singing and using short stories or conversations about church, Jesus, God, and the Bible. Your Christian example to the toddler and her family is the best "church" any toddler can have.

Personal Learning Activities

1. Six characteristics of toddlers are:

   _____
   _____
   _____
   _____
   _____
   _____

2. Three positive ways teachers can help toddlers gain competence are:

   _____
   _____
   _____
   _____
   _____

Twos Gain Control

The two-year-old is beginning to gain control of his body, his motor skills, his language, and his parents!

Physical Characteristics of Twos

Potty trained? Maybe, maybe not. The individual, God-given blueprint is crucial here. Potty learning can only be accomplished when a child's neuro-muscular system has developed enough to control his bladder and bowels.

Twos can take off shoes. Some twos can take off clothing. They cannot put them back on. Getting the right body part lined up to the right apparel opening is too challenging. Buttons and fasteners are too intricate for twos' fingers.

Motor skills of mobility are becoming more stable, but there are still signs of awkwardness. Yet, a two's speed is amazing for his size. He hurries along, touching, exploring, listening to, smelling, and tasting his environment.

The child's two-and-one-half-year disequilibrium can affect his eating, sleeping, mobility, and vision for a time, which certainly affects his emotions and behavior.

Meet physical needs by not pressuring for potty training. A conflict in management can occur between potty training and talking. This is a critical time for making words into sense and sentences. To expect him to also concentrate on, and manage, his bladder and bowel functions is too much! Gentle guidance toward potty training will enable twos to do what comes naturally when their neuromuscular systems are ready. *Toilet Learning* is a helpful book for the child and adult to "read" together.

A two's disequilibrium may cause times of food aversion. Trying to force a two-year-old to eat can be a bitter battle, and the forcer often loses. Provide small servings of nutritional food, and do not give attention to "not eating."

A busy board of locks, buckles, snaps, and zippers will help strengthen the small muscles in the two's hands and fingers and his eye-hand coordination.

Like his former self, the two still needs more "unstructure" than structure, more movement than quiet, more doing than listening, and an environment that provides for exploration and choices.

Mental Characteristics of Twos

Two-year-olds begin to "think things through," rather than going by trial and error. They have a short attention span, but if they are really interested in something they stay with it much longer than they did a few months earlier. Twos are still mostly in the here and now. As they get closer to the third year, their minds will comprehend a broader span of both time and space. Twos will also begin their trek into numbers. The number "two" is significant, and all sums may be "two" for a time.

The younger two is speaking in three or four-word "sentences." By the time he is through this year, he will be speaking in "paragraphs." "Vocabulary increases to more than five-hundred words during the year."[5]

Meet mental needs by capturing twos inquisitive attention with creative art materials, blocks, books, puzzles, and musical and manipulative toys. Answer twos' many questions simply and clearly.

Accept twos' inadequate pronunciations. Ignore stuttering. Give the child time. He will improve. Enunciate your words clearly as a good example.

Emotional and Social Characteristics of Twos

Two is often in emotional disharmony with himself and others. He carries over some of his toddler traits of tantrums and negativism. However, a two-year-old can be such a joy. How much joy may depend on how adults interact positively or how they over-react negatively.

The two-year-old still does not play "with" another child, but he can play alongside a child. He enjoys being with his peers. He is beginning to understand the meaning of taking turns and sharing.

The disequilibrium of the two-and-a-half-year-old is a shake-up of his very being. It brings vacillation between affection, anger, jealousy, frustration, fear, delight, independence, and dependence. "No" is automatic.

Tell a two not to do something, and it may become an irresistible challenge — he may do that very thing! Ask him to hurry and he may slow down.

Meet emotional and social needs by telling a two more of what he *can* do rather than what he *cannot* do. Twos love attention any way they can get it. Give attention to the good times. Ignore negativism. Redirect. Hug the tantrum child, and if that does not work, ignore the tantrum. Be positive. Make statements rather than ask yes or no questions. "It is time to put on your coat," will get a better result than, "Do you want to put on your coat?"

Twos are ready for simplified Learning Centers. The activities and social togetherness in the Centers help keep twos emotionally and socially content.

Spiritual Characteristics of Twos

Observe twos and you may see some of the following spiritual characteristics:[6]

- Enjoys holding and looking at the Bible
- Recognizes the Bible as a special book
- Likes to hear age-appropriate songs and stories about God, Jesus, the Bible, and church
- Begins to recognize Jesus as a special person
- Begins to recognize that God loves people
- Likes to look at books and pictures about God, Jesus, the Bible, and church
- Enjoys many of the things God made in nature

Meet spiritual needs by placing a Bible where twos can handle it. Sing to a child as she carefully turns pages in the Bible. Tell short stories that relate to the Bible. Place Bible-related books in the Book Center. Share safe nature activities.

Personal Learning Activities

1. List six characteristics of twos:

   _____
   _____
   _____
   _____
   _____
   _____

2. Three Bible activities used with twos this week are:

   _____
   _____
   _____
   _____
   _____
   _____

THREES
DEVELOP IMAGINATION

The third year brings calm. Disequilibrium hits, but without the struggle to walk, talk, and make sense of others and the environment. Threes can give more time to socializing, pretending, creating, and (if needed) completing potty training.

Physical Characteristics of Threes

She is steady on her feet. She runs, jumps, climbs, tumbles, walks backward, and catches a ball. And she is proud of it. "Look at me!" is a call of her delight in physical accomplishments. There is a reason. The three's body is more balanced. The three-year-old is more capable of doing what she intends to do physically. She is nimble. She walks confidently and swings her arms with ease. Her coordination allows her to use her feet and hands to make this a tricycle year!

The disequilibrium around three-and-a-half brings some insecurity physically. Vision is affected during this physical growth. The older three may fear heights or complain she cannot see well and move closer to a book or picture.[7]

Improvement in finer motor skills allows the three to control her arms and hands better. She begins to paint more than up-and-down strokes. She can make large, crude circles. Later she may add eyes and a mouth to a circle, then add stick arms and legs. Creativity is ready to express itself!

Meet physical needs by providing a safe space to run, jump, and tumble. Provide low steps, slides, and inclines. Large boxes make inexpensive motor-skill exercisers. Make sand, mud, and water-play available for threes to enjoy.

Threes may see pictures in a book better by being alone and holding the book. A book nook or tent encourages privacy and book looking.

Large paper and large crayons or brushes are good art tools for threes' drawings or paintings.

Mental Characteristics of Threes

Threes recognize such concepts as big, little, up, down, where, there, here. A three-year-old can count one, two, three, or four blocks (and maybe more).

Growing imagination and creativity help the three-year-old child enjoy fun songs and rhymes. She likes make-believe. A three likes to create with art materials and building blocks. She pretends with dolls and house-keeping materials. There is an increase in vocabulary and in her ability to make complete sentences.

Monsters, "bad guys," animals, storms, and the dark may be troublesome fears of threes' growing imaginations. What happens on television is real.

Meet mental needs by helping threes count blocks or objects less than ten. During play, use directional words like *up, down, over,* and *under* as you relate the words to actions or objects.

Dress-up props in Homeliving, and transportation toys and wooden figures in the Block Center, lead to pretending.

Encourage threes to play out short stories you read or tell them. Threes may want to tell or play out stories of their own. Distinguish between pretend stories and stories from real life or the Bible. Bible stories are better understood by preschoolers if they are not in cartoon characters or cloaked in nursery rhymes. Literal-minded preschoolers have difficulty distinguishing theology from the fantasy.

If a child expresses a fear, talk about it calmly and reassuringly. Separate the fears of imaginary monsters that cannot harm the child and real dangers such as storms or fire that can. Regulated disaster drills, explained and conducted regularly, help ease preschoolers' fears.

The joy of wonder-filled Learning Centers can meet many needs of the growing minds of threes.

Emotional and Social Characteristics of Threes

Threes can talk and make conversation. They are becoming aware of the feelings of others. Both improvements make them emotionally and socially better company to themselves and to others.

Threes enjoy children their own age. Cooperation and give-and-take are not uncommon. The interaction can be very personal. The concept of "friends" becomes more meaningful. Also, excluding others from play (not friends at the time) may become evident.

The three-and-a-half-year-old is amidst a disequilibrium time, but this growth period

may not be as erratic as in the past. Now words may replace flaying hands and bodies. And some reasoning, not seen before, is possible. Sharing is often negotiated and agreed upon within a play setting. Threes are helpers and like to please. This is evident with peers as well as adults.

Meet emotional and social needs by giving these preschoolers opportunities to verbalize feelings. This may allow them to rid frustrations that caused earlier tantrums. Move calmly with threes.

They have progressed considerably in their emotional and social behavior in the last six months. Hurrying them may cause stuttering and a reversion to earlier, less stable behavior.

Spiritual Characteristics of Threes

A Bible was open on the floor in the book area. Dana sat beside it and began turning the pages. She stopped at a picture and said, as she pointed to the page, "Mary, Baby Jesus, and, and, and . . . ." Then, with great pleasure, she remembered and patted the page with, "Jofeth, Jofeth, Jofeth."

Threes can build a spiritual foundation if adults provide the spiritual ingredients.

Meet spiritual needs by using age-appropriate Bible stories and Bible activities. *Read-to-Me Bible for Kids* (Holman) contains pictures preschoolers like to see and touch.

Personal Learning Activities

1. List six (or more) characteristics of threes:

   _____

   _____

   _____

   _____

   _____

   _____

2. What are positive ways adults can relate to threes' developing imagination?

   _____

   _____

   _____

   _____

   _____

   _____

FOURS EXUDE CONFIDENCE

Out-of-bounds, cocky, confident, and *fearless* are words attached to fours. The blueprint built into his creation will determine to what extent each four meets the criteria.

Physical Characteristics of Fours

The maturing, physical characteristics blending across the body and face of the four-year-old replace baby characteristics seen earlier. Because of increased physical abilities, fours may get out-of-bounds with running, jumping, climbing, throwing, hitting, and yelling.

Finer motor skills now allow fours to fasten some fasteners and button some buttons. The four-year-old can comb his hair and brush his teeth. He uses scissors more accurately and paints and draws with more detail. However, his hands and fingers and eye-hand coordination are not yet mature enough to do close detail work. He can draw a person with a head, a body, and arms and legs. Hands and feet may be exaggerated because detailed digits are difficult.

Meet physical needs with outdoor space and freedom of movement. Tricycles, wagons, and safe climbing equipment help expend the four's energy. If space is limited, remove "things" and give more space for running, jumping, and tumbling.

Although some fours are very trustworthy, the natural out-of-boundness of fours requires careful supervision.

Mental Characteristics of Fours

Memory is good, especially remembering fun songs, silly rhymes, silly words, and his name, address, and phone number.

Time is more than the here and now. The four-year-old may know days of the week. He can speak of his last birthday or Christmas. He can talk about coming events and special days that include him.

The four knows colors beyond primary colors. He can do more than rote count by counting his fingers and objects up to ten or more. He understands such words as: *above, below, beside, behind, around, high, low, same* and *different*.

A four's imagination is so great that he may convince himself of a tale he tells. A bear in the backyard can be real to this child. He may tell an untruth (out-of-bounds), not with the intent to lie, but because he wants what he tells to be true. He may blame his imaginary friend for his own mischief. Some words of profanity or silly bathroom words become a fascination for fours.

Meet mental needs by enjoying the charm of this challenging child. Collect poems of fun and frolic with silly sounds and rhyming rhythms. Sing "All Fall Down" and "Lady Bug Tea" just for fun (pp. 8 and 50, *'Specially Special Songs*).

Answer the many questions from the four's inquiring mind or help him find the answers.

Profanity and naughty words are so prevalent in today's society that preschoolers should not be punished for repeating them. They are likely to repeat words they hear, but do not yet understand the meaning of those words. Calmly say, "That is a word we do not use." Or, "It is not good manners to use that word." Then direct the child to something more wholesome to think about.

Emotional and Social Characteristics of Fours

The four is so sure of himself that he can be obnoxious. He likes to brag (his imagina- tion is out-of-bounds) and almost believes what he tells. He feels strong and stands up for his rights. He likes to keep others in line and may become a tattler and bossy. But, he also likes to help others, especially his teachers.

The four-year-old understands taking turns and sharing but does not always do what he knows. He also understands coop- erative play. He likes to make up games and rules.

The four-year-old boy may plan to marry his mother. The four-year-old girl may plan to marry her father. Curiosity about sex and where babies come from is not uncommon at this age.

Some fears of earlier years are still pre- sent, but the four can now realize that mon- sters are make-believe. This child still needs reassurance about real fears.

Meet emotional and social needs by ap- preciating the four's leap toward indepen- dence. But, reassure and soothe when he needs to be dependent.

Commend fours when they work/play well together. Painting a mural, building a structure with blocks, or caring for pets or plants give you opportunities to recognize cooperation.

"What do you think?" is a response to use when a child asks about sex. Sometimes a child can answer his own question. When an answer is required, make it brief and honest.

You may need to give preschoolers opportunities to talk, draw, paint, or play out (using puppets) their fears. Give calm, sympathetic reassurances when a child is fearful.

Spiritual Characteristics of Fours

Fours can refer to stories in the Bible. Bible-related songs are enjoyed by this age. Finding markers used to locate Bible verses interests this age. They can recall and tell Bible stories. They can understand that Jesus was a baby and grew to be a man who helped others.

Some children at this age may be cocky in their response to theology by saying: "I don't love Jesus," or "I hate church."

Meet spiritual needs by being literal with fours. Talk, sing, and build activities around Bible stories. Help preschoolers build a strong foundation about Jesus.

Ignore negative comments fours make about church-related topics. You may begin a battle of words. Redirect attention to an activity. Be sure to give positive comments when fours pay attention!

Personal Learning Activities

1. List six (or more) characteristics of fours:

   _____
   _____
   _____
   _____
   _____
   _____

2. Some positive ways to teach Bible-related information to four-year-olds are:

   _____
   _____
   _____
   _____
   _____
   _____
   _____
   _____

Fives Desire Challenges

The five is more harmonious than ever before. She loves life and is positive and pleasing.

Physical Characteristics of Fives

A five's finer motor skills now allow greater dexterity in using scissors, art materials, blocks, small tools, and utensils. Large-muscle coordination allows fives to skip on alternate feet, turn somersaults, and maneuver tricycles and wagons deftly. Right or left-handedness is rather well-established. Eye-hand coordination is much improved for now.

During disequilibrium the five seems vulnerable to common illnesses. She becomes restless and awkward. Finer motor skills and visual perception tend to deteriorate for a time. During that "individual time," a child may become discouraged if pressured to do what her body will not allow.

" . . . the child frequently loses his visual orientation and may often reverse his numbers or letters. (This is one of the several reasons why we feel this is not a good age to teach reading or writing. It is just too confusing for the child to work with words and letters when he is already having trouble figuring out the order of things.)"[8]

Meet physical needs by respecting individual growth and development. Provide materials for creative-learning play in Centers and outdoors.

Hand preference is brain controlled. Adults need to accept hand preference without comment. However, be aware of boys and girls who prefer their left hands. Some adjustments may need to be made. Scissors for left hands are available. The left-handed child will work from a different perspective than the right-handed child, such as turning book pages, using art materials, and needing left elbow room at eating and work spaces.

Fives are capable helpers. Get preschoolers involved in clean up, and other tasks, by using positive guidance: "In five minutes it will be time to put away the blocks. Would you rather put away the big blocks or the little blocks first?" Or, "I saw some really good helpers yesterday. I wonder if they are here today!"

Mental Characteristics of Fives

The desire to learn new things indicates the five's readiness for a challenge. She has an expanding vocabulary nearing two thousand words![9] She may recognize letters and words in print. She may make letters at ran-

dom and, by five-and-one-half-years, be able to print her first name. Some fives may be able to print their first and last names.

Matching, sorting, and classifying hands-on objects are fun learning activities. Numbers are becoming more meaningful, especially as they relate to objects.

Fives recognize words, such as their names and other words that are meaningful to them. Curiosity, interest, and neuro-muscular development will enable some fives to read sentences.

The five-year-old is still literal-minded. He is beginning to separate real from pretend. It is still difficult to separate real and pretend on television.

Meet mental needs by providing "readiness" activities rather than academically-oriented skills or drills. A child needs to learn to *listen* before learning to read. A child needs to learn to *follow directions* before working problems on paper. A child needs to *have choices* before he can become a creative, independent thinker. Age-appropriate learning for preschoolers is best through play-related actions that correspond to their everyday world.

Preschoolers need fantasy and pretending. These are ways they can express and increase their creativity. It allows them ways to "escape" to anywhere. Separate fantasy from that which is "real" by reminding preschoolers that "Pretending is fun" or "This is a true story."

Emotional and Social Characteristics of Fives

When a person is happy within himself or herself, it shows emotionally and socially. So it is with the child of five. She is generally content within herself. She is able to give and take and has a sense of others' feelings. She interacts and shares.

This does not mean perfect behavior. There will be the time of disequilibrium, when life is juggled and reactions are erratic. The five, however, wants to be in control of her emotions, especially around adults. She may take out her frustrations in words rather than by physical attacks on her peers. Or, she may move away, even into isolation, when she is upset. Temper tantrums are rare.

Fives continue with a full range of emotions. Each child will surface any one of these emotions according to his or her own personality. Some children go smoothly along the various emotions; others react with drama or trauma.

Meet emotional and social needs by commending the five-year-old when she meets emotional and social challenges. Her verbal ability, her physical balance, her emotional leveling (for now), and her mental alertness make this a rather easy age to affirm. If she does not get affirmation, she asks for it. "Are you proud of me?" is a likely question. The five is growing in her ability to carry on conversations with peers and adults. Listen, enjoy, and learn!

Spiritual Characteristics of Fives

With a growing spiritual foundation, fives recognize that church is a special place where they learn about God, Jesus, and the Bible. They learn about loving others and that God and others love them. They learn about caring for things of nature.

Fives sing songs related to God, Jesus, church, and the Bible. They can recall Bible stories and Bible phrases that are meaningful to them. Fives can verbalize their own prayers, especially thank-you prayers for people and things in their lives.

Meet spiritual needs by teaching Bible stories, thoughts, and verses on the level of the literal-minded child. Fives are still trying to separate real from fantasy. Keep Bible teachings real, with age-appropriate stories from the Bible. When you mix Bible stories with make-believe stories, you lift make-believe to the level of Jesus, or you bring Jesus down to the level of make-believe.

Leading literal-minded preschoolers to want to obey the teachings of Jesus is more appropriate than using symbolic expressions such as: "Let Jesus come into your heart," or, "Give your heart to Jesus." Television and the Internet provide opportunities to see human heart removals. And Granddaddy may need a heart transplant. Using the expressions noted, would cause the child to wonder, "Where does Jesus go?"

Personal Learning Activities

1. List six characteristics of fives:

    _____
    _____
    _____
    _____
    _____
    _____
    _____

2. What does *literal-minded* mean to you? How does that apply to teaching the Bible to preschoolers?

    _____
    _____
    _____
    _____
    _____
    _____
    _____
    _____
    _____
    _____

    +---+
    | **Note:** Sources for specific children's |
    | books, music, toys, and puzzles are |
    | listed in the "Resources" section on |
    | page 345. |
    +---+

3. "When I was a child, I talked like a child, I thought like a child, I reasoned like a child (1 Cor. 13: 11a, NIV)." As you plan and teach, think "childlike."

    I will remember that fives are:

    _____
    _____
    _____
    _____
    _____
    _____
    _____
    _____
    _____
    _____
    _____
    _____
    _____
    _____
    _____
    _____
    _____
    _____
    _____

*"Train a child in the way he
should go, and when he is old
he will not turn from it"
(Proverbs 22:6, NIV).*

Chapter 7

Avenues of Learning

N*urture* too often is in conflict with *nature* when children enter a preschool. Teachers may cast aside what they know about characteristics of preschoolers and submit to pressures to produce "cookie cutter" results. In such cases, the environment does not allow a child's own nature and pace of learning to develop. Rather, it asks the child to change his nature and be like every other child. If he cannot change, he may be labeled *slow* or a behavior problem.

The Christian weekday program must be one that meets the needs of preschoolers and not the pressure of conforming.

"We must teach each child according to how God created him/her. Training up a child 'in the way he should go' could best be translated 'in his own way.' This means that each child is a unique creation of God and will learn according to his natural bents or tendencies present at birth. The learning process must not only be consistent over time, but it must also be consistent with the abilities and talents with which God has endowed each child"[1]

The book, *How Your Child Is Smart*,[2] by Dawna Markova invites the reader to ask, "HOW is the child smart?" not, "How SMART is the child?" Research shows that each child is smart in some way. Howard Gardner's theory of multiple intelligence (MI) is leading educators to recognize the need to teach to all learning styles. For too long, educators have placed greater emphasis on the verbal/linguistic and logical/mathematic "smarts." The visual/spatial (artistic), musical, bodily/kinesthetic (physical/sensitive), interpersonal (through relationships), and the intrapersonal (inward/individual) have been given only bits and pieces related to their styles of learning. Thomas Armstrong, author of *In Their Own Way*,[3] states an eighth intelligence: the naturalistic (through nature).

When a child gains knowledge through *his or her own way* of processing information, it becomes more interesting and meaningful.

ACTiViTY
TeacHiNG/LeaRNiNG

All preschoolers have one thing in common. They are *active* learners. *Activity* teaching through Learning Centers gives middle and older preschoolers choices of activities. The following avenues of learning help each child find his dominant "intelligence" style and build strengths in the less dominant styles:

Play: A circle, a square, and a triangle were formed out of three pieces of rope on the grassy playground. "Take turns. Jump into the square." "Hop into the circle on one foot." "Two of you hold hands and jump into the triangle." The four-year-olds followed directions of their teacher. By the time all children had a turn, they were falling on the ground in gales of laughter. This avenue of learning through play aided growth cognitively (introduction to geometry), emotionally (fun and laughter), socially (being with friends and taking turns) and physically (body movements). Back in the building (and many times thereafter) children looked for, and handled, things shaped in squares, circles, and triangles.

"For children, play is as natural as breathing — and as necessary. When children do not get the chance to play for hours each day — and, today, many do not — their physical, intellectual, social, and emotional development is diminished."[4]

Curiosity: Five-year-old Bertha came to Mr. Ben and told him she saw a new, white fish with round dots on it in the aquarium. Almost every day Mr. Ben added something new to his classroom. It could be a new book, a picture from the newspaper, a stone, or something from his garden. He never mentioned what he brought. If a child noticed it, he commended the child for her discovery. The children's curiosity about the fish prompted a group time in the library looking at fish books. The avenue of learning through curiosity was a lesson in ichthyology, research, and cooperation. It raised the children's level of interest in all kinds of fish. They asked questions and found answers. They became more interested in the care of fish and the waters where fish live.

Doing: Three-year-old Helen liked to watch other children paint at the easel. When a teacher would say, "You may paint now," Helen would shake her head and move away. It was Helen's second week in the classroom when she finally agreed to paint. After her easel paper was limp and covered with green paint, Helen stopped. With brush in hand she came across the room to her teacher and said, "I love it, love it, love it!" Learning by doing taught Helen the joy of paints and creativity. She learned the responsibility of cleaning up after painting. Helen's teacher was wise to let Helen move at her own pace. After her success with paints, Helen seemed less shy about entering into other activities.

Repetition: Toddler Donald tried over and over again to get the correct-shaped piece into its corresponding shape on the shape ball. So many times the pieces fell to the floor. So many times Donald moved away, then moved back again. Day after day he repeated his activity with the shape ball. Through repetition and maturing finer muscles in his hands, Donald increasingly made the matching connection. One day, he did it! Every piece went into the shape ball. The avenue of learning through repetition is high on the activity scale of young preschoolers. Preschoolers like to hear the same story over and over again. Repetition of positive guidelines is necessary for preschoolers.

Imitation: From the Home living Center a little voice ordered: "You be the daddy and sit there and read the paper. I'll be the mommy and cook supper." Preschoolers imitate both good and bad examples. Family members, teachers, and television characters are "models" for young imitators — good or bad. Preschoolers are trying to make sense of their world, and they do this by watching how others act. Is it any wonder they imitate what they see?

Satisfaction: Christopher struggled with a puzzle. It was more difficult than the ones he usually chose, but he persevered. Finally he shifted the last piece into place. Christopher folded his arms across his tummy, and with a sigh of relief he said, "That's good." Christopher's learning through the avenue of satisfaction was self-affirmed. He had probably heard "That's good" from teachers and parents. Such affirmation may have contributed to his determination to continue and complete the task at hand.

Relationships: Two-year-olds Keith and Howard got into a disagreement. Before the more aggressive Howard could use his hands to show his discontent, Keith hurried onto a teacher's lap and said, "That guy's gonna break me!" The learning avenue of relationships is not always an easy one to travel. Relationships with peers and adults are ways preschoolers learn to live socially. Children learn early to hit, fight, tease, or make relationships unpleasant. As a teacher of preschoolers, you have a gigantic challenge of counterbalancing dysfunctional relationships children see at home and on television. You must continually *show* preschoolers how to use kind words, tender touches, negotiation, and to treat others as you would like to be treated.

Senses: Ms. Lib cut and shared an avocado with three-year-olds. Response to the tasting test was less than enthusiastic. Steve, with his nose wrinkled in displeasure, asked, "Did God make THAT?" Through the sense of taste, threes learned that avocados were not their favorite food. All five senses: taste, touch, sight, hearing, and smelling are essential avenues in the child's learning. A vision or hearing loss often increases the learning awareness in other senses. All senses in full awareness increase the ability to learn.

Ding-A-Ling. A bell sounding to move preschoolers from Learning Center to Learning Center does not consider individual learning styles or personalities. A child creating in the Art or Block Center cannot stop his creativity at the ring of a bell. Perfectionist-personality Christopher would have been frustrated if a bell stopped his deliberate work on the challenging puzzle. A child's intelligence style wants, and needs, more time at one Center than another. For example, the verbal/linguistic and the intrapersonal learner may want more time with books and writing. The visual/spatial child may want more time to enjoy music, art, or blocks. A child should have the choice of moving from Center to Center without a strict time limit.

When the schedule requires a change for all preschoolers (outdoor play, group time), give advance notice of ten and five minutes.

Near each of the most active Learning Centers, hang a pocket chart with spaces for the number of children the area can accommodate at one time. Provide a laminated name tag for each child to place in an empty pocket before playing in the Learning Center of choice.

This system teaches each child to make a decision. "Is there room for me in the Center?" If there is, the child must be responsible. She will need to place her name tag in an empty pocket before entering the Center. This system works well with threes, fours, and fives. Twos need gentle redirection when they all want to do the same thing at once.

Personal Learning Activities

1. Eight avenues of learning are:

   _____, _____,
   _____, _____,
   _____, _____,
   _____, _____.

2. List the eight avenues of learning in what you think is the order of importance. Defend your reasoning with other teachers.

   1. _____
   2. _____
   3. _____
   4. _____
   5. _____
   6. _____
   7. _____
   8. _____

FUNDAMENTALS OF LEARNING

FUNdamentals of learning should be just that. If preschoolers can have *fun* learning, they *will* learn!

Four-year-old Sam came home from his new school and said: "I love my new school. I didn't have to learn a thing!" The school was established decades ago based upon the philosophy, "Learning *can* be fun."

Preschoolers travel through the avenues of learning more effectively if the weekday program has five solid bricks in its educational foundation. The bricks are:

The Teacher — Precious preschoolers deserve a teacher who is a Christian example, a continual learner who enjoys the ministry of teaching and is prepared, prayerful, and present.

The Child — The enormity of potential in each child is awesome. Each child deserves to be understood and loved as she is. She must have opportunities for choices to explore and learn at her pace and through her individual learning style.

The Room — The room teaches. If it is set up properly according to age, preschoolers can make choices and become more independent while they learn. They become more involved. Involved children are calm and orderly. An age-appropriate room, set up in Learning Centers, prevents most discipline problems.

The Curriculum — Good curriculum helps preschoolers grow and develop at their own pace through hands-on activities. It relates to the physical, emotional, social, and mental characteristics of preschoolers. Age-appropriate curriculum allows preschoolers to find joy in learning and feel successful and significant.

WEE Learn Curriculum, for ages birth through five, has excellent, age-appropriate learning activities.

The Child's Family — You cannot know the child well without knowing his family. You can teach him better if you know who lives in his home. You can teach him better if you know if he has a huge yard or if he lives in a fourth-floor flat. A child's behavior from day to day may be attributed to what goes on at home.

Personal Learning Activities

1. What are the five foundational bricks in a good weekday program?

   _____

   _____

   _____

   _____

   _____

2. On a scale from 1 (poor) to 10 (excellent), rate the foundational bricks in your weekday program.

Foundational Bricks	Rating
_____	_____
_____	_____
_____	_____
_____	_____
_____	_____

CHILD-CENTERED PRESCHOOL EDUCATION

Technology is essential and marvelous. It can also create isolation and anti-social behavior. It can rush children too soon toward adulthood. In too many homes, the television and computers become "baby sitters." Right now, and never again, you have opportunities to do something technology cannot do. You can provide person-to-person, eye-to-eye, hand-in-hand, loving, caring, active learning for each preschooler.

Stir your inner child and join the exuberance of preschoolers. Capture their innocence and wide-eyed newness. Discover peas with them. "I rescued them peas!" Del exclaimed after he "rescued" fresh peas from their pods to help make soup. What is old to adults can be very new and exciting to children. Allow girls and boys to enjoy their rightful learning stages of childhood.

Learning Centers

Learning Centers are activity areas set up in the room to facilitate the learning process, beginning with the two-year department. Learning Centers are: Art, Blocks, Books, Homeliving, Nature, Music, and Puzzles and Manipulatives. In this environment, several activities are offered at the same time. Preschoolers are allowed to choose which Learning Center interests them. Each child is allowed to change to a new activity whenever he is ready. He is invited to find personal space and express his own ideas and feelings as he plays. Teachers interact with pre-schoolers in small groups or one-on-one. They teach the Bible as it relates to the child's activity.

"It is possible to force skills by intensive instruction, but this may cause the child to use immature, inappropriate neural networks and distort the natural growth process. Trying to speed learning over unfinished neuron systems might be somewhat akin to racing a limousine over a narrow path in the woods. You can do it, but neither the car nor the path end up in very good shape! Moreover, the pressure which surrounds such learning situations may leave permanent emotional debris. There is an order in which learning is programmed to take place; while it can be encouraged, it need not be forced."[5]

Teachers and parents must realize that learning can take place in fun, humor, joy, adventure, movement, and creating with abandon! Learning Centers can be places where boys and girls enjoy learning on their level. Learning Centers are age-appropriate for two through five years of age. Art, Blocks, Books, Homeliving, Music, Nature/Science, and Puzzles/Manipulatives are basic Centers. A Writing Center can be added. Woodworking, sand, and water play are additional Learning Centers that provide hands-on-learning opportunities.

Introduce Infants and Toddlers to Centers

Infants and toddlers can enjoy their own Learning Centers. Simply rocking and cuddling babies help stimulate brain growth. Art is shared through colors, shapes, books, and pictures. Infants and toddlers enjoy vinyl-covered blocks or Blockbusters. A washable doll and blanket represent a Homeliving Center. Songs and music are a must from birth. Safe nature items can be shown to infants and toddlers. Putting things into and dumping things out of are baby's first puzzles. Toys designed for pounding are the beginning of woodworking. What is basic to writing? Words. When you talk to young preschoolers, you are teaching words and speech necessary to writing.

Information under "Wonderfully Made — Children with Special Needs" (Chapter 5) will help you teach special-needs children in Learning Centers.

Learning Through Art:

A great artist is one who has a unique style of creativity. No famous artist copied another's patterns, designs, or portraits. Asking children to paste cotton balls on sheep patterns is not art. It is busy work. It takes up time children could *enjoy* in developing their God-given, artistic talents.

Mrs. Lee's kindergarten room has a long, low table with access to clean, safe, throwaway materials such as scraps of sewing materials, used gift wrapping, boxes, plastic containers, and cardboard. Nearby are paints, crayons, markers, scissors, glue, and tape. Preschoolers are busy creating through play, curiosity, doing, repetition, satisfaction, relationships and senses at the Art Center.

The physical efforts involved in creative arts are valuable as they move large and small muscles. Vision and eye-hand coordination result when children are busy creating from a variety of art materials. The repetition (and imitation) of getting materials and cleaning up after an art experience exercises the body.

A child's brain is "in gear" all the time, especially when the child is doing something he enjoys. In creative art the brain does in-

dependent thinking, is curious, develops imagination, makes choices, solves problems, strengthens giftedness, and becomes more aware of its own idea of beauty.

The satisfaction of creating something for pleasure is a satisfying experience. The sensory experience of colorful textures — rough, smooth, messy, squishy, sticky, wet and dry — is a joy. Such experiences can also release tension and frustration, preventing misbehavior.

As children paint a large box that will become their grocery store, they must learn to make decisions, share ideas, cooperate, and interact. These experiences build relationships and encourage social growth.

Did you know you verbalize math-related terms as you give directions, ask questions, or make statements in the Art Center? Listen for such words as *shape, size, mixing, matching, up, down, over, under, identify, height, length, more, less, measure, how many, count, alike, different, grouping, classify,* and *form.*

Language teaching is everywhere. As you apply math terms to art experiences, you increase the child's vocabulary. Ask a child to tell about his creation. Through telling about his artwork, a child develops a feeling of freedom to express verbally. He may want to make up and dictate a story about his painting or drawing (readiness for reading).

Point out words that relate to what a child is doing. Say: "The color of the paint is red. Do you see the word *red* on the paint can?" Label containers, or shelves, with words describing the contents, such as *scissors, crayons*, and *paper*. Older preschoolers may learn to read certain words because the words have meaning and purpose in what they are doing.

Preschoolers can begin to have good feelings about the church, God, and Jesus as you share related Bible verses (phrases), songs, and conversation during teachable moments in the Art Center. Say the day's Bible phrase as you print it on a child's artwork. Ask the child to say the Bible phrase.

Middle and older preschoolers may begin trying to print on their artwork. Let them do it their way. Words will develop correctly as cognitive and neuromuscular systems catch up with hands and fingers. Five-year-old Chan scrawled the letters "G E U S" on his picture of Jesus. That is a very good writing *and* spiritual beginning.

Infants and toddlers are attracted to colors and designs. They may pick at floral prints or colors in fabric. A mobile of contrasting colors, or black and white, fascinates bed babies. Toddlers who want to look at the same books over and over indicate they are experiencing a pleasure from color and illustrations.

Learning Through Block Activities:
As a child, Frank Lloyd Wright spent hours playing with a small set of blocks his mother had given him. His play in block

building was a foundation for his famous architectural creations as an adult.

Preschoolers stack and restack blocks, increasing motor skills and eye-hand coordination! The many physical movements in block play exercise the whole body, giving pleasure in the process.

Cognitive development increases through the repetition of organizing, building, matching, comparing, and making patterns and shapes with more than one block. The child increases conceptual thinking in areas of size and quantity, shapes and numbers, sorting, and classifying.

Emotionally, block play brings pleasure through visual and tactile stimulation. The satisfaction of building structures and imitation through dramatic play contributes to a child's sense of competence.

Creative preschoolers can turn a box into a boat, train, house, or car as they build relationships and their ability to function socially. A wooden animal or family set and other accessories can stimulate group play. Children learn to share, cooperate, communicate, and coordinate ideas as they play out situations or build structures, bridges, and roads.

Math becomes tangible in block play. The learning foundation for geometry is laid as children recognize the shapes of blocks: cylinders, rectangles, triangles and squares. Guide children in making a triangle with three or more long blocks. If you ask them to use only square blocks to make as many shapes as they can, they will use creative thinking, patterning, finer motor skills, and visual /spatial skills.

Play math-readiness games such as stacking seven blocks. Take away three blocks and ask, "How many are left?" Continue to play as you add one or take away another. As preschoolers play, ask questions such as: "Who has the most blocks? Who has the smallest (biggest, longest) block?" A child can lie on the floor, and other children can place blocks beside her to measure how many blocks long she is.

The tape outlining the area for block play can be measured by how many blocks can be placed (end to end) on the tape. Count the big blocks. Count the little blocks. Outlines of various-sized blocks on the shelves allow preschoolers to match the blocks with the outlines.

Encourage language, reading, and writing readiness by printing signs to identify structures. Provide materials for children to make traffic signs for the block area. Preschoolers will begin to recognize words that are meaningful to them.

Preschoolers will notice a Bible teaching picture near the block area. Listen for conversation about the picture or begin a conversation about it with a child.

Woodworking increases motor skills. It must be well supervised. Teach safety guidelines, such as the use of goggles and one child working at a time. Beginner woodworking might include a rubber hammer and golf tees hammered into a cardboard box.

Babies and toddlers increase motor skills and eye-hand coordination as they play with soft blocks or Blockbusters. Imitation, repetition, and curiosity increase when small blocks are dropped into and dumped from a container. Sitting on blocks and learning to stand on a Blockbuster bring satisfaction to a young child.

Learning Through Books:

Books can be a life-long journey to anywhere! *Fewer* books are better than *many* in the Book Center. Too many books can overwhelm children.

- Select books that meet the children's ages, developmental levels, and interests.
- Select books that are attractive and have easily-defined illustrations. Any text should correspond to the illustration to encourage older preschoolers to follow along.
- Select books with content free of racial, cultural, and disability bias.
- Select Bible-related books with real-life pictures.
- Select books that relate to the unit theme.

Joyous, cognitive learning happens when you immerse preschoolers in a comprehensive, rich, print and verbal environment. Provide age-level reading and writing materials for the blossoming listeners, speakers, readers, and writers.

Preschoolers learn to listen before they read. By listening, children can learn that printed words are important. Letters and words make stories, communicate, and cause laughter and sadness. Stories, poems, and songs in print help girls and boys learn new concepts and specific information.

Reading should be recognized as pleasurable and informative, not a drill to learn words. Stimulate thinking by reading a new story or book and stopping before the ending. Ask boys and girls to make up their own endings to the story. Older preschoolers may enjoy illustrating endings to the story.

When a child sees and hears words, sentences and stories related to her interests, needs, and understanding, she develops a love for books. She begins to make letters as a prelude to meaningful writing.

A child's brain development determines when a child *can* learn to read and write. Pushing can hinder the process. "In Denmark, formal reading instruction is not introduced until the second grade. Before that, children have a rich exploratory and manipulative language experience; they are read to and talked to, encouraged to dictate their own stories and learn sight words. Denmark has almost 100 percent literacy."[6]

Books create sight-word vocabulary through word repetition in an interesting and meaningful form. Give girls and boys freedom to enjoy books and writing materials. Selecting books, handling books, turning the pages, looking at pictures and words, and putting books back on shelves are necessary physical activities. These activities improve eye-hand coordination, vision, and motor skills in preparation for reading and writing.

Older preschoolers can enjoy a writing area near the Book Center. Large pencils, large crayons, and large paper are more adaptable to preschoolers' fingers and hands than small ones. Alphabet stamps (upper and lower case), ink pads, magnetic alphabet letters, cookie cutter letters, colored paper and cards, envelopes, and magazines can stimulate creativity. At first, children will experiment with making random prints. Then they begin printing meaningful words, usually their name first. Magazines may be used for a "writing" game. One or two children can use crayons to circle animals (cars, houses) in a magazine. Related pictures may be cut out and placed in a left-to-right sequence. A child can make up a story about the pictures — readiness for reading.

When preschoolers want to read and write, encourage them. Those who must be pushed are not ready! Give them time.

Preschoolers are using computers at home, at their leisure. Preschoolers' eye development should be of concern in making computers available at weekday. Computer skills of focusing, tracking from left to right, recognizing letters and words, and keeping their place on moving objects are complex abilities for preschoolers.

If a computer is in the Writing Center in your classroom, it must not overpower every other activity. It certainly should be a choice activity, not a requirement. Each Learning Center can be so interesting and inspiring that children will get a balance in activities.

Provide Braille cards for older preschoolers to experience how the visually-impaired read.

Books help babies and toddlers begin picture-reading by recognizing animals and objects in favorite books. Introduce the Bible to the very young. One or more Bibles used in every preschool room teaches preschoolers that the Bible is a very special book.

Learning Through Dramatic Play in the Homeliving Center:

 Children go into all Centers expending physical energy. Dramatic play in the Homeliving Center is a "moving" experience. All body parts and skills can be improved as boys and girls enjoy "home away from home." Families, as preschoolers see them, are acted out in this Center. Storekeepers, doctors, or nurses may intermingle as children imitate relationships through play. Relationships develop with others who are pretending.

A toddler may imitate an adult by rocking a doll or putting on grown-up shoes, if a doll or shoes are readily available. Middle and older preschoolers enter dramatic play deliberately. They plan, gather props, and assign roles.

Cognitive development occurs through dramatic play because of the creative thinking involved. Imitating a health caregiver expands the child's vocabulary as she expresses language relating to the role she is playing. This creative pretending indicates readiness for creative storytelling and creative writing because a child has to visualize characters and events. Mental pictures in dramatic play indicate continuing mental development. Mental pictures of math problems and historic events make understanding those subjects easier.

Playing out situations in life is an emotional release for children. They can often conquer the "bad guy" in pretending. Satisfaction comes in being who they want to be. Preschoolers may develop emotional feelings of sympathy, empathy, or disdain for other pretend characters.

Social skills grow, and all five senses are in action as children cooperate to "cook" their favorite meal of candy, ice cream, and mashed potatoes! Pretending together in the Homeliving Center helps preschoolers get along better in real situations.

Props used during a grocery store study are valuable for math, reading, and writing readiness. Labels and prices on empty food containers give the child letters, words, and numbers to recognize, explain, and print. Making lemonade to serve at the grocery store requires planning and measuring. A few grocery store math words include *how much, what size, weigh, dollars, cents,* and *how many.*

A note pad and large pencil in the Homeliving Center inspire beginning writing and reading readiness. Children can pretend to scribble telephone messages or grocery lists.

A session on going to church needs dress-up clothes in the Homeliving Center. Dress-up play and imitating church experiences help strengthen the concept of church for preschoolers. A Bible, a Bible teaching picture, and an age-level Sunday School booklet give opportunities for recognition of letters, words, and a Bible story.

Babies and infants can have home or family experiences through pictures of families, safe washable dolls, and books relating to the home. As toddlers near two years of age, a doll bed and a small rocker may be added to their room.

Personal Learning Activity

Review the Art, Block, Book, and Homeliving Center activities. List the ways you find the eight avenues of learning in action.

Learning Through Music and Movement:

Children benefit physically as they happily create their own music and rhythmic movements. Babies gurgle and coo their music. Toddlers bounce and sway to musical sounds. Start a musical cassette and preschoolers become musical instruments. Hands clap, thump, drum, or wave, and fingers try to snap. Small feet hop, skip, jump, run, and sometimes walk. You do not have to be a musician to welcome boys and girls into happy musical experiences. Music activities are synonymous with play, curiosity, doing, repetition, imitation, satisfaction, relationships, and all five senses!

Music does not need to be an isolated "teaching time." Make it a part of the whole day. Welcome children with a song. Spontaneously connect a hum, whistle, or song with an activity. Cognitive development goes on as you encourage made-up songs, chants, and rhythms. As Vera patted the play dough, she was saying: "Pat-pat-pat. Pat-pat-pat." Then it became: "Pat-pat-pat. Patty-patty-patty." Her teacher sat near her and joined the chant. Soon other four-year-olds joined in and began clapping to the rhythm. Laughter, and the development of other chants, resulted.

Twos through fives can strum an Autoharp and "compose" music. A few rhythm instruments can bring out preschoolers' natural rhythm. Older preschoolers enjoy creating their own songs. They like to put tunes to favorite poems. Print a Bible phrase on a sentence strip. Post it in the Music Center. Point to each word as you sing the Bible phrase. Older preschoolers can take turns and point to each word, singing their own tunes to go with the Bible phrase.

Label a few rhythm instruments, being careful not to overcrowd the room with labels.

Sing directions. Children will listen! When girls and boys become restless, take a singing, or a musical movement break. Move to the music of Anderson's "Syncopated Clock." March into cleanup time with Rossini's "William Tell Overture." Continue children's love for music by interjecting it throughout the day. Life will be sweeter.

Relationships and social interaction develop because of music. Songs and music from various cultures broaden appreciation for others. Music is filled with language, words, and opportunities for expression.

Music is especially effective in stirring or soothing the emotions. Preschoolers especially like to hear and sing songs that make them laugh.

Music teaches math, too. Songs like "Colors, Shapes, and Numbers" and "Puppies, Puppies" (pp. 18 and 60, *Specially Special Songs*) are happy ways to learn numbers. Think of terms that relate to music and math like *up, down, clap one-two, sequence, grouping, walk in a circle, play the triangle.*

While he was still in the womb, the baby experienced the rhythm of music with the motions of his mother's heartbeat. A ticking clock or rhythmic toy often comforts the newborn. As you cuddle and rock a baby while singing a lullaby, you are giving the best kind of music for him. Playing with musical toys can bring delight to young preschoolers.

Learning through Nature/Science:
Four-year-olds were learning about weather. They learned that evaporation makes clouds. Clouds make rain. For an experiment on evaporation the children put water in plastic jars and placed them in a window. They watched from day to day as the water levels went down. One morning Jeff came in the room and exclaimed: "It worked! It worked! It's raining!"

Hands-on activities, science-related materials, and freedom to experiment bring out the best in those bent toward science and nature. Label items with pictures for young preschoolers. Label with printed words for older preschoolers. Add a book or teaching picture about a nature/science activity to increase interest.

Sensory experiences with sand (sift, fill, and dump), water (wade, splash, sprinkle, pour), or birdseed (scoop, fill, feed) are emotionally satisfying and can be a springboard into three unit studies. SAND — hot, cold, sand castles, other castles, beach, vacations.

WATER — where, how, fun, drink, health, boats, swim, ocean, rivers, lakes, sea creatures. SEED — birds, feeders, sunflowers, other flowers, garden. Children see and touch the seed, soil, and water. They can hear and smell the outdoors. Tasting carrots they grow is a delicious experience — even for children who do not like carrots! Add the book *The Carrot Seed* to the joy of raising carrots.

With close supervision, babies through fives can enjoy water play. Toddlers through fives like sand experiences. Twos (with closer supervision) through fives find satisfaction in the feel of handling, scooping, and dumping birdseed. Preschoolers can develop sensitivity and responsibility as they feed, water, and care for birds. Older preschoolers enjoy social growth as they plant and care for a small garden. Planning, planting, observing, documenting (drawings, dictating, printing), and reporting encourage cooperation and sharing. Creative learning through stories, pictures, songs, books, and dramatic play can follow.

Compete with the technical mouse by housing a live rodent in the Nature Center. Twos through fives will appreciate a guinea pig or hamster. Children learn responsibility and sensitivity as they help care for God's creatures.

Offer a wide range of simple, scientific experiments. Even physics concepts become intriguing outdoors as preschoolers see: the lever (seesaw), wheels (wagon), pendulum (swing), and ramp (slide). The concepts of balance, gravity, weight, and lever-age may be "experienced" right on the playground. Language skills increase because of words such as soil, sprout, gravity, leverage, and experiment. Older preschoolers increase cognitive thinking by sharing experiences and ideas.

Math terms and actions tie right into scientific and nature projects. Measuring cups in sand, water, or seed leads to scooping one cup, two cups, or more. Preschoolers can add more or dip less. All this is play. It is also teaching math. Older preschoolers can make graphs to document experiments. They can estimate: "How many cups of sand will it take to fill the bucket?" They will develop observation skills as they classify, label, and group items.

Cognitive skills improve for young preschoolers as they explore a safe, interesting, but not over-loaded environment. Babies through fives delight in exploring the outdoors. The sky, trees, grass, flowers, birds, ants, and much more of God's creation give limitless opportunities to experience nature and science. The world is your laboratory!

Encourage safety as preschoolers enjoy science and nature. Use safe, plastic containers. Always consider allergies. Be aware of animal and plant safety.

Learning Through Puzzles and Manipulatives:

Puzzles, games and other manipulatives may also be used in places other than a specific Center. They are found in art (fitting pieces on a collage); blocks (those that interlock); books (hold the book and turn pages); homeliving (stacking dishes and dressing dolls); music (instruments); nature/science (scales, tools, and appliances).

Infants and toddlers repeatedly manipulate rattles, fill-and-dump toys, blocks, and large-piece puzzles because it is fun. All the manipulating preschoolers do with puzzles and other objects increases finger and hand dexterity. Access to choices of puzzles, games, and other manipulatives is invaluable. They stimulate cognitive growth (solving problems), emotional satisfaction, and motor-skill development.

Puzzles allow independent play as well as social interaction. Two or more children creating patterns with drinking straws are developing socially and enjoying math.

Picture puzzles use fewer motor skills but whet a child's cognitive skills and exercise visual acuteness. From magazines cut pictures that relate to each other. Preschoolers can match: car and highway; church and Bible, apple tree and apple, mother and baby. Select a series of pictures for grouping: families, animals, cars, fruits, and vegetables. Expand the difficulty and number of pictures according to the age of children you teach. Matching and grouping activities are basic to math and reading. As you ask girls and boys to make up stories about the pictures, the activity expands to creative speaking, reading, and writing readiness.

Math can be fun as preschoolers solve the problem of putting pieces into the right places. They learn to count pieces, distinguish shapes and sizes, observe, compare, and predict. They also classify objects, recognize and sequence objects, identify relationships between objects, and enjoy it all!

Personal Learning Activity

1. Review the activities in the Music, Nature/Science, and Puzzle/Manipulative Centers. List at least one example of the eight avenues of learning in action.

2. Review all Learning Centers and check the words: cognitive (mentally), physically, spiritually (or Bible related), socially, and emotionally. Activity teaching helps children develop in all ways! Read Luke 2:52.

Treat yourself by reading the book *Children Learn What They Live*[7] by Dorothy L. Nolte.

GROUP TIME FOR THREES AND OLDER

Group time gives opportunities for boys and girls to share experiences from the Learning Centers. They can help evaluate activities and plan for the next session.

"There is a time for everything,
and a season for every activity
under heaven" (Ecclesiastes
3:21).

Chapter 8

Developmental Stages

Mother brought two-year-old Jamie to his classroom. Greetings between teacher and Jamie, and teacher and Mother, were happy and cordial. Before Mother left, she said to Jamie, "Let's take off your coat." Jamie said, "No." The mother insisted. Jamie resisted. Teacher kept saying, "Go on, Mother; we will take care of the coat." Mother replied, "He is going to take off his coat!" After too long, the harried mother turned to the stunned teacher and said, "You take care of it," and left.

Jamie's teacher said, "Jamie, when you are ready to hang up your coat, I will help you." And she did.

What would you call the stage of development Jamie is entering?

Understanding basic characteristics and needs of preschoolers sets the stage for a clear perception of growth patterns and developmental stages. Psychoanalyst Erik Erikson outlined three stages of psychosocial development which occur during preschool years. Each stage builds on the prior stage and establishes a frame of time during which a child confronts a basic developmental task. During each stage a child is laying a foundation for future competencies. Ericson's three stages are: **Trust, Autonomy,** and **Initiative**.

Jamie's actions in the incident described above relate to his search for autonomy. (Autonomy \-me\ 1: the quality or state of being self-governing; esp: the right of self-government 2: self-directing freedom and esp. moral independence).

But how do these three stages of development impact the work of a preschool teacher in a weekday program?

The first important stage in human growth is the development of **trust**. The sensitive period for the development of trust is during the first eighteen months. If a baby could express in words his greatest desires, he would say, "I need you!" When a baby cries, he is expressing a need for food, attention, comfort, relief of pain, or some other basic need. When you meet a baby's needs, you help him feel secure and loved.

Autonomy, the second critical developmental stage occurs from about eighteen months to three years of age. During this stage the child is learning that he is a person in his own right with his own identity. He is becoming independent. His independence grows with his gaining new skills. Learning to walk, climb steps, and run brings new freedom and fosters independence. Beginning language allows him to express wants and preferences. Learning to feed and dress himself are other skills he adds as this stage progresses.

Ericson's third developmental stage involves the task of acquiring **initiative** which usually occurs during the years three to six. The desire to initiate action comes with a child's growing ability to think of ideas, imagine situations, and carry out his own plans. If a child could express his focal need in words, he would say, "I have an idea. Let me try it out!"

Moving through the developmental stages is a continuous journey. A baby's need to trust others will continue forever. A baby balances trusting others against her need for autonomy. A baby feels a part of his or her primary caregiver for several months. The first stage of independence is seen when a child can pull away from the caregiver and go scampering on hands and knees. What freedom! Then comes walking, climbing,

and "getting into everything." Parents are delighted, then exhausted. First, it is: "Mom, guess what! Myra's walking!" Later, when independent toddling is in full bloom, it is: "Mom, she is into everything. I have to watch her every minute."

A toddler's independence is a must for the normal growth and development of preschoolers. When asked to do something he does not want to do, the young child's desire to be independent responds, "No." It is best not to ask a young child a question that can be answered with "yes" or "no." He may say "no" even though he wants "yes." Instead, make a statement, "It is your turn to paint." Or, give a choice, "Would you rather paint or help feed the fish?"

Twos have been living in this bewildering world 24 months. Too often, too much is expected of twos! Sometimes they are labeled, "Terrible." A child's personality, his environment, his health, and the demands on him can all contribute to how a two-year-old acts or reacts. His search for independence is as natural as his search for love and acceptance. Some preschoolers resist at this stage. Others may display a great deal of resistance. The adults in his life must act wiser than the two-year-old. Know that any two-year-old may resist demands and threats. For better cooperation, adults use positive guidance with twos. Lead the child to think an action is his idea, and he is more likely to do it. A mother stepped out of the kitchen door to empty trash. Her two-year-old latched the door behind her. What would you do?

A. ____ Have a tantrum, scream, and
   yell.
B. ____ Threaten, "When your dad gets
   home!"
C. ____ Say, "Oh, Kenny, you have locked
   yourself in the house!

"C." is the correct answer. The mother said those very words. Kenny unlatched the door, and with glee said, "No, I didn't!"

A two likes familiar routines and environments. In an age-appropriate room, twos feel secure when the routine is consistent each day. The two-year-old may set up rituals for his way of doing things. Interference may cause a tantrum. Rituals can help twos feel more secure and independent. The world is big and scary. Today's society moves young children in many directions: up early; go to child care; go to the sitter; go to a fast food dispensary; go to bed late; at Mommy's house this week; at Daddy's the next. The routine and the familiar you provide will help give calm and security as two-year-olds seek independence.

The three is a friendly independent. As the two becomes three, her desire for autonomy is more rational. "No" and negativism are less important because the three is better equipped to express her desires and preferences in words. She likes to please. She is more trustworthy, and adults give her opportunities to be independent. The three-year-old can feed herself rather neatly. Potty training is usually accomplished by now, and she can "go potty" all by herself.

The three catches new words and tries to use them in her independent way. She is sometimes demanding and often uses words she knows rather than a tantrum. One angry three-year-old voiced, "You are diswreckable (despicable?)!" The three may show her independence by standing in one spot and pouting.

The four can be out-of-bounds. Just when the child seems content within acceptable boundaries, growth takes him into the realm of four-year-olds. He takes the initiative! His vision is improving and his horizons are expanding. He is stronger and more independent-minded than ever before. "Out-of-bounds" is fours. Individuality, personality, and environment contribute to how the child gets through this out-of-bounds stage. As with all other stages, each child enters and passes through in his or her own way.

Out-of-bounds is not only shown in steps outside physical boundaries, but verbally as well. Telling tall tales, bragging, bathroom talk, and swearing are not uncommon for four-year-olds.

The inner boundaries that helped maintain the three-year-old are not as evident now. Rules and boundaries that are reasonable are appreciated at this stage of a child's life.

The autonomy and enthusiasm for adventure, information, creativity, fun, laughter, and new things make this age a joy to teach!

Fives continue the initiative. As the four becomes five, he evidences more initiative into intellectual pursuits. The five seems to be more self-assured, content, calm, and conforming. She likes the independence of choosing a special friend. Her food choices are plain and simple. Bedtime rituals are not as demanding on parents. The five-year-old likes the independence of getting herself ready for bed. For cleanliness sake, she needs an adult to verify "clean." The five-year-old appreciates a good-night story and prayer with a parent.

The fives' declaration to her kindergarten teacher might be: "Understand me. Enjoy me. Listen to me. I am independent. I am ready for the kindergarten challenge."

Parents want their children to grow into independent, self-sufficient adults. Independence is achieved one stage at a time through safe, positive guidance from people like you.

Personal Learning Activities

1. List two incidents of the search for autonomy you have seen in children you teach:
   _____
   _____
   _____
   _____
   _____
   _____
   _____
   _____
   _____

2. How can you encourage a positive search for autonomy?
   _____
   _____
   _____
   _____
   _____
   _____
   _____
   _____

Stages in Solving Problems

A baby's problems are not all solved for her. A baby's cry of discomfort is her way of solving the problem of discomfort. An adult responds and makes her comfortable. As the baby grows, she will learn to solve some of her problems. She is bored, so she kicks and pumps her arms, and the colorful mobile jiggles and entertains her. Soon, when she needs to turn over, she does just that. Her pacifier or bottle drops away from her, and she retrieves it. Rolling over, sitting up, standing — these abilities of gradual independence lead to an increase in problem-solving.

Toddlers and twos solve problems. The baby-turned-toddler can now move about and get to a desired goal. He can choose which toy, book, or puzzle he wants to handle. The problem of getting food into his mouth is solved in a messy, but satisfying, way. The need for comfort can sometimes be met by hugging a favorite blanket or toy.

The toddler begins manipulating objects in his environment. He becomes creative and entertains himself by using a box for a hat or a book to cover his feet. He stacks blocks, boxes, or other objects, learning what stays and what falls. He is experimenting to see what happens. He is solving problems.

The older toddler continues with creative problem solving. He may experiment by climbing in new places. He climbs and falls. He climbs again and falls again. He cannot yet reason. He acts or reacts. He may fall because he is standing in his wagon. The next time he may fall from a chair. He cannot connect that the greater distance causes the hurt he gets from falling down.

Toddlers and twos make messes. Toys can become "floor covering." Food can be smeared from eyebrows to tabletop. What's the problem? Who is going to solve the problem?

Limiting available toys makes choices easier. A low shelf for a few toys makes clean-up easier for preschoolers to put toys back into place. Suggest, "Now it is time to put away the toys, so we can have juice and crackers." Toddlers begin solving the problem by putting one or two toys on or near the shelves. Other toddlers may pull them back into the play space. Consistent guidance helps toddlers meet the challenge of putting away toys.

Twos can solve the problem of scattered blocks or toys by replacing them on the shelves. They may direct others who put blocks or toys in the "wrong" place. Twos

are beginning to use their ability to think through a problem, rather than random trial and error.

Messy eating is caused by immature eye-hand coordination. The sensory joy of handling and experimenting with food is another cause. Cleanup can be eased with protective covering on both child and floor. Scolding for messiness may increase the activity. Commend a child even for small successes. When a two-year-old tries to be helpful in cleaning up, give affirmation. He is beginning to solve the problem of messiness.

Within safe and reasonable limits, encourage toddlers and twos in their experimentation with toys and materials used in ways other than intended. Remember that they are being creative and learning to solve their own problems.

Threes use more language with problem solving. They are beginning to work together. Two or three children may plan a project (block structure) and carry out the plan with each child involved. "We" and "friends" are words that surface as threes solve problems cooperatively.

Increased large motor skills can now make problem-solving easier for challenges that once required help. The three-year-old can pull a wagon or pedal a tricycle better, thanks to stronger arms and legs.

Threes like to experiment, solve problems, and get approval from others. "See how I made her (the doll) a hat with the paper cup!"

Threes may solve problems by pretending to be someone else or by creating imaginary friends and animals to help them solve problems. A three-year-old may seek a time alone with a book or other materials when a "problem" arises.

Provide creative, open-ended materials so imaginative threes can experiment and solve problems. Each Learning Center must be a place where threes' imaginations are sparked to create and discover their own solutions.

Fours are becoming aware of social interaction and of wanting others to conform. Let fours help solve problems. Print, on a large poster board, the guidelines children suggest for, "What can we do to help keep everyone safe on the playground?" Some possible answers: "No pushing," "Take turns," "Pick up trash," "Keep your hands to yourself." Post the guidelines near the door. Fours will ask you to read the rules, from time to time. Because they "own" the rules, fours will help keep each other aware of the rules.

Fours are intellectually and verbally able to solve thought problems such as: "What if we had wings instead of arms?" "What if all houses were made of glass?" Read a new story to fours and stop before the ending, allowing them to finish the story. Help them make up a story for a silly title like: "Mr. Kingfidingle Went Looking for a Whatchamajig!" If children need guidance, ask: "What did Mr. Kingfidingle look like? What was he wearing? Where did he travel? How did he travel? Whom did he see? What did he find?"

Fours need a rich variety of creative art materials, books, musical instruments, science and nature objects. Fours know how to create and solve problems! At least, they are not afraid to try.

Fives are more adept at planning a project but may overestimate their abilities. Frustration may cancel the project. However, planning and talking about various ways to make something (solve the problems) often lead to success. Fives are happy to share their "great ideas!" They explain their plans enthusiastically. If preschoolers have been given opportunities for independent thinking in earlier years, it blossoms now.

Independently, the five-year-old begins solving the problems of numbers and letters by experimenting with them at his or her level of development. Making music or artistic creations, alone or with others, is problem solving. Fives' cognitive and social abilities indicate the vast problem-solving territory they have covered in just five years!

Support fives in their projects. Celebrate their successes. Show your support when plans do not work out. Ask questions and make suggestions that may get them back on track. A rich variety of materials and opportunities for exploration continues to increase the ability to solve problems.

Personal Learning Activity

List at least three ways you can encourage problem solving at each age level.

(1) _____
_____
_____
_____
_____

(2) _____
_____
_____
_____

(3) _____
_____
_____
_____
_____

THE HEMISPHERES

The brain sets the stage: "The right hemisphere normally controls spatial and postural factors that pertain to how we learn to move . . . through space. It is also the source of . . . intuition, artistic expression, recognition of faces, body image, fantasy, and imagination. The left hemisphere is primarily the source of analytic[al] and logical thinking, verbalization, mathematical ability, and sequencing. Because of the strong emphasis placed on language and quantitative thinking in our society . . . we tend to neglect the functions of the right hemisphere and overemphasize the left."[1]

CREATIVITY

Ask middle and older preschoolers if they can sing, dance, draw, paint, or tell stories. They will enthusiastically declare they can! As these children grow, make certain they continue to know they have creative ability. Individuals are definitely gifted musically, artistically, or with talents to express in writing, acting, or building. These are individuals who use the right hemisphere of their brains. They believe there are not always set ways to do things.

All children deserve opportunities and encouragement to enjoy creative arts, whether gifted in those areas or not. Help girls and boys learn to appreciate those areas in which they may not be highly gifted.

To keep the creative enthusiasm alive in children:

• Provide open-ended time for exploration and creativity.

• Provide art materials so children can freely create paintings, drawings, murals, collages, structures, and sculptures.

• Stimulate creativity by providing musical instruments, CDs, cassette tapes, and songbooks. Taking trips to see and hear a choir, an orchestra, a ballet, or a children's theater production can also stimulate their creative juices.

• Encourage creativity. Preschoolers create for the joy of doing. It is the sensory experiences with creative materials that preschoolers enjoy.

Two-year-old J. P. had been sitting on his foot looking at a book. When he got up, he said, "My foot sparkles." What a creative way to tell that his foot had "gone to sleep." Katie called butterflies "flying flowers." Words children use, their special interest in books, pictures, art, and music activities may indicate that these children are naturally artistic or creative. Take it as your responsibility to present creative opportunities. Nurture whatever degree of creative ability a child may display.

DEVELOPMENTAL STAGES OF ART

Babies and toddlers are *observers* of art. They can enjoy color, shapes, designs, and easily-defined illustrations in books and pictures. Birds, colorful flowers, and butterflies – real or in pictures – attract the attention of babies.

The young child may like a specific picture, book, or toy. Why? Perhaps it is the colors and designs that she sees.

If a toddler is given a crayon and paper, she may make a few random marks and begin to scribble. Her finer muscles have not developed. If allowed, the crayon will be moved more to the mouth than to the paper.

The random/disordered scribbling stage. — Crayon scribbles progress into up and down marks, some bending lines and crude circles. Easel painting consists mostly of up and down strokes. Later the arm can move like a windshield wiper, and the child can add arcs to paintings. Within the latter part of the second year, a child adds large irregular circles to the strokes and arcs. The arcs may become circles.

The controlled-scribbling stage. — A three makes symbols of circles and marks. A large circle may have eyes and a mouth. Instead of a body, stick arms and legs are added to the large-face circle.

The basic-forms stage. — They begin to make people figures with stick or loop bodies on the large circle head. Some children are able to give more detail to the people figures than others.

The pictorial stage. — Fours and fives begin creating drawings or paintings of things that interest them. Their drawings are more recognizable, because improved motor skills allow them to have more control over lines and directions. At this stage the most important thing in the painting or picture may be the largest. Flowers by a house may be as tall as the house! A painting or drawing of a family may show the artist larger than other family members. Yellow sunshine, or a colorful rainbow, 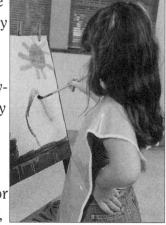 will adorn pictures of the outdoors. Lack of dexterity in the child's fingers will not allow detail work. Hands and feet may be drawn unusually large in order to paint or draw fingers and toes.

Children of this age may try to print their names on their artistic creations.

As a preschool teacher, allow each child to develop his or her own creations. Art can be a way a child expresses hurt, fears, abuse, as well as joy and love. Four-year-old Jay painted a picture of his family. He painted Daddy (the largest) and Mommy (next largest). Between Daddy and Mommy, with his arms linked around Daddy's leg, was Jay. All the way to the far lower edge of the paper was baby brother. It was easy to see that a new baby was in the home. Jay was not going to let Daddy near the baby. In fact, Jay had not fully accepted the baby into his family circle.

Patterns, color sheets, and directed crafts do not give preschoolers the freedom to express themselves. If children are all doing the same "art" work, creativity is diminished. The children do not have to think, or create, only obey.

Each child progresses through each developmental stage of art at his own pace. Encourage each child's creativity as he enjoys each stage.

STAGES IN MUSIC ABILITIES

Introduce great music to children early in life. Edvard Grieg's "In the Hall of the Mountain King" *(Peer Gynt Suite)* pleases even the young preschooler. Music of such composers as Brahms, Bach, Debussy, and Chopin add richness to music education at any age.

Babies, from conception, grew to the music of their mother's heartbeat and the rhythm of her breathing. Babies are musical beings. Keep up the beat! Babies continue to be soothed and entertained with sounds of music. The child who pulls up to the side of her bed, but cannot yet take steps, bounces up and down with or without music. She may listen herself to sleep as she hears a familiar song.

A **toddler's** increased stability on her feet allows her to move her arms up and down when she hears music. The young preschooler is fascinated with musical toys. She may want to hear a special song on a musical toy, or recording, over and over. Musical pull toys are especially interesting to the toddling child.

Two-year-olds delight in showing off newly-developed movements of swaying, jumping, running, and hopping to music. Twos prefer moving to music more than using words to music. They like the repetition of a favorite song or recording. Twos can rap and tap on drums and rhythm sticks with or without music. Sometimes they sing bits of songs to themselves. Provide fun songs and space so children can physically move to music.

Twos like for songs to be sung just for them. Teacher was singing "I Have a Good Friend," and adding Patrick's name. Thea came over to her teacher and said, "Now do me." Sing to children. Weave musical sounds into daily activities.

Three-year-olds may become shy about being noticed as they sing or move to music. This is not a performing age. They are becoming more fluid in motion as they move to a musical beat. Small group singing is likely. They can either sing or move with music. It is unlikely they can do both, at the same time.

Threes are beginning to improvise words to parts of a song they cannot remember. They may hum the forgotten parts. Mother asked three-year-old Keith to sing a particular song for his grandparents. Keith declined by saying, "There's too much humming in that one."

Four-year-olds really take to the musical "stage." They like to be on stage, but only for peers and special adults. They are quick to learn finger plays, chants, fun songs, and songs with body and hand motions. Fours have a good memory for fun words and silly songs. Improved motor skills allow fours a more accurate rhythmic beat and coordinated movements.

Five-year-olds can participate in larger group musical movements and singing. Props and drama can be a part of fives' musical experiences. With guidance, rhythm instruments can be fun as fives create their own songs, chants and dramas.

Provide space and opportunities for preschoolers to express music. Take music outdoors. Children enjoy holding colorful streamers or scarves as they move their hands and bodies to music.

Listening time, or rest time, is an opportunity to introduce a variety of CDs or cassette tapes of orchestras, specific instruments, and music of various voices and cultures.

Personal Learning Activities

1. Which hemisphere of the brain does society tend to neglect?

   _____

2. List ten ways to enrich an environment to encourage art and music creativity:

   _____
   _____
   _____
   _____
   _____
   _____
   _____
   _____
   _____
   _____

STAGES OF
FLUIDITY, FEAR, AND FANTASY

A child's stages of growth might be called fluid. That is, growth tends to move slowly, in spurts and stalls. As mentioned in Chapter 6, the growth spurt is a period of "disequilibrium." It is an erratic time for the child's inner being. The slow or stalled growth period is defined as "equilibrium." The child is more stable. The fluidity of growth places each child on his or her own path of development. All children tend to come and go through growth spurts and stability within six months of the average stage of development.

The growth pattern brings with it increased cognitive, physical, and emotional maturity. With that maturity comes an increase in imagination and fantasy. With growing imagination and fantasy come imaginary fears.

Early fears are not imaginary; they are real. A baby will be startled or cry at loud noises, such as thunder. Fear of the dark may begin in toddlers. This fear may be as much fear of separation from people and happy times as it is fear of nighttime. A night-light can help calm the fear, but recent research indicates that night-lights can later cause certain vision problems, so caution is needed with this choice. A favorite cassette tape or a tape of a parent's voice may also soothe the toddler.

Fantasy and imagination are usually linked to three-year-olds. This can be observed as they express pretending and imagination verbally and physically. However, pretending can begin at a much younger age. A toddler may offer a bottle to a doll that he perceives as crying. He may push a block as a car and make motor sounds.

Imagination enters into a toddler's dreams. Some of a toddler's wakefulness may be an indication that dreams are a factor even before the toddler is verbal. Once a child begins to talk, dream pictures can be shared. Toddler Nyka woke up crying. She had tossed her favorite blanket on the floor saying, "Birds in blankey!" Nyka had to have several nights of assurance before the blanket was again her favorite.

Twos and threes may be able to express their dreams, but they seldom do. Dreams may be real happenings to young children. One morning three-year-old Scott asked, "Mommy, what did I dream about?" His mother replied, "I don't know." He looked puzzled and said: "But, you were in it!"

Preschoolers may have imaginary friends. These friends may develop in children as young as two-and-a-half but more often at three and four. A first, or an only, child may develop imaginary friends, perhaps to fill in lonely places.

The three's fear-stage adds a new dimension to night fears. His imagination creates fantasy monsters, ghosts, and creatures under his bed. Shadows and sounds are turned into unfriendly, imaginary characters. A small flashlight helps the imaginative child clear his mind of such fears.

Fear of separation can be frightening for the older infant. A child's personality may determine the length and intensity of the fear of separation. Fear of separation can become evident when a child has had a hospital stay, a family crisis, change in residence, or other trauma. The separation fear may be evident during the stages of disequilibrium. *The Good-Bye Book* is a book the middle or older preschooler can almost "read" himself, once he hears the story. Help dispel night-time fears for toddlers and twos with a book like *Goodnight Moon*.

Share the security of Bible stories and Bible phrases with fearful preschoolers. The Bible phrase "Be glad and sing" (Ps. 9:2) can remind children to sing happy songs when they are afraid.

Fours and fives are beginning to differentiate between imaginary and real fears. A real fear developing now is the fear of death. Fours and fives especially fear the death of a parent or some other significant person in their lives. If this fear is expressed, listen. Assure the child that there will always be someone to love and care for him. Name some of those special people.

Toddlers and young twos may develop a fear of going down the drain. Rebellion at bath time and potty training may indicate this fear.

The differences in fears of imaginary creatures or events and fears of real animals, storms, fire, and other disasters must be clarified. Encourage preschoolers to talk about their fears.

Preschoolers might put their fears into pretending a scary situation, painting or drawing pictures expressing their feelings. After a recent tornado struck their town, kindergarten children painted a large mural about wind and tornadoes. Without adult direction, over and over they built up and knocked down block structures. What a

relief it was for them to feel in control of the destruction!

Personal Learning Activities

1. What fears do you remember from childhood? _____
_____
_____
_____
_____
_____

2. List ways you can help preschoolers cope with their fears: _____
_____
_____
_____
_____
_____

STAGES IN READING DEVELOPMENT[2]

In Stage One a Child:
- begins focusing and noticing surroundings
- likes to hear spoken words
- looks at pictures or books held or placed in the crib
- enjoys books being "picture read"
- begins to handle books and turn pages
- chooses to spend some time alone with picture books
- likes to be read to
- becomes selective about favorite books

ILLUMINATE THIS STAGE BY showing babies colorful teaching pictures. Talk about the pictures. Point to objects in the picture.

Introduce babies to books that have contrasting colors and easily-defined objects and pictures such as *Baby's First Picture Book*. Point to and say the names of objects in the books. *It's Fun to Be One* and *Let's Play* will help move preschoolers along with first mental imprints of books.

In Stage Two a Child:
- knows that books tell stories
- retells a story from pictures rather than print
- can show the front and the back of a book
- likes books about children, families, animals, trains, and other transportation vehicles.
- is curious about words that are important to him
- recognizes a few alphabet letters
- is beginning to appreciate fun and fantasy in print

ILLUMINATE THIS STAGE by letting the child retell a story by picture reading. Encourage interest in letters and words. Some books for this stage are *Big Friend, Little Friend*; *In a People House*; *Trucks*; and *The Cat in the Hat*.

In Stage Three a Child:
- shows interest in learning to read
- returns to favorite books and pretends to read them
- begins to show an interest in word forms and spellings
- recognizes her own name and familiar words in her environment
- uses sweeping motion to follow print from left to right
- grows in the ability to make predictions
- uses book language when retelling stories
- knows dictated stories can be written down
- identifies some upper and lowercase alphabet letters
- enjoys rhyming

ILLUMINATE THIS STAGE by stopping a story before the ending and asking children to make up endings. This helps boys and girls learn listening skills. It encourages them to create mental pictures. Mental pictures enhance comprehension.

Introduce both upper and lowercase letters to children. A well-illustrated ABC book will help teach the differences in the letters.

Silliness books like *Shake My Silliness Out* and *Silly Tilly's Thanksgiving Dinner* are enjoyed in this stage. A child may want to see and touch a word or words that make him laugh.

Rhymes and riddles are fun mental exercises for children who can repeat them. Thinking about words, understanding the sequence of a rhyme or story, and expressing the words verbally bring depth to readiness for reading.

Read a favorite Bible story and guide children in playing out the story. Use Bible markers to locate Bible verses (phrases). Ask children to touch and say the Bible phrases.

Teach poems, Bible phrases, short stories, chants, and songs from charts. Using a pointer helps teach left-to-right progression as well as letters and words. Some children will begin recognizing and remembering letters and words on the poster.

In Stage Four a Child:
- is interested in many different types of books
- makes predictions about title, pictures, and story content
- pays attention to print when reading
- follows print from left to right, pointing to each word when reading familiar text
- matches words that are alike
- recognizes most alphabet letters
- is beginning to match words with the same beginning consonants

ILLUMINATE THIS STAGE by continuing to provide a rich source of age-appropriate books. A book and other reading materials relating to each Learning Center activity help strengthen this reading stage. Add a child's dictionary, a Bible, or a reference book, as well as a few theme-related books, to the Book Center.

Expand chart reading. Let children volunteer to point to familiar letters or words. Children might point to letters that begin their names, or their friends' names. Color-code charts by randomly printing two or three sets of identical words or phrases in identical colors. Ask volunteers to find special punctuation marks, endings on words, words that rhyme, words with the same beginning consonants, or upper and lowercase letters.

In Stage Five a Child:
- may choose books by favorite authors
- expresses interest in characters and events
- watches the print intently
- begins to develop strategies for reading unknown words (uses cues such as illustrations and beginning consonants; starts at the beginning of a line of print, reads again, and self corrects)
- points to every word accurately when reading familiar text; is not confused by words of more than one syllable
- likes to try to read independently

ILLUMINATE THIS STAGE by regularly taking preschoolers to a library. Preschoolers will find books they have not seen before. They will be able to check out newly-discovered and favorite books.

Preschoolers at this stage may choose to make books. An ABC book is of interest. Place magazines from toy companies in the Writing Center. Boys and girls find "favorite" pictures. Each picture is placed on a page with the letter that begins the name of the pictured object. After pictures are found to match all letters, bind the book with staples, or punch holes and tie with twine.

Print each of the following Bible phrases on separate sentence strips. "Be glad and sing songs to God" (Ps. 9:2); "We work together" (1 Cor. 3:9); "God gives food to us" (Ps. 136:25). During group time, ask preschoolers to place each Bible verse in the Learning Center where it is best suited. Use this activity to relate other Bible verses to pictures, puzzles, or books.

Take children outdoors during any stage of reading. Print a chart of words as middle and older preschoolers name things they see outdoors. All these language builders are the basis for telling, dictating, writing, and reading stories, songs, and poems.

Consider Each Child

Reading readiness is a matter of timing. A child can be as much as six months ahead or behind the "average" growth pattern. The immature child can be just as intelligent as any other child, but he is moving at his individual pace.

"Early readers do not always win the race. The slower starters, with a wide base of experience and problem-solving often pull ahead when thinking skills and application become more important around the fourth grade . . . . Studies in different countries have shown that when five-and seven-year-olds are taught by the same methods, the seven-year-olds learn far more quickly than do the fives, who are likely to develop reading difficulties . . . . Forcing or overloading neural circuits may cause the brain to go into 'idle' because it cannot handle the load."[3]

Active, hands-on learning at any stage of reading readiness promotes curiosity, confidence, independence, and motivation for the next stage.

WEE Learn Curriculum Guide for Five-Year-Olds provides a rich source of age-appropriate reading and other readiness activities that children and teachers enjoy.

It is a resource for Bible stories and Bible activities of interest to fives.

Personal Learning Activities

1. When should reading readiness begin?

   _____

2. Look at the stages of reading. Think of children you teach. Can you see how one age may not fit into any one stage? Explain.

   _____
   _____
   _____
   _____
   _____

STAGES IN WRITING DEVELOPMENT

Hearing words;
Thinking about words;
Saying words that get results;
Seeing words in books and on cereal boxes;
Makes me want to **write** my own kind of words!

Seeing others using pencils, or markers, teaches the young child early writing skills. She knows a pencil or marker makes marks. She then makes her own marks on paper, a wall, or other places. She does not always hold the writing instrument correctly, but she gets results.

All the rich experiences a child has with books, and other exposure to words, increase her desire to "write." Writing readiness comes through manipulatives, puzzles, blocks, paintbrushes, large crayons, and scissors. All of these help develop eye-hand coordination and finger dexterity.

A toddler's attempts at writing are often a few marks. Twos make more scribbles. Some scribbles may have a tendency toward circles and almost "x" marks. The three-year-old begins scribbles with intent. She may tell you what she is "writing."

Middle and older preschoolers like to dictate experiences or creative stories. Seeing you write and hearing you read their creations are motivation for writing.

Two- and three-year-olds' scribbles and "pretend" writing turn into trying to copy letters or words at four and five. At four, a child begins to make efforts at printing his name. Most fives are able to print their first names.

Eye-hand coordination and hand and finger dexterity are not fully mature. Preschoolers still have difficulty holding and moving a pencil or crayon. Because of vision changes, fours and fives tend to reverse letters and create "flying" letters (a letter here and a letter there). Accept a child's own efforts at printing. Accuracy and neatness are not primary goals at this age. As a preschooler's neuromuscular system matures, his management of hands and fingers will improve and so will his printing. Some children will improve faster than other children. Individuality must always be considered as you teach children.

Fives, and some fours, begin to write "words," explaining pictures they draw or writing a story. Children invent words by sound: "GUR" girl, "FKS" fix, "KKEE" cookie. The important aspect of the early stage in printing is making the letters.

PERSONAL LEARNING ACTIVITIES

1. What are four stages that lead a child to want to write?

   _____
   _____
   _____
   _____
   _____
   _____
   _____

2. How can you encourage beginning writing without pressuring preschoolers?

   _____
   _____
   _____
   _____
   _____
   _____
   _____

"We will tell the next generation the praiseworthy deeds of the Lord" (Ps. 78:4, NIV).

Chapter 9

Moral and Spiritual Development

How are we to teach preschoolers from birth about God and His loving plan for us? It is not just *what* we teach, but *how* we teach what we teach that will influence a young child's moral and spiritual development. Christian teachers have a wonderful opportunity to assist children in developing and growing in one of the most important areas of their lives by providing learning experiences that lay spiritual foundations. While children have a capacity for growing and developing physically, intellectually, emotionally, socially, and spiritually, in this chapter we will be concerned primarily with the spiritual development of a child and how a teacher can facilitate spiritual growth and development in the classroom.

Laying Foundations

Christian preschool teachers have a unique opportunity not only to teach but also to provide a spiritual foundation for each child. Preschoolers need a solid spiritual foundation on which to base a future relationship with Jesus Christ. As with a house, if the foundation is faulty, the entire structure will reflect those faults. Most preschoolers begin building that foundation through positive relationships at home, with teachers, and through sharing Bible thoughts and verses.

Preschoolers develop rapidly in the first few years of life. A child's spiritual development begins immediately. An infant can listen as a teacher says, "Thank You, God, for Hanna's hands." As preschoolers grow, their understanding of God grows. A preschool teacher is laying a foundation for moral and spiritual development. When a preschooler begins to understand more about God, he is able to sing songs about God and hear simple Bible stories. An older preschooler can learn to express his thanks to God. Through modeling, teachers show children the importance of the Bible, church, and Jesus. By the time a preschooler is ready to leave a Christian early childhood classroom, he can have a solid foundation on which the rest of his spiritual life and relationships will be built.

How Children View God and the World

The interactions a child has with the adults in his life influence his mental picture of the world or his "world view." During a child's first year and a half, he discovers and orders his world largely through physical experiences.

A teacher of preschoolers needs to provide experiences that foster a child's need to ask questions. Learning experiences planned for the classroom can help foster a child's spiritual development by giving him opportunities to hear God's name, thank God for food, and learn that God loves each child.

By the time a child reaches his fifth birthday, his personality is developed. Since a child grows and changes so rapidly during the first five years of life, he needs many opportunities to experience spiritual truths. His lifelong "world view" is based on experiences during his early years. When a child hears about God while having good experiences in and out of the classroom, he will come to understand that God is loving.

Age-appropriate Bible teaching must be a part of the curriculum to assist children in developing a spiritually-based "world view." Teaching preschoolers about God is vitally important. A teacher can model positive feelings and responses to God by saying, "Thank You, God, for Jennifer." By doing this, the teacher helps the preschooler associate good feelings and a sense of being loved with God.

Personal Learning Activities

1. Think back to your own childhood images of God, the Bible or church. What kind of feelings did you have?

_____
_____
_____
_____
_____

2. Do you remember a teacher, pastor, or other adult who helped you to understand God? Name them and the feelings you had.

_____
_____
_____
_____
_____

3. What are some ways you can develop a good spiritual foundation for the children in your classroom?

_____
_____
_____
_____
_____

Trust and the Preschooler

Spiritual foundations are laid through trusting relationships. A child's personality is developed during his early years based on the relationships he has with the adults in his life. When a child feels she can trust the adult taking care of her to meet her needs, she begins to feel secure. When a child feels secure, she feels loved and begins to know or trust that the adult will love and care for her. When a child learns she can trust the people taking care of her needs, this trust lays a foundation for that child to one day be able to trust and relate to God.

If a child has difficulty trusting a parent or caregiver, he may have difficulty trusting the teacher and diffi-culty understanding that God is trustworthy. It may take several months, perhaps years, to develop a relationship of trust with some children. A teacher must continue to be reliable and trustworthy in many experiences with children. In meeting a child's needs, a teacher will help a child understand that God loves him and that he can trust God.

Meeting the Needs of Preschoolers

Meeting physical needs, especially with younger preschoolers, is extremely time-consuming. Physical needs should be met by loving adults. Holding a child is one of the best ways to meet these needs and to create a bond between the adult and the younger preschooler. Preschoolers need acceptance and approval. Teachers can show acceptance by listening to the child and allowing the child to be himself, allowing for differences in personality and temperament.

At times, it is difficult to take the time to listen to preschoolers. Listening shows the child that he is important to you. When listening to a preschooler, remember to:
- Make eye contact with the child.
- Sit or bend to the child's level.
- Allow a child to express himself.
- Give the child feedback.

Ask open-ended questions that allow for individual expression — questions that cannot be answered "Yes" or "No," or with only one word.

Young preschoolers are very active and require almost constant interaction with adults to meet all of their physical needs. It is this great demand that requires low student-to-teacher ratios, enabling teachers to meet needs and develop trusting relationships. A low ratio of staff to children also allows teachers to spend more time talking and singing with each child as they meet that child's needs.

By the time a preschooler reaches his first birthday, he will also respond more to adult attention. At times, preschoolers will display negative behavior in order to get attention from an adult or other children.

As an infant grows and develops, she needs more toys, manipulatives, and activities to stimulate her growing curiosity. As teachers introduce new objects and activities into the classroom environment, the children learn about the world. When a child encounters new objects, she will learn how these objects relate to her world. When a teacher provides interesting activities, she shows interest in the child.

For a child to have a meaningful pre-school experience, her needs must be met. Preschoolers need to feel safe and secure. We respond to this need by providing appropriate space, curriculum, toys, and loving care for each child. Teachers strengthen a sense of basic trust in each child by showing that they are trustworthy.

Children see that you can be trusted when you are consistent in how you teach as well as how you manage the classroom. When a child feels he can rely on a teacher, he feels he can trust the teacher to meet all of his needs, not just his physical needs. It is important for children to trust adults.

Some children have difficulty trusting adults because the adults in their lives have done things that create mistrust. Teachers can develop a trusting relationship that can be an example to the child.

Personal Learning Activities

1. List three ways you as a teacher can help a child learn to trust the adults in his/her life and eventually trust God.

   (1) _____
   _____
   (2) _____
   _____
   (3) _____
   _____

2. What are some factors that can cause a child to mistrust the adult taking care of his needs?

   _____
   _____
   _____
   _____
   _____

3. Think of a child that may have difficulty trusting. Write that child's name below and begin praying for that child and his family.

   _____

Self-Image and the Preschooler

A positive self-image is closely related to trust. Today, preschoolers often do not receive the message that they are special and loved by God. Christian teachers are able to show children in tangible ways that they are special, not because of what they can do, how they look, or how they behave, but because God created them.  When a child's needs are met, he feels loved. A positive, healthy self-image is a need all people share. Unfortunately, many preschoolers do not feel good about themselves. Our goal should be to help boys and girls to develop a strong sense of worth.

Personal Learning Activities

1. What are some factors that can influence a child's self-image:

Negatively:_____
_____
_____
_____

Positively: _____
_____
_____
_____
_____

A Teacher's Influence

Teachers should prepare themselves spiritually as well as professionally for the classroom each day. We teach out of the overflow of our own personal experiences. To teach even the youngest preschooler spiritual truths, the teacher must be prepared spiritually. Spiritual preparation includes:

1. Spending time alone with God daily.
2. Praying. Taking time not only to talk but to listen to God as well.
3. Scripture reading and memorization.

Set one goal for improving your own spiritual preparation:

_____
_____
_____
_____

Preschoolers learn by imitating other children as well as adults. The values a child learns will be those modeled by the important people in his life. A caring, loving Christian

teacher can make a profound impact on a child's life. Teachers are to be Christian examples everywhere they go. Not only can a teacher influence preschoolers, but she can also influence their parents and family members by showing genuine love and concern for that family.

Attitude Education

A child's "world view" will affect his attitudes. Our goal in Christian early childhood education is to provide foundations for moral and spiritual development. A teacher's words, attitudes, and actions help lay these foundations. When a child hears teachers say, "God loves Nicole," she begins to associate God and Jesus with feelings of love. As the teacher rocks a child and sings softly to him or as she feeds him, she says, "Thank You, God, for applesauce."

Preschoolers also need to develop positive attitudes toward the Bible. Teachers assist children in developing positive attitudes by providing vital ingredients for creating a spiritually-rich classroom environment.

Using the Bible with Preschoolers

Bible thoughts, Bible stories, pictures, and songs introduce preschoolers to spiritual things. We teach that the Bible is a special book and incorporate the use of the Bible thoughts into everyday activities. A preschooler begins to think of the Bible as a special book that tells about God and Jesus. The preschooler learns that the Bible is special by touching and looking at the Bible.

A Bible such as the *Read-To-Me Bible* gives preschoolers opportunities to learn to properly care for and handle the Bible. Using pictures and Bible markers creates interest in the Bible. Bible markers with matching colors or pictures or colorful ribbons can create new interest.  A teacher may laminate a flower and place it in the appropriate scripture reference and then highlight the verse in the Bible.

The Bible can be used throughout the classroom in various Centers to tie the learning activity to a particular Bible thought. The Bible can be placed in the Nature/Science Center with a leaf marking the Bible thought that says, "God made the trees" (Gen. 1:11). The teacher can read the Bible thought as the children water and care for a plant.

Use the Bible in creative ways throughout the day. When teaching preschoolers, use words that are familiar. When using Bible stories and thoughts with preschoolers, use an open Bible to help preschoolers understand that the story you are telling comes from the Bible.

Personal Learning Activities

1. Describe one way you can use the Bible in each of the following Centers:

- **Art** _____

  _____

- **Blocks** _____

  _____

- **Books/Library** _____

  _____

- **Homeliving** _____

  _____

- **Puzzles/Manipulatives** _____

  _____

- **Music** _____

  _____

- **Science/Nature** _____

  _____

Praying with Preschoolers

Is prayer a natural part of your classroom experience? Children can pray at lunch or snack times, when a child is hurt or sad, or during group time. Keep prayers brief. Use simple words the preschooler can understand.

Because preschoolers learn through senses, plan a variety of learning activities. As a teacher is feeding a child, she repeats the Bible thought "God gives food to us" (Ps. 136:25).

Personal Learning Activity

List each child in your classroom. Next to each child's name list one need that you will commit to pray for over the next three months.

Child's Name	Prayer Need
_____	_____
_____	_____
_____	_____
_____	_____
_____	_____
_____	_____
_____	_____
_____	_____
_____	_____
_____	_____
_____	_____
_____	_____

Choose another teacher as a prayer partner. Hold each other accountable for the next three months to pray daily for the children in your class. Also pray for each other during this time period.

Understanding the Preschooler

Developing foundations for moral and spiritual development involves understanding the child as a person. Toddlers are egocentric and insecure emotionally and have a great need to feel secure. At this stage of development, separation from parents is a very difficult process. A toddler needs to feel secure and know she can rely on her teacher, so the teacher must be reliable in attendance and must maintain classroom continuity. Toddlers are able to repeat simple Bible truths, enjoy simple songs, pictures, and books that illustrate Bible thoughts and stories.

As a child approaches his second birthday, he is becoming more social with his classmates and adults. Even though a two-year-old is more social, he still has difficulty relating well to his peers and does not like to share. Teachers can interact with children to assist them in learning how to share and how to show kindness to others. A two-year-old wants to experiment with everything. She wants to touch and look at everything. For the two-year-old, the Bible needs to be "hands-on." Allow preschoolers to handle the Bible. Because preschoolers learn through repetition, they enjoy hearing the same Bible stories over and over again.

The two-year-old is beginning to understand that God made the things in our world and that God made us. As preschoolers grow, they naturally become more curious about the world around them.

As a child approaches his third birthday, he desires to please adults and is becoming more verbal with adults. To please adults, children like to imitate the adults in their lives. It is so important for teachers to model Christian attitudes and interactions with students and coworkers as well.

Preschoolers learn a lot about the world around them and about social relationships by observing adults. We cannot expect a child to learn to share his toys if he hears a teacher complaining about having to share classroom space or materials with coworkers.

Teachers must set a good example and show positive social interactions with others. The three to four-year-old is very imaginative and likes to pretend. He often has difficulty differentiating between real and pretend. Puzzles, pictures, and objects used for teaching about the Bible need to be accurate. Preschoolers are concrete thinkers; abstract thought and symbolism are difficult to understand.

Preschoolers are very inquisitive. It is by asking questions that a child learns. Often preschoolers will ask difficult questions that can make even the most experienced teacher feel unsure. Being at ease can be difficult at times. Be a patient listener and wait for the preschooler to express himself. Remember to be honest; if you do not know the answer, say, "I don't know." A teacher should talk in a relaxed manner with preschoolers and answer questions about God as they arise. Take every opportunity to weave Bible thoughts and verses into conversation throughout the day.

Take advantage of a "teachable moment." When it rains, say, "God sends the rain to help the flowers and the grass grow. Thank You, God, for the rain."

How Children Develop as Moral Thinkers

Children develop a set of moral standards to live by based on what they observe in their world. These moral standards are what the child perceives as right and wrong. Teachers provide classroom examples and expectations so that preschoolers can learn positive behaviors for interacting with their peers, parents, teachers, and others in their world.

Three to six-year-olds view rules as absolute, fixed, and unchangeable. They have not yet made a distinction between actions and intentions. Children use the set of moral standards they have learned from the adults in their lives. The moral standards a preschooler learns will be expanded as he grows so that he can determine appropriate behavior and responses. What a child learns in the preschool years will be the basis of future moral and spiritual development.

Strengthening Families for the Task

Teachers are role models at school and in the community. Teachers can be witnesses not only to the children but also to their families. At home preschoolers often will recall a Bible thought or ask to say the blessing before a meal. Teachers in Christian education have the responsibility and privilege to facilitate and strengthen families. Praying for the children God has placed in the classroom will equip the teacher to assist in this awesome task. Pray in the following areas:

1. Pray daily for each child.
2. Pray for each child's parents/guardians.
3. Pray for patience, understanding, and discernment to be the teacher and the witness God wants you to be.

Personal Learning Activity

1. List some ways you can be a witness to parents and family members:

   _____

   _____

   _____

   _____

   _____

   _____

   _____

   _____

   _____

   _____

Teaching preschoolers about God's love can be a great blessing. Preschool teachers have an opportunity to impact the world for Jesus Christ by building spiritual foundations in the lives of today's preschoolers.

"Love the Lord your God with all your heart and with all your soul and with all your mind and with all your strength" (Mark 12:30, NIV).

Chapter 10

Physical and Mental Development

Demographers tell us there are 15 million American children under the age of 4, a national population of 272 million, and a world population of more than 5 billion.[1] While these statistics astound us, what is even more astonishing is that no two of these individuals are identical! Each person is a unique creation unlike any other.

Thousands of years ago, when the Psalmist wrote, "I am fearfully and wonderfully made" (Psalm 139:14b, NIV), he did not have access to the vast scientific data or medical knowledge at our disposal today. Even then, with his limited perspective, he recognized the magnificence of God's creativity and viewed the creation of mankind with awe and reverence.

Through advanced technology, new information about the complexities of the development of the human brain is being discovered each day. In the last 15 years, scientists have come to recognize that the brain of a human infant is extremely active. Earlier, it was believed that the structure of the brain was genetically determined and could not be altered. We now know that the brain's development is contingent on a complex interplay between the genes we were born with and life experiences.

Research has shown that early experiences have a decisive impact on brain development and on the way the brain is wired. Consequently, those early experiences will directly and drastically influence our capabilities and abilities as adults.[2]

Experience a sense of awe and wonder, a renewed appreciation for the uniqueness and unlimited potential of each child, for we are indeed fearfully and wonderfully made!

The miracle begins with the fertilization of the human egg. In less than a week after fertilization, cell division has occurred. Many of those cells are destined to become the brain and the rest the nervous system. By the nineteenth day, "the future brain is already visible as a bulge on a flat disc of cells."[3] Fifty thousand to 70,000 of the human body's 100,000 genes, will be involved in brain functions.[4]

In a little over a month, the development of the "five embryonic parts that will produce the forty or so major brain structures and hundreds of smaller tracts, nuclei, fibers, ganglia, nerves, bodies, pathways, canals, and membranes that must form for the brain to function normally"[5] has occurred. The emergence of the future brain, the single most critical phase of embryonic development, has happened, often before the mother has suspected or confirmed the pregnancy.[6]

In the uterus, the nerve cells in the fetus' brain proliferate. Twice as many neurons as needed are produced. Through a natural process of elimination, excess neurons die and are shed. Even with this loss, the infant will still be born with over 100 billion brain cells. Most of these neurons are not yet connected. As the baby experiences his world and forms relationships with his parents, family members, and other caregivers, connections among neurons will be formed.[7]

The first few weeks and months after conception, the fetal brain and nervous system are susceptible to permanent damage from a wide range of environmental factors. The fetus can be affected by things the mother is exposed to or things that she may ingest, breathe, or sniff. Even the mother's emotions may affect the fetus. As many as one in five American children have learning behaviors or emotional problems related to the effects of their physical and emotional environment before or after birth.[8]

On the other hand, interaction with the fetus by talking, touching, reading stories, and playing music may stimulate the brain and increase family bonding. According to brain researcher Marion Diamond, "There is no period of parenthood with a more direct and formative effect on the child's developing brain than the nine months of pregnancy leading to the birth of a full-term baby."[9]

While the church and its weekday early education program have no control over this critical developmental period in the child's life, they can help educate parents-to-be on preconceptive care. They can also provide encouragement and support to help reduce family stress and to foster a more positive atmosphere and environment in which the baby can be born.

Once the baby is born, environmental influences have an even greater impact. Although the infant will be born with hundreds of billions of nerve cells, they must be organized into systems for processing, thinking, talking, and remembering. Through the baby's encounters and interactions with the world, over 50 trillion connections (synapses) will be formed. If these synapses or connections are used repeatedly, they will be reinforced and will become a part of the brain's permanent "wiring." Conversely, if they are not used frequently, they will be eliminated.

During the first few months, the number of synapses will potentially increase to more than 1,000 trillion. "It is not the number of brain cells that is important. It is the number of connections that are made between those brain cells."[10]

Current experimental data indicate that early experiences play a critical role in determining which synapses survive. Without a doubt, stimulation reinforces these connections.

When the infant sees something, hears a sound, or is touched, the neural pathway is activated. Chemical changes are produced, which in turn stabilizes the synapse and prevents its elimination. Communication among neurons in the brain and in the body take place, and learning occurs.

Neurons are specialized nerve cells responsible for transmitting messages throughout the body. Neurons relay information via their dendrites, hair-like structures that receive incoming signals from other neurons. As neurons are used over and over, they lay down a multi-layered covering or sheath called myelin. Myelin speeds the nerve impulses and protects the nerves. The thicker the myelin sheath, the faster the signal transmission.

At the same time the "dendrites create increasingly complex interconnecting networks of neural pathways through which reactions and thoughts travel in the form of electrochemical impulses. These ever branching pathways are in a continual state of becoming. As long as stimulation continues, more dendritic branching occurs. If a stimuli stops the branching stops."[11]

At birth, most dendrites in a baby's brain have only one or two branches. Growth (branching) results from environmental stimulation and interaction with the baby through talking, singing, reading, and playing.

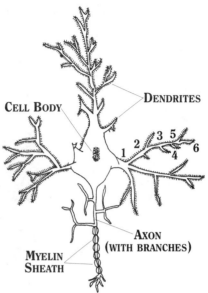

Figure 1
One of over a billion neurons in the human body. The richer the learning environment, the more luxuriant, intricate, and complex the dendrite branching.

The first two years of the baby's life will be a period of dynamic change. Even though the number of nerve cells will have decreased through natural attrition by this time, the brain will have doubled in weight.

How humans develop and learn depends critically and continually on the interplay between nature (an individual's genetic endowment) and nurture (the nutrition, surroundings, care, stimulation, and teaching that are provided or withheld.) Both are crucial.[12]

According to research the infant's brain is far from dormant (See Figure 2). For instance, the preschooler's brain, by the age of two, is as active as an adult's. Its metabolic rate will continue to escalate, and by the age of three, the preschooler's brain will be two and one half times more active than an adult's. This high level of activity will be maintained until adolescence.[13]

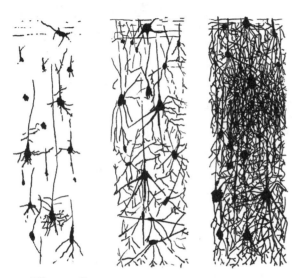

Figure 2
A comparison of a young child's nerve networks at birth, three months, and twenty-four months of age. Dramatic changes can be seen as the brain is stimulated by the child's environment.

The brain will also develop at an incredible rate, in waves rather than in linear fashion. This means there are prime times for acquiring different skills and knowledge. Once the prime time for optimal development has passed, opportunities for forging certain kinds of neural pathways appear to diminish substantially.

Learning is programmed to take place in an orderly manner.[14] However, one will quickly discover that although development occurs in predictable patterns and sequences, there will be a wide variation in the rates of development.

We must not base our assessment of a child's intelligence on his/her physical development. While some children's development will correspond perfectly with the standard growth charts, there will be others, approximately 10 percent, who will not fit within the ranges and yet be perfectly normal.[15] A child may be developmentally-delayed, but have above-average intelligence.

Delays can be attributed to a variety of factors. Prematurity is the most common. Extraneous variables like heredity, glandular and emotional development, sex, personality, nutrition, climate and even the child's birth order within the family may also affect her development and growth.[16]

Developmental delays do not automatically indicate a problem. However, it is always good to confer with parents when a child is seriously outside the developmental ranges and to encourage them to discuss these observations and differences with their pediatrician.

Dr. Kathryn Ellerbeck, a developmental pediatrician, recommends that **all** children who are language-delayed should have a hearing test. Early detection can be critical in intervention and preventing further developmental delays.[17]

Watching a child's skills unfold and develop is one of life's most fascinating experiences. It is the result of an extremely complex pattern of interaction among the various parts and systems of a child's body.

Growth specialists have identified predictable stages or milestones in development, which can be anticipated to emerge at specific ages. Although this emergence is not concrete, typically, certain abilities correspond with specific ages.

Growth specialists have also given us an overall formula for postnatal changes. It is 2-3-4-5, which means between birth and adulthood, the person's head and neck size will increase by two times, the trunk by three times, the arms by four times, and the legs by five times.[18]

Growth and development will proceed based on three principles. The cephalocaudal sequence is first. Based on the Greek word for "head" and the Latin word for "tail," this principle reminds us that the head will grow first, then the trunk, the arms and the legs last.

The proximodistal sequence is second. In Latin, proximodistal means "near to far." From this principle, we can conclude that a child's body will mature from the chest out. The child will have control over his shoulders before his arms and fingers, his upper legs before his lower legs and feet.

Differentiation, the third principle, means that growth will proceed from the simple to the complex. Development will move from the large muscles to fine muscle control. Essentially, this means a child will be able to walk long before he will be able to construct a building with Legos®.

It is recommended that teachers pay close attention not only to the age-level characteristics of the children they teach, but also to the age level which precedes and the one which follows the children they teach. In this way, teachers will be able to recognize emerging skills, identify skills that have been mastered, and anticipate skills which have yet to be demonstrated.

Birth to Six Months

The majority of the baby's time is spent sleeping, eating, and being diapered. In the first few days, one can expect the baby to average three minutes an hour of alertness during the day and less during the night. Slowly, over the next few weeks, the time will lengthen to an average of six to seven minutes per hour. By two months, wakefulness will increase to 15-20 minutes per hour.[19]

During this phase, babies will have very limited mobility and head control. Because the head is disproportionately large, it is best always to provide head support when lifting or holding a baby. By four months of age, he will be able to hold his head in an upright position, and by six months, his head control will be even stronger.

Although babies do exhibit right and left facing postures, a baby's head will be turned to the right 85 percent of the time.[20] With this in mind, mobiles should not be placed directly over the baby, but off to the far right or far left, with the design toward the baby, at a distance of twelve inches. Mobiles should feature bold, contrasting colors and features similar to those of the upper front portion of the human face, since babies are especially interested in looking at the area between the top of the nose and the top of the head. Seven to nine inches from the eyes is ideal focusing range. By three and one-half months, the baby will have near-mature visual capacity. Vision is clearly linked to the learning process.[21]

Teachers will also note that the baby's hands are tight fisted. If his fingers are pried apart, he will grasp a finger or whatever is placed in his palm. While he can hold a rattle, it has no significance. At about six weeks of age, the hands will start to relax. The baby will discover his hands, will spend a lot of time staring at them, and will begin swiping or batting at suspended objects. At this point in development, mobiles will need to be replaced with crib gyms.

At fourteen weeks, the infant begins turning her body up to one side or the other. This will soon be followed by the ability to turn over.

Her interest in the world escalates, and teachers will see her begin to explore her world in several ways. One way she explores her world is through sight. She is all eyes. Faces and pictures of faces are especially appealing. Small, slow-moving, detailed objects are also attractive.

A second way she explores her world is through her hands. She will finger objects,

move them back and forth and touch anything within reach.

Gumming and mouthing objects is another favorite pastime. Her fist will be followed by her fingers and finally anything that can be brought to her mouth will be gummed. Not only is her mouth an organ for exploration, but teeth will be erupting soon, and gumming objects relieves discomfort. Because of the developmental needs of this stage, it is essential that teachers provide a clean and sanitary environment and disinfect toys before and after each use.

Another sign of exploration is listening. She especially likes to listen to the sound she makes with her own saliva. As the months pass, this interest in sounds will become more pronounced.

Experiences during the first year are critical to the child's acquisition of verbal skills. In the early weeks of life, babies do not vocalize. The noises they make are related to eating and mouthing. In the second month, they begin to coo and make light, happy noises.

Babbling begins in the fourth to fifth months. The baby will begin to repeat syllables over and over again. Even before babies learn to speak, the sounds they make will have inflections that express emotions.

Language development will be influenced by the quality of the interpersonal relations in the early weeks and months of an infant's life.

Six to Eight Months

This phase has sometimes been described as "the lull before the storm."[22] Life will change dramatically as soon as the baby acquires the ability to move on her own. The child will no longer be content to sit and look. Around six months of age, the child will begin to gain control of his torso and be able to turn over from back to stomach and from stomach to back.

Sitting up will not be far behind. Sitting independently is a huge developmental step. This new control will motivate the child to explore the rest of his environment.

The young child will begin exercising leg muscles in preparation for walking. When held in an upright position, he may begin bouncing up and down.

Teachers should limit the use of swings and bounce chairs. To develop coordination, the child needs time on the floor and freedom to move in order to gain experience in creeping, crawling, and making his arms and legs work together.

Another major step in gaining control of her environment is refining the ability to open and close fingers around objects. Small objects, toys, keys, and jar lids are especially interesting to children of this age. The child will hold the object, mouth it, and pass it from hand to hand to discover all its possible uses and properties.

The discovery of object permanence is a major achievement at this age. It is the beginning of abstract thought. This accomplishment is necessary for the development of fantasy play, imagination, and the use of symbols to represent objects, as needed in reading.[23] This is not something which can be taught but happens naturally.

Eight to Fourteen Months

Physical development dominates everything else at this stage. No longer is the child one who sits and watches. As the child learns to sit up and crawl, she will begin pulling up to a standing position and will begin walking alongside objects, using them for support. As the child feels confident "cruising," the next step is standing alone and then walking unaided. Because of her increased mobility, she requires constant attention.[24]

The Toddler

This is one of the most difficult stages because the toddler is into everything. The toddler will probably have extremes in moods and be demanding, egocentric, and highly energetic.

A toddler's energy is boundless, and he hates to be confined. Toddlers need open spaces, both indoors and outdoors. They also enjoy activities which involve their senses. Water play, sand, play dough, music boxes, and smelling activities intrigue toddlers.

Language is also at its apex. Toddlers seem to say new words every day. Although their pronunciation is frequently incorrect, it is better to model correct language than to correct them at this time. There is also a discrepancy between the language they produce and the language they receive. The child will understand more words than she will produce in her own speech.[25]

One of the best things teachers can do is to surround the child with meaningful talk. Build on the child's words. For instance, if the child says, "cat," the teacher may add, "See the gray and white cat sleeping in the sun?"

The greatest benefit occurs when teachers speak directly to the child about routines, activities, and events which relate specifically to him.

Toddlers also enjoy books, music, and nursery rhymes. The toddler stage is an excellent time to get children interested in books. Books with clear, realistic, uncomplicated illustrations and photographs work best. Sturdy, homemade books can be even better than ones purchased commercially, because they can be tailor-made to the child's interest and vocabulary.[26]

In these early years, music and language are closely related. Even though the toddler may not be able to carry a tune or sing along, the exercise of singing will model another way of utilizing his voice to express himself. "A room that has singing in it is usually a happy room."[27] Music communicates even when children may not understand the meaning of words.

Two-Year-Olds

Like toddlers, twos are still working to establish their independence. Although their attention span is short, it is considerably longer than that of a toddler.

By two years of age, the motor and sensory areas of the cortex are well developed. The cortex is the thinking and reasoning part of the brain. Teachers can see the results of this development in the child's increasingly complex motor behavior.

The child's steps become longer, and the width of the stepping gait is reduced and smoother. At about twenty-one months, the child may begin running. Both running and walking will become automatic by the age of three.

Manipulative skills are still being refined. Because control over finger extension occurs only after reaching and grasping are well developed, the two-year-old will experience some difficulty in building towers with blocks. The process will become smooth by three years of age.

Teachers should provide a variety of activities to give practice for fine motor control. Large beads to string, pegboards with large pegs, and wooden puzzles are especially fun.

Art activities can also be fun. However, it is the *process* and not the *product* that produces enjoyment. The two-year-old likes the cause-and-effect experience. He presses a crayon on a piece of paper and makes a mark. Early marks will be mostly zig-zags. Later, he will begin making circular motions. Through this process, the child is learning how to use his hands for different things at the same time. For the two-year-old, art is primarily a sensory experience. Because twos will probably sneak a taste, materials and supplies should be simple and non-toxic.

Two-year-olds should not be "sat down" for any learning activity. Instead, the teacher provides the materials, supervision, and guidance which allows the child to work at his own pace and as long as his interest is sustained.

Two-year-olds generally have a vocabulary of about fifty words. Vocabulary will continue to increase an average of about nine new words per day. By the age of three, the child's vocabulary will have increased to approximately 900 words and to about 14,000 by the age of six.[28]

Three-Year-Olds

Age three is an exciting year of development. Although the rate of physical growth of both the body and the brain are beginning to slow, growth increases will be seen in the control of voluntary movement, alertness, attention and memory, and in motor and cognitive abilities as well.

By this age, balance is much more refined than when the child was two. Even though threes may alternate feet climbing up the stairs, they may continue to walk down the stairs one by one.

Fine motor skills are also being refined. Since it is still difficult to hold a pencil between the thumb and index finger, the three-year-old may hold the pencil, crayon, or paintbrush with his whole fist. When he draws, lines are less repetitive and have more definite direction.

Because of its novelty, cutting with scissors is a popular activity. Some children will still have difficulty manipulating scissors. Practice improves this skill remarkably. Threes can practice and improve their cutting skills by cutting play dough, cutting fringes around the edge of paper, or cutting on a line. Close supervision is needed, especially to discourage the temptation to cut their hair or someone else's hair.

Three-year-olds are also capable of a wide variety of movement. They have a fluency of movement they have not had before. Running, galloping, jumping, and dancing bring them pleasure. By three years of age the child will also be able to jump from a height of about 18 inches, pedal a tricycle, and throw a ball fairly accurately.

While threes enjoy activities with balls and bean bags and are beginning to gain skills at rolling and bouncing the balls or tossing the bean bags, catching them remains a challenge. More and more, the hand muscles are cooperating with the brain.

The typical three-year-old is full of questions. The child's inquisitiveness is punctuated with where, what, and why questions. Until their sense of time is strengthened, questions beginning with "when" will be rarely heard.

Threes especially enjoy hearing stories read over and over. They prefer stories about everyday life, books about the seashore, farm, modes of transportation, and different seasons. Short books are appropriate for short attention spans. Threes cannot sit still and listen for long periods of time. "A child who develops an adversarial relationship to books early on is a child in academic trouble."[29]

Four-Year-Olds

In the four-year-old, teachers will see a budding sense of initiative. Having mastered basic skills successfully, the four-year-old is ready to undertake new tasks and bring them to completion. Boldly, she will attempt new and exciting feats, such as climbing up a slide the wrong way.

Another prominent characteristic of the four-year-old is his curiosity. "Why" questions are endless. Teachers need to keep in mind that questions are intended as a way to get the adult's attention and not just to get a meaningful answer.[30]

Many four-year-olds will be interested in naming letters and finding words they know. If the child's interest is spontaneous, encourage it. It is a great age for stimulat-

ing imagination. Karen Miller, author of *Ages and Stages,* maintains that imagination should be dominant. She states, "If you can encourage and stretch the natural imagination and curiosity of four-year-olds and not squelch them, you are giving the child a valuable gift and a tool for later life. You have created 'eager learners,' children who want to know more."[31]

Five-Year-Olds

By age five the child's body proportions have changed. His head is about one-fourth of his body size. His brain is 90 percent of its adult size. His body configuration is beginning to more closely resemble that of an elementary-aged child.

He is becoming more skillful in both large and small motor activities. Handling spoons, forks, pencils, and paintbrushes is done with ease. He can also pour from a large container and unwrap small pieces of candy. While he may have little difficulty with buttons and snaps and can basically dress and undress himself, he may still have difficulty tying his shoes.

Manipulative activities such as lacing cards, sewing with burlap and yarn needles, peg boards, and fit-together blocks encourage hand-eye coordination.

The five-year-old's large muscles have also matured. Not only can she walk and run with speed and grace, but she has control over stopping, starting, and turning. She can stand on one foot with her eyes closed and can execute somersaults. Some children can ride both a tricycle and a bicycle.

The five-year-old has a high activity level. This is made possible by his rapid metabolism and heart rate. It also explains why preschoolers are less sensitive to temperature extremes. Because of their high level of activity, they need lots of space and freedom to move, as well as a variety of activities that will occupy not only their bodies but also their minds.

The conception of time and space are more clearly differentiated. She is beginning to move toward realism and comedy and away from make-believe and magic.

By five, right or left-handedness is evident. Accommodate children who demonstrate left-handed dominance by providing left-handed scissors and seating them at the left end of the table.

The five-year-old is growing in self-control and self-direction. Fives can stay on task longer and work until a project is finished. "Sitting at a table or desk doing workbooks is not the way in which young children learn best," contends Dr. David Elkind, a professor of child study at Tufts University.[32] Fives enjoy a variety of hands-on learning experiences which allow children the freedom to move and explore in Learning Centers.

Movement is essential to learning.[33] Using hands-on experiences during the learning process greatly increases learning

efficiency. More of the brain is activated, thus building more complex nerve networks. Whenever touch is combined with the other senses, one's learning potential is dramatically increased.

According to Dr. Carla Hannaford, nerve cell networks, which are actually the essence of learning, are created through physical movement. "Movement activates the neural wiring throughout the body, making the whole body the instrument of learning."[34]

Dr. Hannaford maintains that we custom design our nervous systems to meet the challenges of our world and interest.[35] "Fifty percent of one's potential brain capacity is developed in the first five or six years of life."[36] Because the first five years are the most critical of all, it is imperative that preschoolers be provided an environment which stimulates brain activity.

Edward Zigler, a Yale psychologist, says, "If any stimulation is effective it's plain old talking."[37] Evidence shows that reading books to a baby will increase his love for reading far more than flash cards, and if the reading is done while he is in the arms of a loved one who is also enjoying the experience, his appreciation of reading will be augmented even more. A baby will be stimulated through his daily routine and encounters with siblings, parents, and caregivers.[38]

In other extensive research, Craig Ramsey, a University of Alabama scientist, determined that the cognitive, motor and language development are enhanced by old fashioned measures like peekaboo, blocks, and beads.[39] "Many experts believe that wooden unit blocks in graduated sizes and shapes are the best toy of all."[40]

A baby is born to learn. At birth, he begins a life-long journey of discovery. This journey will become a never-ending process of organizing and classifying information. Children need constant interaction, a variety of experiences, and an enriching environment.

Learning specialist Dr. Jane Healy says learning occurs best if the child feels rested, in control, and secure. "Infants need safety, love and conversation from their parents, or from capable consistent caregivers. They need an environment that stimulates them to do their own exploring, manipulating, and wondering."[41] It is the quality and the amount of adult-child interaction which is important, not the toy or how much it costs.[42] Our challenge is to help each child meet his or her highest potential.

One way teachers can do this is to present information in the learning style in which the child learns best. The preschooler begins to develop a preferred or individual learning style. While he can learn in a variety of ways, it is through his preferred learning style that he learns best. There are at least three styles or modes. They are auditory (need to hear it), visual (need to see it), tactile (need to touch or feel it).

Listening is the most difficult mode for young children (and many adults) to learn.

Yet, most of our teaching is verbal instruction. Young girls tend to be better listeners than boys. This tendency generally continues throughout life.

Boys, on the other hand, tend to be visually stronger. However, most preschool children remember best what they touch, handle, and manipulate.

Dr. Dawna Markova reminds us that we don't all think and learn in the same way. To properly educate our children, we must understand the nature of the different ways they think and use their brains. She maintains that children suffer tremendously when their natural way of thinking, absorbing, and processing information is mocked, criticized, or ignored.[43]

As one closely watches a child, the child's preferred learning style will become apparent. For example, if his strongest mode is auditory, he will gravitate to things related to hearing. He needs to actually hear it or hear himself say it to remember it. Auditory learners talk out loud without realizing they are talking or making noises. They enjoy books on tape, quiet music, happy songs, or listening to someone read. Visual learners need to see it. They like mobiles, pictures, photographs, colorful objects, nature items, or demonstrations. Kinesthetic/tactile learners need to move or to touch or feel it. They are constantly moving and changing positions, tapping toes, nodding their heads, or looking around the room. They enjoy an assortment of textures, blocks to stack, and space to crawl, walk, sit, run, and jump. The kinesthetic child cannot sit still for long periods of time. If they can do something or move while they listen, learning is easier.

There is no single learning style that is better than another or makes a person smarter or more capable. Each child is a mixture of learning-style strengths. "Learning will be most effective if every lesson taught includes an auditory, visual, and kinesthetic component in how information is conveyed. In other words, knowledge should be transmitted by reading and demonstration through action and by verbal instruction."[44]

Every child also has gifts and abilities. Our challenge is to discover that giftedness and to also use it as another means of helping develop the child's fullest potential.

Howard Gardner, a developmental psychologist, has created a revolutionary Multiple Intelligences theory.[45] His model provides valuable information on the many ways a child can exhibit intelligence. Gardner maintains there are eight kinds of intelligence located in different parts of the brain.[46]

Although they may be in different proportions, each person has all eight kinds of intelligence. In this way, everyone has an opportunity to excel in some area of life. Children who are taught through their natural learning styles become achievers in school. The Multiple Intelligence Pie (*Figure 3 on the next page*) describes each of the intelligences and suggests ways teachers can incorporate activities to support each intelligence.[47]

Teachers of infants and young children must realize the significant role they play during the most critical period of growth and development in a child's life. Teachers can be instrumental in helping a child reach his greatest potential in order to become the unique person God created him or her to be. The more freedom the child has to explore his world, and the richer his environment, the more complex will be the pattern for learning, thought, and creativity.

Without a doubt, we can give thanks to God, for we are fearfully and wonderfully made!

Personal Learning Activities

Choose the better statement:

A. The structure of the brain is genetically determined and cannot be altered.
B. Brain development is contingent on the complex interplay between the genes we are born with and life experiences. Early experiences have a decisive impact on brain development.

A. An array and variety of expensive toys and equipment are needed to provide a stimulating teaching and learning environment.
B. The most effective stimulation is not through specialized toys, but through daily routines and encounters with loving, caring teachers and parents.

A. Auditory instruction is used most frequently because it is the most effective style of learning.

B. Learning will be most effective if every teaching session includes auditory, visual, and kinesthetic components.

- -

A. A teacher needs to know how intelligent each child is to teach the child most effectively.

B. A teacher needs to know how each child exhibits intelligence to teach the child most effectively.

(The Bs are the better answers.)

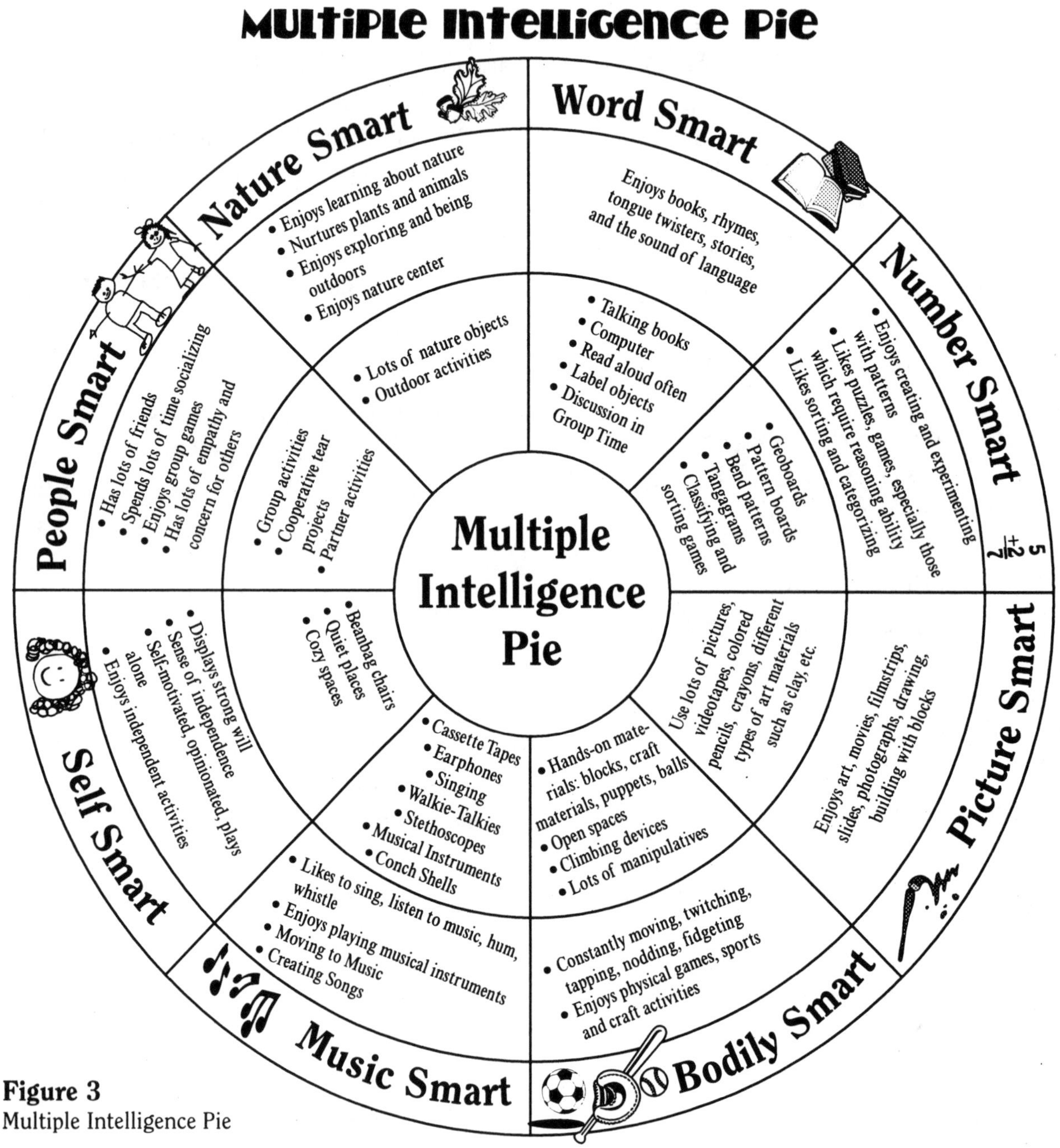

MULTiPLE InTELLiGEnCE PiE

Figure 3
Multiple Intelligence Pie

Teaching in Christian Weekday Early Education

PHYSICAL DEVELOPMENT OF THE YOUNG CHILD

AGE	LARGE MUSCLE	SMALL MUSCLE	MATERIALS AND ACTIVITIES
Birth to Eight Months	• Controls Neck and Back Muscles • Rolls Over • Sits Alone	• Learns to Reach • Grasps and Drops Objects • Holds Objects • Puts Objects in Mouth	• Live Singing • Interesting Things to Look At • Objects Which Make Sounds • Unbreakable Mirror • Textured Objects • Rattles
Eight to Fourteen Months	• Crawls and Scoots • Stands • Climbs • Takes First Step	• Uses Hands Together • Feeds Self with Spoon	• Balls • Nesting Toys • Objects with Hinges • Pop-Up Toys
Fourteen to Twenty-Four Months	• Walks and Climbs • Creeps Upstairs • Climbs Forward into Chair, Then Turns to Sit • Kneels on Floor	• Eats Finger Foods • Turns 2-3 Pages of a Book at a Time • Unzips Zipper • Removes Shoes and Socks • Beats Two Spoons Together	• Fill and Dump Toys • Push and Pull Toys • Tug and Lug Toys • Pegs in a Hole • Shape Match • Rocking Boat
Twenty-Four to Thirty-Six Months	• Runs • Kicks Large Ball by Walking Into It • Jumps in Place • Walks on Tiptoe	• Scribbles • Learns to Potty • Folds and Creases Paper • Unscrews Caps	• Sand Play • Play Dough • Balance Ropes • Jumping Games • Magnet Fishing • Clothespin Play
Three-Year-Olds	• Nimble on Feet • Rides Tricycle • Jumps from Steps • Catches a Large Ball	• Cuts with Scissors • Builds with Blocks • Can Draw a Circle • Stirs a Liquid with a Spoon	• Ring Toss • Ball Pass • Stringing Beads • Spooning Beans
Four-Year-Olds	• Hops, Gallops, Balances • Climbs Ladders • Stands on One Foot for Five Seconds or More • Hangs from Top of Jungle Gym	• Draws Recognizable Pictures • Cuts a Straight Line with Scissors • Holds Fork and Spoon Adult-Fashion • Drops Small Objects into Small-Necked Bottle	• Beanbag activities • Bottle Bowling • Braiding • Paper Mosaics
Five-Year Olds	• Skips, Somersaults • Balances on Either Foot for Ten Seconds • Jumps Backwards • Hops Forward Four to Eight Times on Either Foot	• Ties Knots • Draws a Square • Can Thread a Needle • Spreads Peanut Butter and Jelly on Bread	• Hopscotch • Coffee Can Stilts • Lacing and Threading • Jacks

*"... since God so loved us, we
also ought to love one another"
(1 John 4:11, NIV).*

Chapter 11

Social and Emotional Development

Just look around. The world is filled with beautiful and incredible things created by God. Genesis 1:31 (NIV) states, "God saw all that he had made, and it was very good."

Look in the mirror and you will see one of God's finest works. The manner in which God created you and the rest of mankind implies the significance and importance of each individual to God.

The fact of being created in God's own image and being blessed by Him promises each person the potential of an unlimited and glorious future. Much depends on how we develop and use the resources God has given us.

God has given each human being characteristics and abilities which distinguish him from His other creations. Man's ability to talk, feel, think, and interact with others make him distinctive.

We are emotional and social beings. God did not plan for man to be alone. From the beginning of time, God planned for man to live in relation to others. Whether we are adults or children, we need socially and emotionally-satisfying relationships. While we have always been aware of our need for each other, we are just beginning to realize the tremendous effect our social relationships and emotional state have on our lives.

Researchers have found that even more than intelligence, a person's emotional awareness and ability to handle feelings will determine success and happiness in all walks of life, including family relationships.[1] Furthermore, children with high emotional and social skills or emotional intelligence (EQ) are happier, more confident, and more successful in school.[2]

The importance of healthy emotional and social relationships and self-discipline is an important part of teaching preschoolers. May you, the reader, recognize that God's great love for you and your importance to Him is directly connected to your emotional and social health. The same is true for everyone.

The Relationship of Body, Thought, and Emotion

Distinctions between body and mind and thought and emotion are nonexistent. It is now apparent that emotions, body, and reason are physiologically inseparable.[3] Body, thought, and emotion are intimately connected through intricate nerve networks and function as one to enhance our learning.

The human body actually has three distinct brains wrapped in one. The cerebellum lies at the base of the brain and produces instinctive behaviors like finding food, staking territorial boundaries, social group formation, and personal care. Conceivably, some of children's most disruptive and irritating behaviors could be instinctive, like fighting or mimicking peers, and may originate from this lower brain center.[4]

Subsequently, when the child feels threatened, he has the capability of closing off higher levels of thinking. Therefore, for optimal learning to occur, the child must feel safe and secure. Effective learning takes place in a positive emotional climate where the child is able to make choices and express feelings.[5]

The "second brain," the limbic system, houses emotions, motivation, and regulates impulses. Aspects of memory, certain drives, and attentiveness are also regulated here. For years, its importance has been underestimated. Every experience is run through the emotional filter of the limbic system. This process assesses its value, meaning, and survival potential in light of past experiences. Socially, our actions stem from our need to survive and to be accepted within our group.

The "third brain" or the cerebral cortex, also known as the thinking brain, is located above the limbic system. "The cortex allows us to have feelings about our feelings. It allows us to have insights, analyze why we are feeling a certain way, and then do something about it."[6]

Each child is born with a physical brain structure and certain chemical and electrical response patterns that strongly influence the way in which the brain responds to stimuli both from within and outside the body. Genetics and environment work together to determine the child's sociability, emotional state, and personality.

The emotional experiences the baby has while his nervous system is still developing will impact his emotional stability later in life. If a caregiver responds when the infant feels intense distress, anger, or fear and restores feelings of comfort and recovery, the infant will soon learn self-soothing behavior. Because the teacher took him from distress to comfort, he will learn to employ his caregiver's soothing responses.

However, if he cries out in fear, sadness, or anger and no one responds, he will experience more fear, more sadness, and more anger. Hence, he will become passive and non-expressive. When the baby gets upset, he will lack a sense of self-control and will experience negative emotions, fear, and anxiety.

While teachers and parents cannot control the child's genetic make-up, they can influence environmental factors and can teach children techniques to control their emotions and emotionally-distressing situations.

Even though the brain comes into the world preprogrammed, many aspects of learning, emotional responses, and behavior are susceptible to alteration by different biochemicals produced by the brain. To illustrate this point, the brain produces biochemicals to which the body reacts. One of these chemicals is serotonin. Blood pressure, digestion, sleep and body temperature are just a few of the body systems influenced by serotonin.

The body naturally produces serotonin when a person smiles. Serotonin can help children deal with stress by inhibiting an overload of input into the brain. Serotonin has also been known to decrease aggression and impulsivity. Smiling contracts the facial muscles. The blood flow to nearby vessels is decreased, which cools the blood and lowers the temperature of the brain stem. This, in turn, triggers serotonin's production.[7] A simple smile can make a big difference.

Yet another biochemical is associated with aggression and can increase a person's arousal and likelihood to fight. But the simple action of relaxing and taking a deep breath, sends a message to the brain to slow the production of the chemical. This simple action greatly reduces the desire to be aggressive; therefore, telling a child to relax and take a deep breath can have positive results.

A child's emotional circuits are formed by the emotional lessons learned at home and at school, making him competent or incompetent at the basics of emotional intelligence. Babies who receive warm, responsive care tend to thrive and show more resilience in later life. Children who have developed strong social skills generally have been the recipients of consistent, responsive care during the first years of life.[8]

The chart below gives an overview of a preschooler's social behaviors, according to age, to help teachers better understand what social behaviors are developmentally appropriate.

Social Development of the Young Child

Age	Social Behavior
6 Weeks	Responsive to smiles and conversation
12 Weeks	Recognizes mother
14 Weeks	Interested in father
16 Weeks	Solemn with strangers
32 Weeks	Inhibited by strangers
40 Weeks	Responsive to "bye-bye"
52 Weeks	Responds to "no-no"
52 Weeks	Enjoys pat-a-cake
52 Weeks	Can wave "bye-bye"
1.3 Yrs/Mos	No longer inhibited by strangers
1.3 Yrs/Mos	Imitates adults (talking on phone, etc.)
1.6 Yrs/Mos	Intrigued by another child but treats him like an object
1.6 Yrs/Mos	Plays by himself/herself
1.6 Yrs/Mos	Retrieves things for an adult
1.9 Yrs/Mos	Begins to understand personal possessions
1.9 Yrs/Mos	Willing to help with household tasks

Social Development...*continued*

Age	Social Behavior
2 Years	Fascinated by other children
2 Years	Participates in parallel play
2 Years	Dependent and passive with adults
2 Years	Shy around unfamiliar faces
2.3 Yrs/Mos	Antisocial
2.6 Yrs/Mos	Ritualistic in behavior
2.6 Yrs/Mos	Domineering
2.6 Yrs/Mos	Resistant and independent
2.6 Yrs/Mos	Assertive, difficult to deal with
2.6 Yrs/Mos	Conflicts with peers
3 Years	Subordinate
3 Years	Receptive to suggestions
3 Years	Independent
3 Years	Reverts to infancy
3.6 Yrs/Mos	Forms friendships
4 Years	Assertive
4 Years	Prefers peer mates
4 Years	Shows off
5 Years	Obedient, cooperative, pleasing
5 Years	Seeks approval
5 Years	Prefers own age group

*Adapted from L. H. Stott , *The Longitudinal Study of Individual Development* (Detroit: Merrill Palmer School, 1955)

Studies show early care and nurture have a decisive, long-lasting impact on how children develop, on their ability to learn, and on their capacity to regulate their emotions. "Children who feel safe because they can depend on an adult are able to reach out to new experiences."[9]

An unwholesome physical environment can cause adverse effects. Studies show, when children have been neglected in early life, brain-mediated functions like empathy and attachment are impaired.[10]

Children who receive highly-erratic care are more prone to becoming very anxious later in life. When they persistently receive unresponsive care, children tend to shut down emotionally and distance themselves from others.[11]

Even an overly-restrictive caregiver, who controls and limits the child's activities, can retard the child's thinking and problem solving skills as well as his willingness to take initiative. Children learn by acting on their world. They are driven by exploration and curiosity. They naturally poke, prod, and ask questions. When a toddler unrolls a whole roll of toilet tissue or a three-year-old splatters the paint, such exploration does not mean the child is "bad." It simply means his boundless curiosity has led him to this action.

The more freedom the child is allowed, within reasonable and safe limits, the more capable he becomes. Children need to feel capable and proud of themselves. A positive self-image is built by celebrating with babies when they discover something new and cheering their efforts to try new things. We boost a child's self-image when we allow the child to explore, discover, and think and do for himself.

Personal Learning Activities

1. List the characteristics of children with high emotional intelligence (EQ):
   (1) _____
   (2) _____
   (3) _____

2. For optimal learning to take place, a child must feel _____ and _____.

3. Three ways the physical environment impacts a young child emotionally are:

   _____
   _____
   _____
   _____
   _____
   _____

The Stages of Emotional and Social Development

The First Year

Since childhood, especially the first six months, is an opportunity for establishing emotional habits, it is imperative that teachers and parents be attentive, responsive, prompt, and consistent when teaching and caring for children.[12]

Even in these first weeks the baby begins to understand the importance of communication and the pleasure of contact with other human beings. The baby desires to be held and touched. He will wiggle, jerk his body, and move his tongue and mouth. He moves to attract attention from adults who can be attentive to his physical needs. The baby's cries and his helplessness are important in the beginnings of social development.

The baby's first smile usually surfaces between six and ten weeks of age. According to Swiss Psychologist Piaget, these first smiles are linked to the baby's familiarity with whatever he is seeing at the time.

By four months of age, the child has become vocal and giggly. He will cry when left alone. His social interaction with others has greatly increased.

By five or six months of age the baby's intentional cries are used to get what she wants. Her cries of despair lead to feeling better. She uses sounds, gestures, facial expressions, and crying as methods of communication.

The period of life between eight and twelve months is of primary importance. Through interaction with adults, the child develops lifelong competencies. He learns to express affection, annoyance, and to show pride in achievement. He begins to have his own sense of self as separate from others.

He takes a great deal of pleasure in being with other people. He is beginning to understand certain words and phrases and use them to interact with others.

The child responds to her own name. Social rituals, like saying "bye-bye," are common. She is affectionate and particularly enjoys hugs and warm, infectious smiles.

One and Two-Year-Olds

Although a twelve to fifteen-month-old enjoys being in groups, he will tend to play alone or near another child rather than with her. Despite his outgoing attitude, he still needs reassurance and security. When meeting new people or going to an unfamiliar place, it is quite normal for the child to withdraw and even become tearful.

Up until now the child has looked to his primary caregiver as the main provider of affection and care. As he gets older and his self-awareness increases, he will begin to see the adult as a separate person.

As a toddler, he will strive to establish his individuality. Simultaneously, the child needs the attention and support of trusted adults to sustain his need for security. One of his first words and one which is repeated frequently is, "No!"

It is unrealistic to expect toddlers to share or to put themselves in another child's shoes. Piaget's preoperational stage of development, which includes the preschool years, has significant relevancy for understanding another aspect of a child's social development. Piaget asserted that preschoolers cannot understand another child's perspective; they only understand their own. When they behave self-centeredly, they are not being selfish and unkind. They are only seeing the world from their perspective.

Since they have few words to express frustrations and often feel powerless, they may react intensely and resort to tantrums. Their short attention spans make it easy to distract them and to redirect them to another interesting object or activity.

Another developmental milestone is the ability to fantasize. Toddlers often engage in pretend play. They pretend to be animals or to use an object, such as a telephone, to mimic an adult.

During the second year, the child will become even more independent and outgoing. She will form stronger friendships with adults and children. Dramatic play with dolls, dishes, and dress-up clothes in pretend play will emerge.

Two-year-olds are becoming more aware of their feelings and the feelings of others and will show signs of sympathy when others are in distress.

Three-Year-Olds

After passing through the turbulent twos, the child settles into a period of equilibrium. He is beginning to learn how to share, to take turns, and to be patient. He is at peace with himself and his world.

This stage is a highly "we" age. The child often begins sentences with, "Let's . . ." Not only is the child beginning to play alongside other children, but she is beginning to interact with others in cooperative play and is eager to please.[13]

Threes are able to come up with solutions to problems and begin to use language to express displeasure. This is an opportune time for teachers to encourage preschoolers to use their words and think of their own ways to solve problems. This can be done by working with the child to identify the problem, working together to generate solutions, evaluating the solutions, selecting the best option, making and implementing the plan, and evaluating the outcome.

Preschoolers need to learn to resolve preschool-sized problems so they will be able to solve larger problems as they get older. When children successfully solve problems, they begin to construct a belief system which says, "I can think for myself. I can solve problems."

Dramatic play becomes more imaginative. It now includes cooking, feeding, and putting the doll to bed. Everyday life experiences are often reenacted with different children playing different roles, including the family cat.

Teachers will want to encourage threes to do as much for themselves as possible. Allowing the child to zip his own zipper, button buttons, or snap snaps not only saves the teacher precious minutes, but the practice helps the child develop self-help skills, boosting self-image and fostering a sense of independence.

Three-year-olds can also assist the teacher in other ways, such as passing out snacks, feeding the class pet(s), wiping the table, straightening books, and putting away toys. Involving the child at this age helps him feel important and needed.

During this year, if not earlier, successful toilet training will likely occur. The teacher can help the parent look for obvious signs. For example, when a child is ready to begin training, he may remain dry for long periods of time, and his facial expressions may indicate readiness to eliminate. Another indicator of readiness is when the child can follow simple instructions and can communicate personal needs. Teachers should work closely with parents in this process and be as consistent in their expectations and procedures as possible. Expect many accidents and be as low-key and non-punitive as possible.[14]

Fears, especially night terrors and animal phobias, are very common among three-year-olds. They are often threatened by ordinary events, which they have misinterpreted. These misrepresentations occur because of their budding imaginations, their inability to separate fact from fiction, and their need to protect their sense of identity.[15]

The best approach to dealing with their fears is to acknowledge the fear and to stay close enough that the child feels safe and protected.

At times the three-year-old seems insecure. This is evidenced in his physical demeanor. He may stutter, tremble, or stumble. He may need a security object, like a blanket or stuffed animal, for emotional security. One may also notice he releases tension through sucking his fingers, biting his nails, blinking his eyes, chewing at his clothes, or picking his nose.

The three-year-old also engages in magical thinking. In magical thinking, the child wishes for something to happen. If his wish becomes a reality, he begins to believe he has the power to make it happen and begins to feel responsible for its occurrence. Threes are literal-minded and are easily confused by metaphors and figures of speech. Teachers must be careful to avoid symbolism and say specifically what they mean.

The ability to lead and to follow his peers and to express emotions freely becomes apparent. By the end of the third year the child has become a very sophisticated social being.

Four-Year-Olds

The four-year-old enters an age of extremes. "Out-of-bounds" is a key phrase to describe him.[16] He is out-of-bounds in his motor behavior, personal relationships, and verbal execution. Hitting, kicking, throwing fits of rage, running, slamming doors, defying orders, chafing at restrictions, and incessant talking are to be expected. It is not uncommon for the four-year-old to experiment with swear words or bathroom language. Consequently, the four-year-old needs firm supervision and someone who can regain control when the situation gets out of hand.

A four-year-old may enjoy playing by himself or with other children. Fours enjoy

dramatic play and will be more elaborate in dressing up. They create more roles and settings such as restaurants, airplanes, trains, and the post office.[17]

Boys enjoy fantasy play as much as girls, so props and dress-up clothes should accommodate both male and female roles. "Time spent in pretending is time well-spent."[18] Fantasy play has many benefits. It not only enhances the child's social development, but it helps a child rehearse life experiences and develop flexibility in thinking and coping with life changes and stress.[19]

The four-year-old begins to realize that girls grow up to be women and boys grow up to be men. Precocious sexual behavior is not uncommon and is just a way of exploring and understanding the mysterious differences between males and females.[20]

Teachers can enrich the child's experiences by presenting an age-appropriate or Learning Center-based curriculum which gives equal opportunities for boys and girls to participate in all learning activities. For instance, woodworking should be available to girls, just as sewing should be available to boys. Non-sexist, multicultural puzzles, books, and pictures can be used to broaden a child's awareness and acceptance of gender and racial differences.

Five-Year-Olds

Compared to the out-of-bounds four-year-old, the five-year-old is calm, serene, composed, and together. Five-year-olds pre-fer playing with friends to playing alone.

Evidence shows that children learn social behavior by watching adults and other chil-dren and imitating their behavior.[21] Conse-quently, it is imperative that teachers model the behavior they wish to encourage.

Socially acceptable behavior is also the result of positive reinforcement. Positive reinforcement in the form of praise, recogni-tion, or personal satisfaction may encourage socially acceptable behavior.

It has been said that the most fundamen-tal thing the teacher can do to foster mental health in young children is to provide oppor-tunities for healthy, emotional attitudes to develop.[22]

Personal Learning Activities

1. Socially and emotionally, the first year of a child's life is: _____
_____
_____
_____

2. The one and two-year-old are:
_____
_____
_____
_____

3. The three-year old is:
_____
_____
_____
_____

4. The four-year-old is:
_____
_____
_____
_____

5. The five-year-old is:
_____
_____
_____
_____

ERikson's Stages of Emotional Development

Erik Erikson has contributed significantly to our understanding of these basic attitudes. He believes that individuals pass through a series of emotional developmental stages which form their basic attitudes.

Three of these stages occur during early childhood. They are: the stage of trust ver-sus mistrust, autonomy versus shame and doubt, and initiative versus guilt. He stress-es that the successful completion of each stage is necessary before progressing to the next stage.

Trust vs. Mistrust

The first developmental state is that of trust versus mistrust. Trust develops as the baby learns he can depend on other people to meet his needs. Trust is closely connect-ed to the quality of care provided by the mother and other caregivers, and the man-ner in which they meet the baby's needs, especially in diapering, feeding, and providing physical affection. The mother's responsiveness assures the baby that he is of great value and importance.

When the baby's basic needs go unmet, he learns mistrust. The baby then perceives the world as undependable, unpredictable, and potentially dangerous. While the balance between trust and mistrust has been decided before the child enters preschool, the need for trust to be affirmed and reaffirmed continues throughout life.

At the weekday education program, the child needs the assurance that the teacher is dependable. Being consistent in policies and class rules, being reasonable, and being sensitive in meeting the child's needs as they arise establishes the teacher's trustworthiness and strengthens the teacher-child relationship.

Autonomy vs. Shame and Doubt

Autonomy versus shame and doubt is the next stage. This stage generally coincides with toilet training. The drive to become independent and to express independence by making choices is part of the child's need to exert control and to assert himself. This stage of development becomes most obvious to teachers of a two-year-old who says, "No!" and "Mine!"

The child who is deprived of the opportunity to establish independence, self-sufficiency, and autonomy may become overcome with feelings of shame and self-doubt. The

result is negative self-image, defiance, and manipulative behavior. To promote autonomy and self-assertion, teachers need to provide opportunities for the child to make his own choices and to practice independence.

Initiative vs. Guilt

With practice, the child develops the ability to act independently. He is then able to tackle the next developmental challenge, which is initiative versus guilt.

The older preschooler is interested in reaching out to the world, doing things, and being part of a group. He will try things out in order to see how others react. For example, he may experiment with profanity. He will also develop attitudes about appropriate sex roles, become curious about the world, and enjoy imaginative play in this stage.

Fostering Self-Discipline

As the child explores, experiments, and interacts with others, the teacher's primary goals will be to help the preschooler act responsibly and to develop self-control and self-discipline.

To each teacher, discipline can mean something different. Technically, the word *discipline* comes from the root word "disciplina," which means teaching and learning.[23]

At its best, discipline is positive instruction and guidance given to children to teach important life lessons: lessons in correct principles, lessons in respectful communication, and lessons in healthy relationships. There is a big difference between discipline and punishment. Punishment has negative connotations in the sense that we **do** something negative to a child to improve behavior. Punishment is an act of force to stop an action. It incorporates emotional or physical hurt to teach a lesson. The outcome breeds resentment and an adversarial rather than a cooperative working relationship.[24]

Research shows that punishment is ineffective. Over time, the punishment must become harsher and more punitive to continue to work. Too, constant monitoring and supervision is needed. Children who are punished do not own their behaviors, they just pay for them.[25]

A more worthwhile goal is to see misbehaviors as opportunities for teachers to give instruction and guidance and for children to learn. This type of discipline leads to self-discipline, the ability of a person to discipline himself, to base his decisions on outcomes and to own actions.[26]

Madelyn Swift, author and an authority on discipline, says the critical question in disciplinary action is deciding what you want to accomplish. What is your vision or goal for each child?

Swift recommends a four-step, disciplinary process. Step one is to determine the lesson to be taught. Identifying the concept or what the teacher wants to teach the child is an important beginning.

Step two is to identify the real problem and address the concern with respect and authority. In the third step, action is taken as needed. Finally, in step four, the process is evaluated. The teacher determines what lessons and principles were learned and assesses their effectiveness.

Cooperation is a critical factor in this entire process. Adults often fail to inspire cooperation because of the words they use and the manner in which words are delivered. Instead of promoting cooperation, words can produce resistance.

Swift identifies ten barriers to promoting cooperation. They are blaming and accusing, put-downs and belittling, threats and intimidation, commands and orders, lecturing, reminding and nagging, guilt, labeling and name-calling, comparisons, and sarcasm.[27]

These obstructions to cooperation violate dignity, creating disrespect and resistance. Once obstructions have been identified, they become easier to eliminate. To produce cooperation, teachers must maintain each child's dignity.

Several techniques can be used to enhance cooperation.[28] One technique is to give children the opportunity to be helpful. Even toddlers can help pick up the toys. Helping makes children feel important. Requests prefaced with, "It would be helpful," will increase compliance and cooperation. A dividend of helpfulness is a more positive self-image. When helpfulness becomes a choice, a child's self-image rises. Children begin to see themselves as capable, competent, helpful, and cooperative. By making a significant contribution to the classroom, children develop attachments to the group. "I belong" is an important message to a child.

The use of descriptive language is another technique which can be used to facilitate cooperation. Teachers avoid accusations and negative comments when they describe what needs to be done rather than what went wrong.

Descriptive language tells the child what he needs to do. It teaches ownership of problems and mistakes and then helps a child assume responsibility for rectifying them. An example of descriptive language is, "Your empty cup and napkin belong in the trash can."

Another useful method of phrasing statements is "I-messages," an approach developed by Thomas Gordon. I-messages help others know how the person feels as a result of the behavior. Responsiveness, empathy, understanding, compassion, and sensitivity are taught through their use. "I am frustrated because I can't find the missing puzzle pieces," is an example of an I-message.

Giving alternatives is always more helpful, which benefits children as they get to make a decision in the process.

Establishing rules, policies, and rights is another way to teach responsibility and own-ership. Positively stated, rules, policies, and rights help children know what **to do** rather than what **not to do**.

Use of natural and logical consequences, problem solving, redirection, and limiting the environment are disciplinary strategies which teachers can incorporate to help children learn self-discipline and control.

Consequences teach children that they are responsible for what they have chosen to do and for what happens to them or others as a result of their actions and decisions. The use of consequences helps a child think ahead. As a result, they learn that whatever they do, it is their responsibility to make it right. The teacher may say, "The milk spilled on the table. The paper towels are above the sink."

For children under three, redirection works well. It is gentle and subtle. Because the attention span of younger preschoolers is so short, they can easily be directed to alternate activities. For example, Julie wants to work a puzzle. As she waits, the teacher may say, "Julie, all the puzzles are being worked. Would you like to build with the blocks or look at a book while you wait?" Not only is she being directed to another activity, she is also being offered a choice of activities.

Limiting the environment is another discipline tool which works especially well with younger preschoolers. Teachers remove, limit, or postpone the use of certain objects until a child is older and more mature.

Handling anger and frustration is a job each person must learn to deal with appropriately. A typical way young children deal with anger and frustration is through temper tantrums. Teachers have been told to ignore them and they will cease; perhaps this is not the wisest response.

There are two very similar behaviors which appear to be tantrums. In one situation, the child is in perfect control and is seeking attention and directing his behavior.

In the other situation, it is obvious the child is not in control of his actions. When anger takes over, the lower brain responds. The production of adrenaline accelerates and shuts down that part of the thinking brain responsible for reasoning, logic, and language. This explains why attempting to reason with a child in the midst of a tantrum never works. Until the child regains control, rational thought is impossible. Ignoring a child in this state says, "You are on your own."

Instead of ignoring the behavior, steps must be taken to help the child regain control. Unfortunately, there are no pat answers. What works to calm one child may not work for another. Some children may need to be held and rocked. Rocking, patting, and swaying motions are controlled by the right brain. Singing softly is also calming for some. Other children reject touching; they want to be left alone. There is a difference between giving a child space and ignoring him.

After calmness has been restored, the next step is to return to the incident which precipitated the behavior. Children must be taught that tantrums do not get them what they want, nor do they solve problems.

There is no loftier goal than to help each child develop high emotional and social skills, be self-controlled, happy, confident, and successful.

A positive self-image is the key to a child's behavior. When we help a child to like himself because God created him, to be self-sufficient, and to believe there is no problem he cannot handle, we boost his emotional and social intelligence and move him closer to realizing his God-given potential.

"Our children come into the world with a spark that is uniquely their own. We are the caretakers of that flame. Even if it is reduced to a tiny ember buried in a charred timber, it is our responsibility to provide the wind that will help it rekindle."[29] Keep the fire burning.

Personal Learning Activities

1. Discipline is _____
   _____

2. Ways a teacher may see a child's misbehavior as an opportunity include:
   _____
   _____
   _____

3. My definition of self-discipline is:
   _____
   _____
   _____

section 3:

The Teacher
You Can Be

Teaching in Christian Weekday Early Education

"I have raised you up for this very purpose" *(Exodus 9:16, NIV).*

Chapter 12

Your Call

WHOM DOES GOD CALL?

A weekday teacher shared, "Teaching preschoolers in our weekday program is where God has called me to be. Ministry to families brings me great joy!" How committed are you to obeying what God has called you to do? Are you ready to answer God's call?

JESUS' CALL TO TEACH

Teaching was Jesus' life's work; it was His ministry. Forty-five times the gospels tell us that Jesus taught; forty-six times Jesus was called teacher. How do you know God would have you teach preschoolers in Christian weekday early education? How has God called you?

YOU ARE CALLED FOR A PURPOSE

"I have raised you up for this very purpose, that I might show you my power and that my name might be proclaimed in all the earth" (Exodus 9:16, NIV). Your very being was planned with a purpose — God's purpose.

He was calling you as He created you by giving you your abilities, your personality, and your gifts. The call on your life began in the mind of God even before your conception.

DETERMINING YOUR CALL

Following are questions that may assist you in determining if you have a calling for teaching in Christian education:

1. Am I a learner?
2. Do I have a passion for teaching?
3. Am I enthusiastic about teaching?
4. Do I desire to meet the needs of preschoolers and their parents?
5. Am I living my life in such a way that I would want young children to imitate me?
6. Do I plan for using Bible thoughts and verses with preschoolers?
7. Am I willing to commit my life to God's call to teach?

God initiates the "call"; we choose whether to respond. Ministry is not simply a vocational choice; it is a lifetime commitment and a response to a call.

ACCEPTING GOD'S CALL

You may have a growing awareness of God's leading you to teach in Christian education. You know God has given you your abilities and your desire to teach. If you have sensed God's call on your life as a preschool teacher, you should give your life to doing just that — serving God by teaching preschoolers.

You are a preschool teacher, handmade by God. The timing of your life is unique. You were made for this time, this moment, to be a radiant preschool teacher, glowing with the love of the Lord.

If He has chosen you to teach His young children and to lead as a teacher in Christian weekday education, may you respond to His call.

THE JOURNEY OF YOUR CALLING

God first called you as He asked you to allow Him to be Lord of your life. Your salvation experience is the first calling God placed on your life.

As you accepted God's call, He began to reveal His purpose and plan for you.

Think back to the day you accepted Jesus as your Saviour. Write your testimony in the space provided and answer the questions about your salvation experience. Retrace the steps that led you to be called "teacher" in a weekday ministry:

MY TESTIMONY

How I Came To Know The Lord:

_____
_____
_____
_____
_____

How My Life Changed:

_____
_____
_____
_____

Becoming A Teacher Called By God:

The Beginning — How did you sense God directing you to become a preschool teacher?

_____
_____
_____
_____

The Process — What events in your life led you to become a preschool teacher?

_____
_____
_____

The Present — What makes you want to teach today?

_____
_____
_____

GROWING IN YOUR CALL

A preschool teacher called by God reflects Jesus Christ. He or she exhibits a meek and quiet spirit, is gracious, discreet, controlled, and pure, putting the needs of others first. He or she knows the preschoolers who arrive each day. This is God's beautiful preschool teacher. Although there are many who teach preschoolers, your call is unique. Celebrate the preschool teacher that God called you to be!

ACCOMPLISHMENTS OF SOME WHO ANSWERED GOD'S CALL

Let us look at several people who answered God's call and fulfilled God's purpose in their lives:

- MOSES led the Israelites out of bondage.
- GIDEON delivered Israel from Midian.
- DAVID was Israel's greatest king.
- MARY was the mother of Christ.
- ESTHER saved her people from being killed.
- NEHEMIAH led the rebuilding of Jerusalem's wall.
- JEREMIAH served as a prophet to Judah.

Did any of these people question their abilities to do what God asked of them? The answer is yes; they did. When God called Jeremiah to be a prophet to Judah, he told the Lord that he did not know how to speak and that he was only a child. But God told Jeremiah that before he was even born, He knew him and had appointed him to be a

prophet. He also told Jeremiah not to say that he was only a child. God asked Jeremiah to tell the people whatever He commanded him to say. Jeremiah answered that call and faithfully did as God said.

Personal Learning Activity

Does God's calling on these ordinary people inspire you? Write your own insecurities and feelings of inadequacies in what God has called you to do.

_____
_____
_____
_____
_____
_____
_____
_____
_____

Ask God to quiet those feelings and bring confidence and strength to your character.

One thing these people had in common was the fact that they had a passion for serving God. When God calls us to be teachers, He trusts us to minister to the children and their families in His name. We are to teach with a passion. We are to teach with a purpose.

OUR RESPONSIBILITY IN OUR CALLING

Remember God has chosen you to be a weekday teacher of preschoolers. Equip yourself to climb to the highest level of your ability and to do the best job in the area of ministry to which God has called you. How have you prepared for your calling of preschool teacher?

1. Have you shared your "call" with others? List the people you told about your "call."

   _____
   _____
   _____
   _____
   _____
   _____
   _____
   _____
   _____

2. Are you studying God's Word regularly?

   _____
   _____
   _____

3. Have you used all opportunities to further your education?

   _____
   _____
   _____

Test the growth of your "call" by rating the following areas on a one-to-five scale, with one representing the lowest and five representing the highest level on the scale:

1. I am growing in my personal relationship with Jesus Christ.

   1——2——3——4——5

2. I am growing by learning from a more experienced preschool teacher.

   1——2——3——4——5

3. I am growing in knowledge by furthering my education.

   1——2——3——4——5

4. I am growing through experiences with the preschoolers I teach.

   1——2——3——4——5

5. I am growing through my prayer life and Bible study.

   1——2——3——4——5

You will be successful if you strive to live up to your purpose.

Checking Your Heart

Give your heart a checkup; Galatians 5:22-23 (NIV) says: "The Spirit gives love, joy, peace, patience, kindness, goodness, faithfulness, gentleness, self-control." List the characteristics which preschoolers see in you as you teach:

_____
_____
_____
_____

Some qualities a teacher should possess are:

- A desire to help
- An interest in the welfare of each preschooler

- Unconditional love of preschoolers
- A shared interest in their problems
- The knowledge that the most effective lesson is the teacher, herself
- The knowledge that truth is *caught* more than *taught*
- The knowledge and desire to seize each teachable moment
- The knowledge and desire to use Bible thoughts and verses throughout the day

Are you giving your best to the preschoolers you teach?

FULFILLING YOUR CALL AND COMMITMENT

Because I am committed to God's call, I will live a life of: *(check all that apply)*

_____ Servanthood
_____ Humility
_____ Consistency
_____ Going the extra mile
_____ Caring for others
_____ Sacrifice
_____ Prayer
_____ Sharing Jesus Christ

Because I answered God's call to teach, I will:

_____ Make my classroom a learning environment filled with love and joy
_____ Pray for boys and girls in my class
_____ Pray with parents about their children
_____ Live my life so that others may see a resemblance of Jesus Christ
_____ Share what Jesus has done in my life as God opens windows of opportunities
_____ Love my students unconditionally as God loves me.

"I have raised you up for this very purpose, that I might show you my power and that my name shall be proclaimed in all the earth" (Exodus 9:16, NIV).

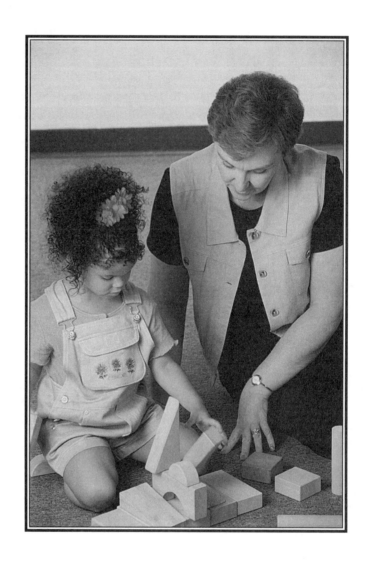

"For none of us lives to himself alone"
(Romans 14:7, NIV).

Chapter 13

Your Influence

WHAT IS INFLUENCE?

Influence is that moral or spiritual capacity by which we have the power to produce an effect upon a person or development without using authority or force. Every step of the way we are consciously or unconsciously exerting an influence upon those with whom we come in contact.

THE INFLUENCES OF A TEACHER[1]

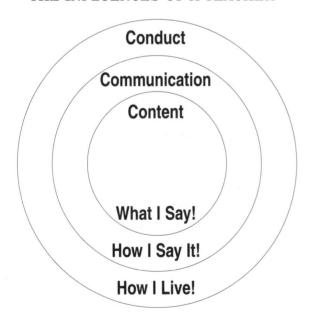

A Christian teacher has a great impact on preschoolers through her Christlike influence.

Your influence as a Christian teacher will continue long after the preschooler leaves your class.

What lasting impressions will you leave with your boys and girls and their parents? What kind of foundation will you build in their lives?

HOW IMPORTANT IS YOUR INFLUENCE?

Our lives have an impact. Others are depending upon us. How important is your influence? It is important enough to significantly impact the lives of young children and families who are in Christian weekday education programs. Prepare your own heart and mind before you enter the classroom each day.

Complete the following statements:

• I will show God's love by _____
_____
_____

• I will use Bible thoughts today when I
_____
_____

• I will show patience as I _____

_____

_____

• I will show concern to each child by

_____

_____

• The new activity I will provide this week is

_____

_____

Name other ways you can use your influence.

Jesus described two approaches to life: the first is the person who made the right choice about where to build, and the second is the person who made the wrong choice about where to build. He makes the appeal to His listeners that everyone who hears His words and puts them into practice will be the kind of person who builds his or her life on a firm foundation. Jesus offers us the blessing of being a different kind of person, one who builds his life on Him and lives by Kingdom principles. The teacher who builds her life on Jesus Christ can influence children and their families to build their lives on that same foundation, also.

What is important to you? What best describes the primary foundation of your life?

• Your work?
• Your talents and abilities?
• Your intelligence?
• Your common sense?
• Your great personality?
• Your family and friends?
• Your possessions?
• Your relationship with Jesus?

The contrast between the wise and foolish builders points to the difference made by choosing the right foundation on which to build life. Deciding to build your life on Jesus Christ, believing in Him, and committing your life to seek to be obedient to His teachings equips you to use your influence in ways that will matter for eternity.

How can a Teacher use Her Influence?

Jesus said, "You are the light of the world" (Matthew 5:14, NIV).

If we are to be "light," consider these characteristics of light and ask, "As a teacher of young boys and girls, how can I be 'light' to these children and their families?"

Light . . .

. . . illuminates
. . . reveals
. . . comforts
. . . guides
. . . warns of danger
. . . awakens you to a new day
. . . shines for others' benefit
. . . heals
. . . connects to a power source
. . . burns sacrificially (costs)
. . . is conspicuous
. . . is visible
. . . is pure

Considering *each* phrase above, think of a way you can be "light" to your class.

HOW IS YOUR PERSONAL CONDUCT AN INFLUENCE?

The teacher is a role model. How she lives will influence children. The values and lifestyles he embraces will reflect on future generations. Every step of the way we are exerting an influence upon those with whom we come in contact.

The teacher plays a major role in determining the child's attitude and actions in life.

Teacher, You Are What You Teach

If you are courteous and considerate, your students learn to be kind.

If you are generous and caring, your students learn to be giving.

If you attend to your students' needs, your students will be thoughtful of others.

If you speak kindly to your students, your students learn to be kind.

If you praise your students for trying, your students will have confidence.

If you raise your voice and talk angrily, your students will become rebellious.

If you model God-like traits, your students will learn what God is like.

If you give unconditional love, your students will give love as God does.

If your life teaches trust in Jesus Christ, your students will come to know Him.[2]

Using a scale from one to five with five being the best rating, rate yourself on how you are influencing the preschoolers in your class :

1. I am courteous to and respectful of my students.

    1——2——3——4——5

2. I am generous and giving.

    1——2——3——4——5

3. I am caring and thoughtful.

    1——2——3——4——5

4. I speak kindly to my students.

    1——2——3——4——5

5. I give genuine praise to individual students.

    1——2——3——4——5

6. I use a kind tone of voice with my class.

    1——2——3——4——5

7. My students can learn what God is like by seeing my actions.

    1——2——3——4——5

8. I love my students unconditionally.

    1——2——3——4——5

WHEN ARE WE TO TEACH?

Deuteronomy 6:6-7 (NIV) tells us, "These commandments that I give you today are to be upon your hearts. Impress them on your children. Talk about them when you sit at home and when you walk along the road, when you lie down and when you get up." In other words, we are to teach about God through Bible thoughts and verses at every possible opportunity.

List five times you could use Bible thoughts, Bible verses, and songs to teach about God in your classroom:

1. _____
_____
_____
_____

2. _____
_____
_____
_____

3. _____
_____
_____
_____

4. _____
_____
_____
_____

5. _____
_____
_____
_____

THE INFLUENCE OF CURRICULUM

The Teacher

The curriculum involves everything that a child experiences while attending a Christian weekday education program. The teacher's major role is to plan for every activity that will take place during the day.

A teacher who *plans* to use Bible truths and stories as he teaches will be more likely to actually use them while he is teaching.

Watching and Learning

No written word nor spoken plea
Can teach young hearts what they should be,
Nor all the books upon the shelves,
But what the teachers, parents, friends are themselves.

Author Unknown

"Fathers (mothers and teachers) . . . bring them up in the training and instruction of the Lord" (Ephesians 6:4, NIV).

The Environment

Does your room say, "Come in, touch, explore, find, enjoy"? Planning for an age-appropriate environment will affect the way a child learns.

These components influence learning:

- A well-lit room
- Neutral or soft, pastel-colored walls
- Unit teaching picture
- Age-appropriate toys and equipment
- Well-ventilated room
- 35 square feet of space per child
- Learning Centers for hands-on learning

The Influence of Content Plus Communication

With the Child

The influence of content is what the teacher says; the influence of communication is how the teacher says it. In the book, *The Five Love Languages of Children*, Chapman and Campbell have much to say about the power of words. They talk of communicating love through affectionate, praising, and encouraging words — words that say, "I care about you." Consider their description:

"Such words are like a gentle, warm rain falling on the soul; they nurture the child's inner sense of worth and security. Even though the words are quickly said, they are not soon forgotten. A child reaps the benefits of affirming words for a lifetime. Conversely, cutting words, spoken out of short-lived frustration, can hurt a child's self-esteem and cast doubts about his abilities. The tongue has the power of life and death."[3]

With the Parent

When a child witnesses a friendly, warm relationship between his parent and teacher at the Christian weekday education program, it enhances his self-esteem and creates a desire for learning. A teacher must build warm, caring relationships with parents to assure quality education for their child.

To communicate and to encourage involvement with parents, a teacher can:

1. Show equal respect and friendliness to all parents.

2. Listen to parents to obtain information about their child.

3. Arrange parent/teacher meetings at times of the day convenient to parents.

4. Use parent pages from the *WEE Learn Curriculum* to provide activities for parents and children to do at home.

5. Be open to problem-solving sessions related to their child.

6. Encourage parents to visit your classroom.

7. Encourage parents to keep you informed about their child.

8. Keep the lines of communication open.

Affectionate Words

When babies come into this world, they do not know the meaning of words. They do understand what an adult's facial expression, voice tone, and demeanor communicate. Because young children cannot think abstractly, they cannot "see" love, but they can "feel" love. These boys and girls receive love through what adults say with body language. Your tone of voice is part of your body language.

The Tone of Voice

It's not so much what we say
As the manner in which we say it.
It's not so much the language we use
As the tone in which we convey it.

"Come here!" I sharply ordered;
And a child cowered and wept.
"Come here," I softly whispered;
And into my arms he crept.

Words may be mild and fair,
But the tone pierces like a dart.
Words may be soft as summer air,
But the tone can break a heart.[4]

Author Unknown

Words of Encouragement

When we use encouraging words with children, we are giving them courage to try new things and to move up a level in development. Teachers can be encouragers by the words they choose to use.

Young children have the natural drive to take the toy they want when they want it. A teacher can encourage by observing when a child shares or does any other kind deed and gives praise for the good behavior.

The Bible says in Proverbs, "A gentle answer turns away wrath" (Prov. 15:1, NIV).

Make a list of all the children in your class. Beside their names write positive words that describe them. Also, write words that will encourage each individual child.

_____
_____
_____
_____
_____
_____
_____
_____
_____
_____
_____
_____
_____

Words of Guidance

Children need to be guided by the adults in their lives. Observing a child behaving appropriately, and praising him for it, encourages desired behavior.

 170

In a positive manner, practice explaining the behavior you desire in a child. Use as few words as possible. Some examples are:

- "The chair is for sitting."
- "Our feet belong on the floor."
- "Use your inside voice."
- "We walk inside."
- "We draw on our own paper."
- "It is kind to share."
- "We will go inside in five minutes."
- "Keep the dishes in the Homeliving area."
- "Return the blocks to the shelf."

Words of Wisdom

Proverb 22:6 (NIV) says, "Train a child in the way he should go, and when he is old he will not turn from it." In other words, what you teach a child will be a part of him for his entire life.

Luke 2:52 (NIV) tells us "Jesus grew in wisdom (mentally) and stature (physically), and in favor with God (spiritually) and men (socially)." A teacher has a profound impact on a child's life as he develops in all areas.

Influence in Ministry

Ministry is meeting the physical, social, emotional, and/or spiritual needs of an individual. There are numerous ways a teacher can see that ministry takes place. Read the list below and put a check by the areas in which you are already ministering to students and parents. Place an "X" by the areas in which you would like to begin ministering to families that are in need.

Partner with your church and ask for support and assistance for the following:

____ 1. Providing supplemental food supplies

____ 2. Obtaining clothes for children and family members

____ 3. Helping with gifts at special times of the year, such as Christmas

____ 4. Making scholarships available for the children of single-parents or low-income families

____ 5. Conducting Christian-parenting classes

____ 6. Offering a parent's night out

____ 7. Preparing meals for new moms

____ 8. Taking a gift(s) to the new baby and big brother or sister

____ 9. Providing classes which include special-needs children

____ 10. Providing support meetings for parents of special-needs children

____ 11. Sharing local services offered to special-needs children

____ 12. Letting your church staff know when there is a crisis such as hospitalization of a child on your class roll or a family member of that child

____ 13. Communicating with parents about their child and his progress by holding parent conferences

____ 14. Working with parents to have consistency in discipline at home and school

____ 15. Inviting your children and their families to attend your church services and special events

AM I a "WWJD" Teacher?

Circle the dots beside the statements that would help any teacher be a "What Would Jesus Do" Teacher.

- I teach by example and love boys and girls unconditionally.

- I know what the home life of each child is like.

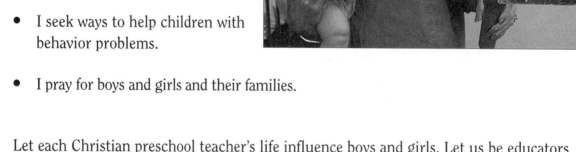

- I take time to listen and acknowledge what children say.

- I laugh with my class.

- I think about individual children's differences as I make lesson plans.

- I seek ways to help children with behavior problems.

- I pray for boys and girls and their families.

Let each Christian preschool teacher's life influence boys and girls. Let us be educators that pass on the knowledge of Jesus Christ to future generations, enabling them to pass this knowledge on to their children. Let us be eternity influencers.

"Do your best to present your-self to God as one approved, . . . who does not need to be ashamed and who correctly handles the word of truth" (2 Timothy 2:15).

Chapter 14

Your Professional Image

THE PROFESSIONAL

Being professional means a person is skilled, proficient, trained, capable, adept, and learned in his or her field.

THE EARLY CHILDHOOD PROFESSIONAL

Early childhood teachers are in a profession of service, a service that helps children reach their highest level of potential. Service includes helping parents enhance the quality of their children's lives.

A Professional Teacher:

- Illustrates an understanding of the growth and development of young children
- Implements a plan to teach using developmentally-appropriate practices, practices which are individualized and age-appropriate
- Records observations of each child's growth and development; knows each child's progress
- Establishes and maintains a safe, sanitary environment
- Develops and nurtures positive relationships with students, co-workers, and parents
- Maintains a professional appearance
- Uses time wisely
- Maintains high ethics
- Is an advocate for children
- Seeks training opportunities
- Sets personal goals
- Is a life-long learner

PROFESSIONAL APPEARANCE

Teachers are role models. Young children learn from their role models; what you wear will be an example to them. When you are appropriately dressed, you are saying to the boys and girls, "I will show my respect for you by dressing my very best each day."

After the first or second week, your class will decide how they are going to behave throughout the year. Young children will decide based on the signals they receive from you. If you expect boys and girls to behave, make good choices, take turns, and share, then you as the teacher must model these behaviors. The way you choose to dress will affect your class; the way you behave will affect your success. The teacher is a powerful influence!

The book, *How to Be an Effective Teacher The First Day of School* says this about how we dress, "Clothing may not make a person, but it can be a contributing factor in unmaking a person."[1] You do not get a second chance at a first impression.

"Whether or not we want to admit it, our appearance affects how we are perceived and received in definite ways. Clothing has nothing to do with students liking a teacher, but clothing definitely has an effect on a student's respect for a teacher. Respect is what a teacher must have if learning is to take place. Research reveals that clothing worn by teachers affects the work, attitude, and discipline of students. You dress for four main effects:

1. Respect
2. Credibility
3. Acceptance
4. Authority

The effective teacher uses these four traits as assets in relating to students, peers, administrators, parents, and the community."[2] Having these traits will assist young children in learning more in the classroom because their teacher dresses as a professional.

Personal Learning Activity

Read the list below and put an "X" beside the items you are presently wearing to class. Write beside that item a better choice to wear:

_____ 1. "Jogging" or High-Heeled Shoes
_____ 2. Sweatshirts
_____ 3. Stretch Slacks or Leggings
_____ 4. Trendy Clothes
_____ 5. Blue Jeans
_____ 6. Excessive Jewelry

Choosing appropriate dress for a preschool teacher is a challenge. The teacher must think about sitting on the floor, bending over, and sitting in low chairs when deciding on appropriate clothing to wear. Young children notice a teacher who is dressed in an attractive skirt or slacks and a blouse. Shoes are also important; low-heeled shoes are practical and comfortable.

If a church weekday education program provides shirts or smocks with the program logo on them, policies should be communicated to employees regarding dress codes.

A child laid a photograph on his teacher's desk. The teacher was in the photo, along with many of the children. The teacher could not believe how poorly she looked in the photograph. The next day she decided to dress differently. She chose clothing that was much more appropriate and more professional. To the teacher's surprise, the children responded in a very positive manner, creating a happier learning environment.

Ask yourself the following questions:

1. Would I want my child's or grandchild's teacher to teach him or her dressed the way I dress?

2. Does my appearance say that I am glad to be a teacher?

3. Does my appearance enhance my communication with parents?

4. Does my choice of clothes send a professional message to the community?

USE OF TIME

In today's culture, people are usually accomplishing multi-tasks simultaneously, and the multi-tasked professional is nothing new to preschool teachers. For example: When the teacher is working with an indi-vidual child, she is also aware of what is taking place in the total classroom.

To conquer this multi-task oriented society, the teacher must be prepared. Ecclesiastes 8:6 (NIV) tells us, "For there is a proper time and procedure for every matter." Ask God for wisdom in your teaching and planning for individual children's needs. Use a developmental check-list to serve as a guide in teaching. This checklist will give guidance as you prepare to meet the needs of each boy and girl.

Teachers must take time for young children. In the book *Train Up a Child*, Gary Smalley's foreword mentions time in reference to family: "Parents . . . struggle with weighty burdens of finance, schedule, . . . and spirituality. Frequently, parents have little time for their children, so demanding is their lifestyle . . . ."[3] Tragically, more than half the time, divorce shatters homes, and single parents desperately try to serve as both mother and father, provider and comforter, teacher and spiritual mentor. Time is important to children. The time you spend with young children as their teacher will impact the rest of their lives.

ETHICAL STANDARDS AND ADVOCACY

Ethics are what ought to be. A person of high ethics might be called conscientious, honest, decent, or good. Ethical issues for teachers can include:

Children:

1. Keeping current on characteristics and needs of young children through training and continuing education

2. Respecting the uniqueness of each child

3. Creating and maintaining a safe and healthy environment

4. Being knowledgeable of the symptoms of child abuse and neglect and the procedures for reporting

5. Supporting inclusion of special needs children in regular classrooms when it is consistent with their abilities

Families:

1. Establishing relationships with parents

2. Reporting each child's progress to the parent

3. Assisting parents in understanding developmental stages

4. Involving parents in decision-making

5. Giving open access to their child's classroom

6. Informing parents of any accident involving their child or any contact with a contagious disease

7. Protecting confidentiality and the disclosure of a child's records

8. Being knowledgeable about resources and professional services available to families

Colleagues:

1. Establishing a trusting and cooperative relationship with co-workers

2. Assisting in deserved recognition of co-workers' professional development

3. Refraining from talking about co-worker's behavior to other employees

Employers:

1. Making the program the highest quality possible

2. Refraining from speaking for the organization without permission from the right authority

3. Being constructive in trying to make changes in the organization

4. Carrying out the mission of the church

Community and Society:

1. Providing the community with a high-quality program for young children

2. Promoting cooperation among the agencies that can help families and their children

SEEKS TRAINING OPPORTUNITIES

A professional early childhood teacher will seek out opportunities to learn about the preschoolers she teaches. Opportunities exist through videos, reading current early childhood books, workshops, being mentored by an experienced teacher, or taking classes to receive your Child Development Associate (CDA) certification. Check with your state agency to learn the requirements for teachers in childcare centers.

Parents today are more informed about their child's development and needs. These parents ask questions and appreciate a teacher who is a lifelong learner.

Personal Learning Activities

"We ought to have inspirational dissatisfaction — a restlessness of heart that comes from recognizing the distance between where we are and where we want to be."[4] Is there a place in your life that you would like to improve?

1. List three areas in which you would like to become more competent *(Examples: time management, wardrobe, organizational skills)*:

   _____
   _____
   _____
   _____
   _____
   _____

2. Write goals and objectives for achieving your desired growth.

   (1) _____
   _____
   (2) _____
   _____
   (3) _____
   _____

3. Set dates to accomplish your goals and objectives.

   Goals   *Date to Accomplish*

   (1) _____
   _____
   (2) _____
   _____
   (3) _____
   _____

Would you like to grow in your relationship with the Lord? Would you like to know better ways to positively guide young children? You can improve by setting goals and using them as a guide to become a better teacher. Why should we set goals? Consider these reasons:

- Goals are a statement of faith in what we have been called to do.
- Goals are a commitment to our relationships with family and co-workers.
- Goals give us a sense of fulfillment and accomplishment.
- Goals help us focus on our resources of time, talents, and energy.
- Goals contribute to our better health as they reduce anxiety and tension.

Our personal goals should:

- Be written down
- Include a deadline for reaching them
- Be measurable
- Be challenging, yet attainable
- Relate to circumstances we can control
- Be specific

Self-Evaluation

Evaluation is a significant part of the learning process. Learning takes place when objective evaluation is done. Teachers who evaluate themselves learn how to be a better teacher as they prepare each day. Ask yourself these questions:

1. Did the discipline problems in the class today occur because I was not ready when the first child arrived?

   _____
   _____

2. Were there challenging activities in all the Learning Centers?

   _____
   _____

3. Was there a written lesson plan?

   _____
   _____

4. Were materials for activities gathered in advance?

   _____
   _____

How Professional Am I?

Evaluate yourself by placing a dot, reflecting your professionalism, between "low" and "high" after each statement:

In teacher-to-child relationships, I . . .

1. . . . individualize teaching for preschoolers in my class to enhance learning and to develop self-esteem.

   Low _____ *High*

2. . . . observe and record progress and developmental stages.

   Low _____ *High*

3. . . . study to understand the age group I teach.

   Low _____ *High*

4. . . . refrain from embarrassing students before the group.

   Low _____ *High*

5. . . . create a friendly atmosphere in the classroom.

   Low _____ *High*

6. . . . redirect in a positive way as much as possible.

   Low _____ *High*

7. . . . seek ways to improve by evaluating my preparation each day.

   Low _____ *High*

8. ...have my classroom ready when the first child arrives.

   Low _____ *High*

9. ...greet my children as they enter the room by looking them in the eye, speaking to them, and calling them by name.

   Low _____ *High*

10. ...interact with boys and girls on the playground.

    Low _____ *High*

11. ...attentively listen to boys and girls.

    Low _____ *High*

In teacher-to-parent relationships, I ...

1. ...regularly greet parents with a friendly smile.

   Low _____ *High*

2. ...ask parents to assist with special classroom projects.

   Low _____ *High*

3. ...show an interest in the entire family.

   Low _____ *High*

4. ...acknowledge parents' concerns by listening sensitively to complaints.

   Low _____ *High*

5. ...communicate with parents through personal visits, phone calls, and notes.

   Low _____ *High*

6. ...ask parents to assist with field trips, picnics, or special outdoor events.

   Low _____ *High*

7. ...ask parents for suggestions for topics for parent meetings, workshops, or programs.

   Low _____ *High*

8. ...have periodic open house for parents.

   Low _____ *High*

9. ...make sure parents feel welcome to observe my class at anytime.

   Low _____ *High*

10. ...express appreciation to parents for their assistance.

    Low _____ *High*

In teacher-to-teacher relationships, I ...

1. ...recognize accomplishments of colleagues and tell them so.

   Low _____ *High*

2. ...refrain from criticizing.

   Low _____ *High*

3. . . . learn from a good teacher.

Low _____ High

4. . . . avoid gossiping about and with co-workers.

Low _____ High

5. . . . exhibit a positive attitude and willingness to share ideas.

Low _____ High

In teacher-to-director relationships, I . . .

1. . . . support the policies and programs of the center.

Low _____ High

2. . . . relay information about children and families such as crises, behavior problems, and accidents in a timely, professional manner.

Low _____ High

3. . . . refrain from complaining.

Low _____ High

4. . . . contribute to positive working relations with parents by communicating regularly with the director.

Low _____ High

In teacher-to-community relationships, I . . .

1. . . . represent the church and Jesus Christ in the community.

Low _____ High

2. . . . realize I can make a difference in young children's lives as a Christian teacher.

Low _____ High

In teacher-to-profession relationships, I . . .

1. . . . keep myself informed about early childhood issues.

Low _____ High

2. . . . encourage capable persons to become preschool teachers.

Low _____ High

3. . . . have a mentor who helps me grow.

Low _____ High

A professional demonstrates Christ's love to young children and families. She shares Bible thoughts and verses at every opportunity. She shares Jesus with parents by:

- Meeting the needs of the child
- Praying with parents during a crisis time
- Inviting parents to church events
- Celebrating special times with a family

Matthew 4:18-20 states, "As Jesus was walking beside the Sea of Galilee, he saw two brothers, Simon called Peter and his brother Andrew. They were casting a net into the lake, for they were fishermen. 'Come follow me,' Jesus said, 'And I will make you fishers of men.' At once they left their nets and followed him."

The vocation one chooses can be a channel through which God uses an individual to make a difference in the lives of people. You have a marvelous opportunity for God to use you to minister to young children and their families.

PRAYER

Pray for each child in your class. Plan to meet the needs of each individual child. Pray for each child and his family.

Presence

Reflect Christ through your speech, patience, forgiveness, kindness, faithfulness, creativity, and self-determination. You are made in God's image. As a Christian teacher, you help children feel secure, safe, and loved. Your presence every day contributes to a preschooler's continual development. As a professional in Christian weekday education, you have an awesome task of touching young lives, ministering to families, and being a role model to the community.

Personal Learning Activity

A true professional attempts to keep balance in life. How do you establish your priorities? Spend a few minutes thinking through each of the following questions:

1. What do I spend most of my time doing?

   _____
   _____
   _____
   _____
   _____

2. What do I consider most important in my life?

   _____
   _____
   _____
   _____
   _____
   _____

3. What do I believe about who I am?

   _____
   _____
   _____
   _____

4. What are my goals for my life?

   _____
   _____
   _____
   _____
   _____

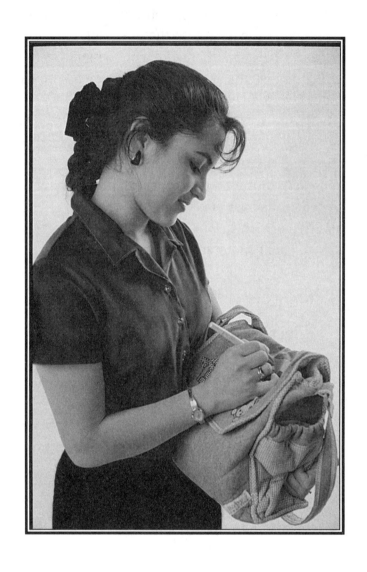

"We gave different gifts, according to the grace given us" (Romans 12:6).

Chapter 15

Your Role, Your Style

Teacher Know Yourself

For many years, early childhood educators have recognized the importance of teaching the individual child. Teaching has focused on developmental growth patterns and individual needs of children. There are also stages of development for teachers. The focus on adult development should be as progressive. For you to grow and mature in your teaching abilities, it is important to know your developmental level, your learning style, and your role as a teacher in Christian weekday education.

The knowledge of individual experiences, abilities, and skills enhances the teacher's understanding of herself as well as her understanding of the children in the weekday program. The recognition of different learning styles assists in developing lesson plans based on the individual needs of each child. As you become aware of the individual traits that make you unique, you will become more aware of the differences in the children. Teachers and preschoolers will benefit as you celebrate the uniqueness of each person.

Developmental Stages of Adults

"We, as adults, continue to develop and change in adulthood just as children grow and change during their childhood."[1] Research confirms that adults continue to develop in cognitive, language, and social areas throughout life.

Research and Adult Developmental Stages

Much research has been done on adult developmental stages. Leading theorists in professional development are Loevinger, Erikson, and Levine. Each researcher gives his definition of adult development. Ask yourself the following questions as you read the research:

1. Where am I in my development?

2. Am I coming out of one stage and going into another?

3. What can I do to raise my level of development to enhance the learning experiences of children in my class?

Loevinger's Research

Loevinger states that the first stage of adult development is the self-protective area. Adults in this area or stage are impulsive, they blame others or circumstances for their problems, and they depend on others for decision making.

The second area is the conscientious-conformist stage. These adults are beginning to develop a self-evaluation process and understand there can be more than one style of teaching and learning.

The third area of adult development is integrated and autonomous. This area or stage respects individuality, others, and self. Disharmony decreases, intelligence solidifies, and information is better processed and understood. Reactions are slower, but problem-solving is more thorough.[2]

Where do you think you are? Explain why you think you are in that particular stage. How can recognizing these stages help you relate to other staff members?

Erikson's Research

Erikson's view: a person makes decisions during his life, and these decisions affect and control the rest of his life. The decisions affect all relationships in the person's life. The experiences a person has with others will affect his decision to interact with others. For example, if a teacher has lost some of the significant people in his life, he may shy away from developing relationships with the staff with which he works.[3]

Do you know staff persons who either withdraw from relationships or are drawn to relationships? Within your staff, who is least likely to develop active friendships? Who is most likely to develop active friendships? Do you know why these staff persons withdraw from relationships or are drawn to develop relationships? Would having this knowledge help you relate to the other person?

Levine's Research

Levine describes the adult developmental levels in these three stages: early, middle, and late. In the early stage the adult is examining various relationships and roles and is feeling indestructible. In the middle stage the adult is established in the work arena and wants a home and family. The late stage shows the adult taking an appraisal of priorities and rearranging his life activities and energies.[4]

Play, the Missing Piece of Adult Development

David Elkind says that the occasions for play are disappearing for children and adults. "For adults, play has been replaced with increased workloads, although, play is important for continued adult learning. Learning takes place as adults are "playing" with possibilities, being flexible, staying loose when things go wrong, being curious, thinking creatively, and problem solving. Continued learning is critical for early childhood professionals."[5]

Many healthy results occur when people take time to have fun and laugh. Teaching is a serving profession, a giving profession. Everyone needs to refuel, regenerate, and reduce stress. Early childhood professionals need to arrange for a little play in daily routines.

Planning Play

The activities need not take much time; the important thing is that adults take time to play. Find a friend with whom to do fun activities or start a "fun" group and include recreational activities at staff meetings.

Fun activities may be to play board games such as "Monopoly" or "Pictionary," celebrate ordinary happenings, exchange humorous childhood experiences, or play at the park. You may even slide down the slide.

Write down three fun things you can think of to do that would allow you to play or relax.

1. _____
   _____

2. _____
   _____

3. _____
   _____

The Teacher and Learning Styles

Just as children learn in different ways, adults have different learning styles. "Teachers' learning styles will also influence the selection of activities and learning situa-

tions."[6] Individuals are born with an inclination toward the right side or left side of the brain-approach to learning. One teacher may be stronger in auditory learning while another teacher will be stronger in visual learning. One may solve problems in an orderly, organized fashion (left brain preference) and the other may be more perceptive and take a wait-and-see attitude in solving the problem (right brain preference).

Factors Affecting Learning Styles

1. Flexibility or Openness to Change
2. Dispositions and Temperaments
3. Self-Image
4. Past Achievements in Teaching
5. Mentoring by a Good Teacher
6. Expectations and Needs

DeTeRMiNiNG YOUR LeaRNiNG STYLe

Environmental Elements

Sound — Do you learn best with music playing in the background, or do you need absolute quiet to concentrate? Are you able to screen out people's conversations and other extraneous environmental noise when you read and concentrate on a task?

Light — Do you find either bright or dim lights distracting? Do you work best in natural filtered daylight? Describe your preference.

Temperature — Are you affected by extremes in temperature? Do you prefer cool, warm, or moderate temperatures in which to learn?

Design — When you read something that requires your full attention, do you prefer to sit in an easy chair, a hard back chair, or do you like to stretch out on the carpet? Do you prefer formal or informal room arrangements when you attend a workshop or lecture?

Emotional Elements

Motivation — Under what conditions do your sources of motivation differ? When do you need reinforcement to encourage you to tackle new knowledge and ideas (praise, grades, bonus)? Under what conditions are you motivated to learn something new?

Persistence — How would you describe yourself with respect to your level of persistence in learning new things? Do you prefer short, achievable goals or do you have a level of persistence that allows you to tackle long-range goals and objectives?

Responsibility — Under what conditions are you most likely to take responsibility for your own learning?

Structure — Do you like to have new areas of learning highly structured and tightly supervised or do you prefer to set your own goals and monitor your own progress?

Sociological Elements

Grouping — What types of things do you learn best on your own, in small groups, or in large groups? What kinds of staff-development experiences do you find most rewarding?

Physical Elements

Perceptual Preference — If you rely on a visual perceptual style when you learn new things, you learn best when information is written out, when there are diagrams, charts, and tables, and when visual media such as films, videos, and pictures are used. If you have an auditory preference, you learn best by hearing things spoken. You like discussions and lectures. If you are primarily kinesthetic in your perceptual preference, you learn best by touching, moving, and feeling. You like to be active and involved in learning new things. Describe your perceptual preferences.

Intake — How important is it to you to have something to eat or nibble on when you focus on new task? Do you like to chew gum or drink something when you master something new?

Time — Some people are more alert in the morning; others prefer to tackle new learning tasks in the afternoon or evening. Describe your preference.

Mobility — When you attend a staff development workshop, do you need to get up and move around at regular intervals?

When you work at a computer or when you read, do you like to take frequent breaks to stretch your muscles, or can you sit and concentrate for long periods?

Your thinking style will be closely related to your learning style. The book *Blue Print for Action* gives an assessment to assist in the discovery of learning styles and thinking styles as well as your brain dominance.[7]

STYLES OF THINKING

1. **In a problem situation do you . . .**
   a. write down and consider all alternatives, then choose the best?
   b. wait to see if the situation will right itself?

2. **Do you think daydreaming is . . .**
   a. a waste of time?
   b. a viable tool for planning your future?

3. **In making decisions, are you more apt to . . .**
   a. rely on facts, information, and logic?
   b. trust feelings and intuition?

4. **In planning a typical day, do you . . .**
   a. have a plan for everything and a system to keep things organized?
   b. just let it happen?

5. **With respect to organization, do you . . .**
   a. have a place for everything and a system to keep things organized?
   b. feel comfortable with clutter — believe organization can stifle spontaneity?

6. **Do you learn new sports and athletic skills by . . .**
   a. learning the sequence and repeating the steps mentally?
   b. imitating, getting the feel of the sport?

7. **Do you express yourself well verbally?**
   a. Yes
   b. No

8. **Are you goal-oriented?**
   a Yes
   b. No

9. **When you want to remember directions, a name, or a news item, do you . . .**
   a. write down notes to help you remember?
   b. visualize the information?

10. **Do you remember faces easily?**
    a Yes
    b. No

11. **In attending meetings and keeping appointments, are you . . .**
    a. on time?
    b. often late?

12. **In an argument, do you tend to . . .**
    a. find an authority to support your point?
    b. become animated, talk louder, even pound the table?

13. **Do you have a sense of how much time has passed without looking at your watch?**
    a. Yes
    b. No

14. **Do you gesture to . . .**
    a. make a point?
    b. express your feelings?

15. **In preparing yourself for a new or difficult task, do you . . .**
    a. prepare notes and gather data regarding the task?
    b. visualize yourself accomplishing the task effectively?

16. **Which handwriting position do you prefer?**
    a. right handed
    b. left handed

17. **When you sit and clasp your hands comfortably in your lap, which thumb is on top?**
    a. left
    b. right

18. **With respect to mood shifts, do you . . .**
    a. experience almost no mood changes?
    b. experience frequent mood changes?

19. **In a conversation with another person, do you . . .**
    a. focus on what people say?
    b. interpret their body language?

20. **Do you enjoy taking risks?**[8]
    a Yes
    b. No

INTERPRETING STYLES OF THINKING

The assessment provides a profile of your cognitive style or brain dominance. We sometimes refer to this as left-brain or right-brain thinking. To determine your orientation, count the number of times you circled the (a) response to a question. These are associated with left-brain thinking. The (b) responses are associated with a right-brain orientation. If you had a 10 point difference between your (a) and (b) totals, you probably have a strong preference for that orientation. If you have a balance between both orientations, you have an integrated style. This means that your orientation draws on both the left-brain and right-brain in terms of your preference in cognitive style. Below is a summary of the characteristics of left-brain and right-brain dominance.

Left (Analytic)	Right (Global)
• trusts logic	• trusts intuition
• remembers names	• remembers faces
• responds to verbal instructions	• responds to demonstrated or symbolic instructions
• systematic/sequential	• random
• solves problems by breaking them down into parts using logic	• solves problems by looking at the whole, looking for patterns, relying on hunches

Left (Analytic)	Right (Global)
• makes objective judgments	• makes subjective judgments
• planned and structured	• fluid and spontaneous
• prefers established, certain information	• prefers elusive, un-certain information
• analyzer	• synthesizer
• relies on language in thinking and remem-bering	• relies on images in thinking and remem-bering
• prefers talking and writing	• prefers drawing and manipulating objects
• prefers multiple choice tests	• prefers open-ended questions
• prefers carefully-planned work and study	• prefers open-ended work and study
• prefers hierarchical (ranked) authority structures	• prefers collegial (participative) authority structures
• controls feelings (reflective)	• free with feelings (impulsive)
• plans ahead	• spontaneous
• speaks with few gestures	• gestures when speaking
• punctual	• less punctual
• responds to facts and dates	• recalls images and patterns
• appears tidy and organized	• appears disorganized[9]

YOUR ROLE

For your program to have maximum effectiveness, each staff member needs to understand her job requirements. When job requirements and center policies are clear, each teacher can do her best job of teaching. A staff questionnaire pertaining to role responsibilities can be very helpful.

STAFF ROLE QUESTIONNAIRE

Circle the number which represents your best response in relation to your staff role.

1. I know what my responsibilities are.

Seldom————Sometimes————Always
   1   2   3   4   5

2. I receive the support I need to do my job well.

Seldom————Sometimes————Always
   1   2   3   4   5

3. I understand the objectives of the center.

Seldom————Sometimes————Always
   1   2   3   4   5

4. I receive training to help me grow as a teacher.

Seldom————Sometimes————Always
   1   2   3   4   5

5. **I have ample supplies and resources to do my job well.**

Seldom————Sometimes————Always
   1   2   3   4   5

6. **I have opportunities to use my special abilities as I teach.**

Seldom————Sometimes————Always
   1   2   3   4   5

7. **The staff policies are fair and clear.**

Seldom————Sometimes————Always
   1   2   3   4   5

8. **I use the staff handbook as a guide to do my job well.**

Seldom————Sometimes————Always
   1   2   3   4   5

9. **I have enough time to prepare adequately.**

Seldom————Sometimes————Always
   1   2   3   4   5

10. **I am supported by the director and other staff.**

Seldom————Sometimes————Always
   1   2   3   4   5

ROLES OF THE TEACHER

Not only does the teacher teach, but she assumes some other secondary roles which may include:

Substitute Parent — The child sees the teacher as a "substitute parent" when he is at the weekday program.

Communicator and Relationship Builder — The teacher relays information about the child and develops relationships with the child, the child's parents, and with coworkers.

Advocate — The teacher must be an advocate for each child. She must report cases of child abuse or neglect. She must enthusiastically teach, using age/developmentally-appropriate practices with hands-on learning experiences to meet the needs of each child.

Facilitator — The teacher is a guide to children in the learning environment. She sets up the environment with a variety of activities from which children may choose.

Coach — The teacher is a coach as she encourages children and co-workers to solve problems and develop social relationships.

Model — The teacher is a role-model to children. Boys and girls learn values and morals from their teachers. Children learn about Jesus and His love through the words and actions of their teacher. The teacher is a model to the community as she influences parents and families in the community.

Individual Needs Assessor — The teacher must observe and look for specific developmental and educational needs of each child and suggest appropriate steps toward intervention or change. This assessment is best when it is begun in the preschool years.

Social Services Coordinator — The teacher needs to be knowledgeable of the agencies and services available to meet the specific needs of children and families. The teacher can direct parents to professionals in the public school system or in the community who are qualified in early childhood assessment.

Disciplinarian — The teacher must know the developmental stages of children and have the ability to guide children's behavior in a positive manner.

Health and Safety Director — The teacher needs to look for signs of childhood illnesses and unsafe toys and equipment and to keep the environment as sanitary as possible.

Parent Educator — The teacher assists parents in learning about child development and is eager to communicate positive parenting skills.

THE ROLES AND STYLE OF JESUS

Jesus gave Himself names that portrayed His unique roles and style. These names gave a picture of who He was:

- *Son of Man* (John 6:27) — Jesus referred to Himself as humanity and divinity.

- *Bread of Life* (John 6:35) — Jesus lived the life-role of giving; He is the only giver of eternal life.

- *Light of the World* (John 8:12) — Light symbolizes spiritual truth. Jesus guides us to spiritual truth.

- *Gate for the Sheep* (John 10:7) — Jesus is the only passageway for eternal life.

- *Good Shepherd* (John 11:25) — Jesus is like a shepherd who protects his sheep from harm. Jesus protects those who profess Him as Lord and Savior and gives His assurance of eternal life.

- *The Resurrection and the Life* (John 11:25) — Jesus is the authority over death.

- *The Way, the Truth, and the Life* (John 14:6) — In this title, Jesus gives the total meaning and purpose for His coming to earth.

- *The Vine* (John 15:1) — Jesus explains that we have to be connected to Him for spiritual development.

As the leaders in the early childhood profession move into the 21st century, we must know who we are, what children need, our learning styles, and the roles we fill. We can make a difference in the lives of boys and girls.

Let this be our prayer today and every day:

"God, give us wisdom to see that today is the day with our children. That there is no unimportant moment in their lives. May we know that no other

career is so precious. No other work so rewarding, no other task so urgent. May we not defer it nor neglect it, but by thy Spirit accept it gladly, joyously, and by thy grace realize that the time is short and our time is now, for children won't wait!"[10]

Section 4:

The Process You Can Implement

Teaching in Christian Weekday Early Education

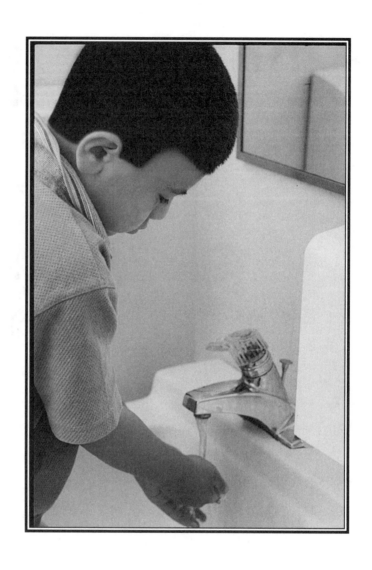

*"Everything should be done
in a fitting and orderly way"
(1 Cor. 14:40, NIV).*

Guidelines for Hygiene, Safety, and Security

Providing a secure environment in a weekday education program where young children can grow and learn safely is an increasing challenge in today's world. Unfortunately, a child's world is beset by a multitude of dangers. Ensuring the health and safety of each child is a teacher's *most fundamental responsibility* to the child, the family, and the church sponsoring the weekday program.

Our Lord expects us to be accountable for the children in our care. The Gospels of Matthew, Mark, and Luke all record Christ saying, "'Let the little children come to me' . . . And he took the children in his arms, put his hands on them and blessed them" (Mark 10:14,16, NIV). Matthew also records Jesus commending the disciples if they give "even a cup of cold water to one of these little ones" (10:42, NIV).

Jesus further indicated in the Sermon on the Mount that ensuring the well-being of children is a basic assumption: "Which of you, if his son asks for bread, will give him a stone? Or if he asks for a fish, will give him a snake?" (Matthew 7:9, NIV). A few words later in verse 12, Jesus then gives us what

many call "The Golden Rule": "So in everything, do to others what you would have them do to you." Thus, Christ's instruction and example are clear: we are to give complete and loving attention to meeting the needs of young children.

Just as Luke 2:52 assures that Jesus "grew in wisdom and stature, and in favor with God and men (NIV)," children today can be nurtured properly only when the environment is safe and loving.

To emulate Jesus' example in loving and protecting children, we must follow appropriate safety and security guidelines in weekday preschool programs. In addition to protecting children, such guidelines also will provide reassurance to their parents, demonstrate the professionalism of the staff and teachers, and meet legal requirements which safeguard host churches as well as the children.

Several steps are necessary for developing and implementing guidelines regarding hygiene, safety, and security. As a teacher, can you answer the following questions affirmatively?

Write "Y" (Yes) or "N" (No) beside each:

____ Does your church-elected weekday early education committee include members from the health and legal professions who assist in formulating and implementing policies to safeguard children?

____ Were standards of care consulted as recommended by the state child care licensing agency; the state child protective services (for child abuse reporting procedures); and other agencies governing fire, electrical, and building codes?

____ Were state and federal guidelines followed regarding the weekday program's policies on the screening and hiring of teachers and other staff?

____ Has the advice of an attorney and the weekday program's insurance carrier been consulted regarding all policies?

____ Have policies been posted as appropriate and provided in written form to all teachers, employees, volunteers, and parents?

____ Are you receiving ongoing training and supervision to ensure that established policies are properly implemented?

____ Are you diligent in following all guidelines and policies and committed to protecting the health, safety, and security of all the children?

Although your diligence in implementing policies is essential, these policies also must include guidelines in the following areas:

• Hygiene procedures for hand washing, diapering, disinfecting toys and equipment, laundering linens, handling food, and preventing infectious diseases.

• Safety precautions regarding children's personal files; staff-child ratios; facility and classrooms; equipment, supplies, and toys; pets and plants; snacks; playgrounds; field trips and transportation; medications and first aid; emergency responses (fire, tornado, etc.); and abuse prevention.

• Security safeguards regarding the screening, hiring, supervising, and training of staff; procedures for the arrival and departure of children; and protection in today's legal climate, including documentation and confidentiality.

If you are unsure about your child care center's policies regarding any of these topics, ask your supervisor or director to provide you with specific written guidelines. If your center does not have written policies on all of these topics, you are within your rights to insist that guidelines be formulated and made available to you and other employees.

A number of resources exist for policies on standards of care. The director in your program should consult with your state child care licensing agency. The preschool and weekday education consultants in your state's Baptist convention offices or at LifeWay Christian Resources in Nashville, TN, also can provide help. The Centers for Disease Control and Prevention (CDC),[1] the National Association for the Education of Young Children (NAEYC),[2] and other health or education agencies and professionals can provide published materials regarding guidelines.

Even if your state's laws do not require licensing for the program where you teach, the policies and practices for every child care center should reflect recommended standards of care. In fact, all teachers and staff members should work to ensure that church-sponsored weekday early education centers reflect a *higher* standard of care consistent with Christ's call upon our lives and our service.

HYGiene PROCEDURES

Hand Washing

One of the most basic responsibilities for all child care staff members is providing a clean environment. Many experts agree that the most basic deterrent to the spreading of germs is effective hand washing. The following procedures are recommended by the Centers for Disease Control and Prevention.[3]

Always wash your hands **before:** your day's work begins at the center, handling food, preparing bottles, feeding a child, giving medication, eating, and going home.

Always wash your hands **after:** diapering, toileting, or assisting children with toileting; contacting body fluids (mucous, blood, spit, vomit, tears); wiping mouths, eyes, noses, or sores; handling pets and pet accessories; cleaning anything; handling soiled items (tissues, linens, clothing); removing latex gloves; and when hands are soiled.

Besides washing your own hands, assist all children in washing their hands when involved in the circumstances indicated above. Additional times for washing children's hands also include before and after their play with clay, play dough, sand, or water, and following their time on the playground.

How to Wash Hands

Post procedures near bathroom sinks. Hand-washing procedures include the following:

- Wet hands in warm, running water and apply a dime-sized squirt of liquid soap to your hands.

- Lather hands vigorously, rubbing all sides of fingers, nails, and hands for 15 seconds or longer.

- Rinse hands under warm, running water.

- Dry hands with a clean, disposable towel, using the towel also to turn off the faucet and open any doors.

- Discard used towel in a trash can with a disposable plastic liner.

- When you assist children with these same procedures, wash your own hands again.

If you do not have warm, running water easily accessible to each teacher and child, check with your state child care licensing agency for other approved procedures. Do not rely on pre-moistened cleansing towelettes or liquid hand sanitizers as replacements for hand washing. These alternatives are not effective in combating many infectious diseases.

Diapering

Diapering is best done with a positive attitude and in an organized setting. An orderly diapering area will keep you happy, and your positive attitude will help children feel happier. *Never scold a child or show disgust while changing his diaper, and never leave a child unattended.* You will need: (1) a designated diapering area with a moisture-proof surface a minimum of three feet above the floor and near a sink; (2) supplies (within reach of teacher) including waxed paper; fresh diapers and clean clothes (if needed); moist disposable wipes; child's personal lotion or cream provided by the parent and labeled with his name; disposable latex gloves; plastic zip-lock bags; disposable trash liners; and trash can with cover.

How to Change a Diaper

- Put on gloves. Place a clean diaper on the diapering surface. Place a sheet of waxed paper on top of the diaper, and lay the child on the paper-covered diaper.

- Remove soiled diaper and any soiled clothing. Seal cloth diaper and clothing in separate plastic zip-lock bags to give to parents. Or, fold disposable diaper with contents taped inside and place in a covered trash can.

- Clean child's bottom, wiping front to back only once with a moist towelette. Use fresh wipes as needed. Dispose of used wipes in trash can.

- Remove waxed paper under child and discard.

- Fasten the clean diaper securely.

- Remove and dispose of gloves. Clean hands with a fresh moist wipe, then clean the child's hands with a fresh wipe. Dispose of these.

- Dress child in clean clothes (if needed).

- Wash child's hands under warm, running water before he returns to activities.

- Wash and disinfect diapering area and all items and equipment touched.

- Wash your own hands under running water.

Disinfecting Equipment and Toys

Younger preschoolers routinely place toys and other items in their mouths. Although most older preschoolers are not as likely to put items in their mouths, they do place their hands near their mouths, noses, and eyes. Therefore, cleaning and disinfecting procedures are essential for reducing the spread of germs and infectious diseases. While the following procedures are consistent with current recommendations from the Centers for Disease Control and Prevention, your director should keep you informed of any updated or revised recommendations which might be issued.

When infants and toddlers place toys or other items in their mouths, these toys should not be shared with other children until they have been washed and disinfected. Therefore, provide only toys which can withstand rigorous cleaning and disinfecting procedures. Once a child is finished with a toy, retrieve it and place it in a tub reserved for dirty toys which will be washed and disinfected later.

Even though toys and equipment used by older preschoolers may not receive daily disinfecting, a weekly washing of items is recommended using soap and water, followed by rinsing in clear water and air drying. Items which may need this treatment include blocks, dolls, transportation toys, manipulatives, and other such toys.

How to Clean and Disinfect Items

Consistent and regular washing of items with soap and water is the first best defense against the spread of germs. The mechanical process of scrubbing surfaces and toys with soap and warm water physically loosens germs, and rinsing removes them. Once toys and eating utensils have been properly washed, soaking items for 10-20 minutes in a weak solution of one tablespoon of household bleach (5.25% sodium hypochlorite) to one gallon of cool water provides further protection.[4] Rinsing, then air-drying items on a clean surface completes the process.

When toys and other items can be washed in a dishwasher, use of a disinfectant is unnecessary.

For crib rails and other surfaces which are "mouthed" by babies, this bleach solution should be used after the surfaces have been thoroughly washed. Cover or drench the surfaces for at least 10 minutes with the bleach solution before "rinsing" off with a wet (with tap water) disposable towel. Allow surface to air dry. The use of this mild bleach disinfectant is effective but is harmless to babies.

When disinfecting diaper-changing surfaces, bathrooms, and other areas potentially soiled with body wastes, however, a stronger solution of 1/4 cup of bleach to one gallon of water (same as 1 T. bleach to 1 qt. water) must be a part of the cleaning process. However, chlorine-containing scouring powders or other commercial disinfectants may be used in bathrooms; these should be used several times a day, if possible.

Although commercial products which meet the standard for "hospital grade" germicides by the Environmental Protection Agency (EPA) may be used, household bleach often is preferred because:[5]

- It is inexpensive and easy to obtain.
- It is easy to mix and to use.
- It is nontoxic and effective when properly mixed.
- It kills most infectious agents. (Cryptosporidia is killed only by hydrogen peroxide or ammonia.)

How to Mix and Use Bleach Solution[6]

- Use *one tablespoon* bleach to *one gallon* of water for disinfecting toys, eating utensils, crib rails, and other items which children place in their mouths.

- Use *one tablespoon* of bleach to *one quart* of water for disinfecting bathroom, diapering area, etc.

- Mix bleach solution fresh each day, using cool water, since it loses "strength" easily by exposure to heat, sunlight, organic material, and evaporation. Therefore, to maintain potency, discard *used* solution often during the day, refreshing with *fresh* solution.

- Wear disposable latex gloves when disinfecting items with bleach solution. Gloves will protect your hands from germs and from sensitivity to the bleach.

- Never use bleach solution in combination with other chemicals since a reaction may occur which could release toxic chlorine gas.

- Discard any leftover bleach solution at day's end.

- Keep all containers of bleach and bleach solution in a safe place out of the reach of children.

Laundering Linens

Many child care centers provide a washer and dryer for teachers or other staff members to use in laundering linens. In addition to detergent, staff members should use bleach and hot water. Items which need to be laundered daily include the sheets, blankets, and other linens used by infants.

Bedding for older preschoolers should be labeled with each child's name and washed weekly. Each child's bedding should be reserved for his use only. If items are inadvertently used by another child, bedding should be laundered before another use.

Cots, mattresses, and other bedding surfaces should be washed and disinfected weekly. When storing cots, do not stack them in such a way that surfaces are contaminated. Mattresses used by infants should be disinfected daily.

Do not launder cloth diapers or a child's personal clothing which is soiled with urine or fecal material. Instead, place such items in waterproof zip-lock bags and give these to the parents. Also, do not place a child's urine-wet clothing in the dryer to dry before redressing him. This will contaminate the dryer and other surfaces. Ask parents to provide extra clothing to be kept at the center for toileting accidents.

Handling Food

To prevent foodborne illnesses in your child care center, follow regulations for food safety and sanitation provided by your local health department. If a dishwasher is not available or cannot be installed, follow guidelines for washing, rinsing, and disinfecting eating utensils as provided by the health department and the state child care licensing agency.

Another source of helpful information is a reproducible sheet, "What You Should Know About Foodborne Illnesses in the Child Care Setting," found in the CDC's handbook, *The ABCs of Safe and Healthy Child Care*.[7] Several basic guidelines include the following:

- Always use proper hand washing procedures when you handle and serve food, and assist children in washing their hands before they eat.

- Do not allow children to share food or utensils that are not individually wrapped, nor food that is brought from a child's home.

- Accept only commercially-prepared food (from a source inspected and approved by the health department) when parents bring snacks to celebrate birthdays or other special occasions.

- Remove leftover food from the eating area, and discard food which has been dropped on the floor.

- Require clear labeling on each child's lunch which has been brought from home: child's name, date, type of food. Store lunches at appropriate temperatures.

- Accept expressed breast milk only if it is labeled with the date and the child's name. Send all unused milk home with the parent at the end of the day.

- Do not serve foods containing raw eggs, such as homemade ice cream.

Preventing Infectious Diseases

Hygiene procedures which prevent the spread of infectious diseases include the previous instructions. However, several other factors are critical. Observe children carefully upon arrival for signs of illness which might include fever, sore throat and swollen glands, diarrhea, vomiting, severe coughing, body rash, earache, eye discharge, yellow tinge to skin or eyes, or unremitting crying and irritability.

Follow your center's written policies regarding exclusion of children (and staff members) from the child care center when they show signs of illness. These guidelines should be included in policies parents receive upon enrollment.

If a child (or teacher) becomes sick during the day, take him to a prepared area isolated from other children where he can be assisted until a parent or other approved person is called to take him home.

Check with your local health department for a list of diseases which require that your center follow control measures in reporting and monitoring exposure to these specific diseases. The health department can provide guidelines on when it is safe to readmit a child or staff member.[8] In addition, follow health department guidelines on immunizations required and records to be retained on each child.

SAFETY PRECAUTIONS

Although sanitation and *hygiene procedures* must form a firm bedrock of protection

for children in child care settings, *safety precautions* become the foundations upon that bedrock for providing a happy and developmentally-appropriate environment. Providing complete and exhaustive guidance on safety is impossible within the limits of this chapter. However, many of the fundamental precautions are included below.

Children's Records

Keeping each child safe in a weekday child care setting begins with having basic and accurate information. Although records should be treated as confidential, all teachers must know how to access a child's complete records should an emergency occur. Individual files should include:

- child's complete name, date of birth, name of parent(s), home address, parents' employers and job locations, and telephone numbers;

- name and telephone number of person(s) permitted to pick up child and to be con-

tacted in an emergency if the parent(s) cannot be located;

- health information, including current immunization record, name and telephone number of physician, name of insurance company, list of food and medical allergies as well as any special medical needs, and blood type (if known);

- names and ages of siblings, pets, fears, church, and any other helpful information;

- signed permissions authorizing emergency medical care, field trips, transportation, administering medications (if applicable), and any other needed consent;

- date of acceptance and withdrawal from program.

As a service to parents, some weekday centers also provide a complete set of fingerprints on each child. The fingerprint files often are maintained by the child care center, then given to parents to keep when a child is withdrawn from the program.

Staff-Child Ratios

Of primary importance in creating a safe environment for young children is an adequate number of teachers. If your weekday center is licensed by the state child care licensing agency, your center must at least abide by the minimum requirements. However, most child care centers should try to exceed the minimum standards in order to provide the best possible environment for children.

The following staff-child ratios are recommended by the American Academy of Pediatrics and the American Public Health Association:[9]

Age	Staff-Child	Max. Group Size
0-24 mo.	1:3	6
25-30 mo.	1:4	8
31-35 mo.	1:5	10
3-yr.-olds	1:7	14
4-5-yr.-olds	1:8	16

When mixed age groups are together, the staff-child ratio and group size should be determined by the age of the majority of the children present. If the group includes infants and toddlers, follow the recommendations for the younger ages. Volunteers or substitute teachers who are properly supervised also may be used to maintain appropriate numbers.

Facility and Classrooms

Maintaining safety standards in the facility and classrooms is the responsibility of all staff members. The state's child care licensing requirements, along with fire, electrical, and building codes must be consulted by your center's director. However, a safety checklist for your center might include:

General Facility Check List

___ Infant and toddler rooms are on ground floor.

___ Stairways are well-lighted and have handrails.

___ Stairways, doorways, and halls have non-slip surfaces and are unobstructed.

___ Doors have slow-closing controls or safety edges to prevent pinched fingers.

___ Unused electrical outlets are covered with caps, and electrical cords are out of reach of children.

___ Cleaning supplies, medications, and other hazardous items are stored in locked areas.

___ The kitchen is inaccessible to unsupervised children.

___ All areas are free of toxic or lead paint, cracked or falling plaster, and crumbling asbestos.

___ Heating units are isolated from classrooms.

___ Heating or cooling equipment and hot water heaters are inspected by professionals at specified intervals.

___ Adequate exits are provided with lighted signs, and exit doors have emergency bars.

___ Emergency lighting is in operating order.

___ All areas are equipped with regularly-inspected fire extinguishers, smoke detectors, and sprinklers.

___ Emergency response and evacuation information is clearly posted in all rooms occupied by children.

___ Telephones are easily accessible to all staff members with emergency numbers clearly posted.

Classroom and Rest Room Check List

___ All areas are maintained in a clean and orderly fashion, free of insect and rodent infestation.

___ Classroom doors have small, one-way glass openings for viewing activities in the rooms.

___ Walls have durable, washable coverings, and all surfaces are free of mildew and mold.

___ Windows cannot be opened more than six inches from the bottom and have screen coverings.

___ Window coverings are safe and dust-free; any cords are short and out of reach of children.

___ Fluorescent lighting is fitted with color-corrected bulbs (i.e. 3500 degrees Kelvin) so that objects in the room appear as natural as possible under an artificial light source.

___ Floors are smooth with nonskid surfaces; carpets and area rugs are firmly anchored and skid-proof.

___ Safe and adequate ventilation, heating, and cooling are provided in each room.

___ All trash cans have disposable plastic liners, are self-closing, and are out of young children's reach.

___ Rest rooms are easily accessible to children and always supervised.

___ Rest room doors do not have locks but are kept closed when not in use.

___ Rest room doors can be opened to allow visibility needed for the protection of children and teachers.

___ Child-sized toilets and sinks are provided, together with child-height toilet paper, soap, and paper towel dispensers.

___ Safe, stable step stools are available if needed.

___ Water temperature is no hotter than 120 degrees.

___ Rest rooms for adults are located separately.

Equipment, Supplies, and Toys

Teachers are the front line of defense regarding the safety of all equipment, supplies, and toys. Your observant diligence is required in order to ensure that any item which is in disrepair, is inappropriate for the age of the children, or is potentially hazardous is removed from their use. Young children do not have the innate judgment to understand the dangers of misusing items, inappropriate climbing on, or throwing equipment. The consistent guidance you provide for children in the safe and appropriate use of all equipment and supplies is essential.

The Consumer Product Safety Commission (CPSC), Washington, D.C. 20207, is a helpful resource for teachers and parents concerned about equipment and toy safety. Product safety guidelines also can be obtained through the CPSC Internet Web site and telephone hotline.[10]

Safety Guidelines for Equipment, Supplies, Toys

- Discard, repair, or replace broken or worn items.

- Provide child-sized equipment and items which are developmentally-appropriate for each age.

- Provide only items painted with lead-free paint.

- Remove items with sharp points or edges, splinters or chipped paint, small parts, loose bolts or nuts, or hinged pinch points.

- Provide cribs which meet CPSC standards with slats or rails 2 3/8 inches apart or less, tight-fitting mattresses, and without protruding corner posts.[11]

- Use high chairs with a wide base for stability, safety belt and crotch strap, and firmly latching tray.

- Do not use baby walkers.

- Use hot water in a crockpot to warm bottles for infants. (Do not use microwave ovens for this.)

- Do not "prop" bottles when feeding infants, and do not place infants on their tummies in cribs.

- Do not use the following with children under four years of age: marbles, coins, safety pins or push pins, balloons, plastic bags, Styrofoam®, or any objects with parts smaller than 1 1/4 inches in diameter and 2 1/4 inches long.

- Use a choke tester to check the size-safety of all toys and removable toy parts.[12] (If a toy or its parts are smaller than 1 1/4 inches in diameter and 2 1/4 inches long, preschoolers may be able to swallow it.)

- Use only commercial art materials labeled *nontoxic* and stored in original containers out of children's reach.

- Use water-based markers, glues, and paints; permanent markers, epoxy, or glazes may contain toxic solvents.

- Use liquid rather than powdered tempera paints.

- Provide durable toys which can withstand cleaning and disinfecting procedures.

- Do not use stuffed toys, dolls with hair, or other items which cannot be easily disinfected.

- Provide only rattles, squeeze toys, and teethers with handles too large to lodge in a child's throat; avoid toys with ball-shaped ends.

- Remove toys if the squeeze squeaker or other items could become detached and swallowed.

- Do not allow projectile toys, electrical toys, battery-operated toys, or toys with loud noises.

- Do not use strings longer than 12 inches on pull-toys; do not hang toys across a crib or around an infant's neck.

Plants and Pets

Activities with plants and pets provide important nature experiences for young children. However, because of allergy and safety concerns, teachers should make careful choices and closely supervise children during activities with plants and pets. For younger children, place flowers or leaves of plants inside a sealed, clear plastic bottle so children can safely observe the plant without directly handling it. Since a number of plants are toxic, obtain a list of poisonous plants from the state health department or regional poison control center.[13] Avoid using such plants in any way, and also make sure all such plants are removed from playgrounds and other areas.

Plants Generally Considered Not Poisonous

A list of plants considered safe for preschoolers to handle include the following.[14] However, any plant can cause reactions in some individuals. Therefore, check with the poison control center anytime a child ingests a plant or displays any unexpected reactions.

African Violet	Hen and Chickens
Airplane Plant	Honeysuckle
Aloe Vera	Impatiens
Begonia Species	Lily, Easter/Day/Tiger
Christmas Cactus	Marigold
Chrysanthemum	Mimosa
Coleus	Petunia
Daisy	Roses
Dandelion	Rubber Plant
Dogwood	Scheffelera
Ferns	Wandering Jew
Forsythia	Weeping Fig
Gardenia	Zinnia

Precautions with Pets and Animals

Check with the state health department or child care licensing agency for information on appropriate pets in the child care setting. Your director will need to make sure that local ordinances are followed if animals are kept on the premises. Parents always should be advised when children will be in the presence of animals. In planning activities involving pets or animals, provide continuous supervision when children are with the animals. Additional guidelines include:

* Do not allow ferrets, turtles, reptiles, birds of the parrot family, or wild animals in the center.

* Do not bring newly-purchased birds to the center until they are observed for 30 days for any illness.

* Allow only animals which are visibly clean; healthy in appearance; friendly to children; have up-to-date vaccinations; and are free of ticks, fleas, and worms.

* Use only approved animal cages which can be easily cleaned and maintained.

* Assist children in washing their hands after handling or feeding animals.

Snacks and Cooking Activities

When preparing and serving snacks for preschoolers, follow this chapter's sanitation and safety guidelines in the section, "Handling Food." Consult the health department and state child care licensing agency for additional information. Other precautions include:

- Consult parents to avoid serving foods or snacks to which children are allergic.

- Even with parents' permission, be cautious in serving foods (peanut butter, peanuts, orange juice, oranges, bananas, and strawberries) to which many children develop early sensitivities or allergies.

- Serve nutritious and wholesome snacks, avoiding high levels of sugar, salt, and fat.

- Avoid foods that can cause children to choke easily such as hot dogs, hard candy, seeds, nuts, popcorn, peanuts, raisins, raw carrots or celery, whole grapes or olives, apples with peelings, and peanut butter.

- Guide children to remain seated while eating.

- Carefully supervise children during cooking activities with metal utensils or small appliances such as toasters, toaster ovens, or blenders.

Playgrounds

Most state child care licensing agencies require that centers provide at least 75 square feet of outdoor play space per child. When only a minimum of 1,800 square feet of playground space is provided, no more than 24 children may use the space at one time. The area must be fenced, with secure gates. A fence height of at least four feet or higher is required. Preschool rooms which open directly onto fenced play areas provide the advantages of good security and easy access to rest rooms and drinking water.

Direct sun and shade provided by trees, awnings, or the building are needed. Good drainage and a variety of grassy levels with slopes provide an interesting area for children. At least 25 per cent of the playground should be an open area.

Impact-absorbing materials at a depth of 8-12 inches or more should be placed under climbing, swinging, or revolving equipment and cover a fall zone area extending six feet on all sides. Impact-absorbing materials might include shredded hardwood or rubber, washed concrete sand, or safety-approved compact rubber surfacing.

For specific playground safety guidelines, especially regarding construction and placement of equipment, the director of your child care center should consult the *Handbook for Public Playground Safety*.[15] The director or an appointed committee should make sure that age-appropriate equipment is installed, maintained, repaired as needed, and used consistently with the manufacturer's instructions. Hazards to avoid include: equipment with openings that might entrap any part of a child's body or head; equipment that might have pinch, crush, or shear points which can injure children; or equipment that is poorly anchored or with exposed anchoring.

The child care center should provide safe equipment for a variety of play opportunities including climbing, swinging, crawling, riding, rocking, sliding, balancing, tossing, digging, moving, and pretending. The playground should be clean and free from weeds, tall grass, standing water, animal excrement, stones or sharp objects, and litter. Adequate adult supervision is required, and teachers should provide children with guidance to ensure their safety at all times.

Field Trips and Transportation

Well-planned field trips provide great learning opportunities for children, but they require special safety precautions, especially when transportation is needed. Because of safety concerns and the "stranger anxiety" experienced by younger preschoolers, you should plan trips away from your child care center only for children older than three years old. Although the director of your center should have a signed general permission form for each child, granting parents' permission for field trips, you must ask parents also to sign an informed consent form for *each* child prior to *each* trip. You must maintain appropriate staff-child ratios during each trip, excluding the driver in the ratio count. Follow any guidelines provided by your state child care licensing agency, in addition to these:

- Use only vehicles and drivers approved by your child care center and that are in compliance with all applicable state laws.

- Provide the center's director with a schedule showing the travel route, itinerary, and other details of the trip or outing.

- Make sure the destination is appropriate for the age, understanding, and interest levels of the children.

- Prepare and take a copy of the scheduled route for the driver and a trip sheet indicating the name, address, and telephone number of the child care center; names of children being transported; information needed to contact children's parents in an emergency; and emergency treatment release forms for each child on the trip.

- Properly secure each child in approved car seats or seat belts according to state and federal requirements (check with your state child care licensing regulations).

- Keep doors locked while vehicle is moving.

- Check the attendance each time you enter and leave the vehicle to account for the presence of each child. *Never leave a child alone in a vehicle.*

- Make sure each child is wearing identification.

- Carefully supervise children leaving and entering the vehicle and while at the field trip site.

- Carry along a trip emergency and first aid kit.

Administering Medications and First Aid

In many states child care professionals **are not** required to give medications. A child's physician often can arrange dosages at times when parents can give the medications.

However, if your center accepts the responsibility for giving medications, make sure that you follow your state child care licensing agency's guidelines. Requirements generally include detailed written information on each medication, physician and parent consent forms, dosage protocols, and medication logs (child, date, time, medication and dosage, person administering, comments, etc.). For complete guidance, along with sample consent forms and other materials, consult resources such as *Model Child Care Health Policies* and *Healthy Young Children: A Manual for Programs*.[16]

Regarding first aid, specific staff members may be assigned the primary responsibility of administering first aid. However, all staff members should be trained in handling small injuries and in using the first-aid kit. Any time an injury occurs or first aid is given, an incident report form should be completed and filed with the director.[17] The following first-aid supplies should be stored in a location accessible to all staff members and out of children's reach:

- first-aid protocol manual
- disposable latex gloves and sealable plastic bags
- antiseptic soap
- antiseptic wipes and hydrogen peroxide
- gauze squares and variety of adhesive bandages
- adhesive tape and absorbent cotton
- tweezers and stainless steel scissors
- child's thermometer

- triangular bandages (sling-type) and safety pins
- splints (cardboard)
- dosage or measuring spoons and paper cups
- padded tongue blade and tongue depressors
- disposable mouth shield for use in CPR
- bee sting kit
- syrup of ipecac
- instant cold packs and hot water bottle
- eye irrigation saline solution
- pen, pencil, paper

Upon the recommendation of first-aid trainers or local medical consultants, you also may wish to include such items as calamine lotion, burn ointment, a non-prescription antiseptic cream, antihistamine syrup, and other items.[18] In addition to a complete first-aid kit, several smaller first-aid kits should be made available to teachers who take children on the playground, nature walks, or field trips. The most important items, along with a supply of tissues, can be placed in first-aid packs or pouches which strap onto teachers' waists.

Emergency Responses

The training of all staff members in responding to emergencies is essential. Your director should discuss (and post near the telephone) procedures for using the telephone in an emergency. These include stating the caller's name, nature of emergency, name of church and child care center, phone number, address and directions, and location of injured person. The caller should stay on the telephone until the emergency dispatcher hangs up.

A centrally located telephone should be available in the child care center, with these emergency numbers posted: 911; paramedics, fire; police; ambulance; hospital (with address and directions to hospital); poison control center; county health department; and electric, gas, and water companies.

All teachers, volunteers, and other staff members who work around children need training in emergency response, including first-aid and CPR instruction. Teachers and children also need regularly-scheduled practice in certain disaster drills. In an emergency situation, *always count the children* before taking them out of the room and then recheck the count periodically. Also, take the class attendance sheet with you and follow the usual security departure procedures when parents arrive.

Response to Fire

Remain calm, but take charge. Ask children to hold hands as you leave the room. Shut the door. Lead the children along the exit route to a designated location outside and away from traffic areas. (To remove infants, place them in a designated bed with rollers which fits through all doors.)

Response to Power Outage

Make a game out of this situation to help children remain calm. Get one or more flashlights from the pre-arranged storage area in the room. Sing songs and tell stories until further instructions are given.

Response to Tornadoes, Storms, Severe Weather

Close the door as you leave the room. Calmly escort children to a ground floor (or basement) to an enclosed space in the center of the building, such as a hallway. Show children how to sit with their backs against the wall, knees under their chins, arms wrapped around their knees, and heads on their knees.

Response to Earthquakes

Gather children under a supported doorway or under a sturdy table. Hazards to avoid are heavy hanging objects, tall or heavy furniture, hot water heaters, gas lines, electrical wires, and windows.

Follow-up Activities

When teachers and parents help children to feel free to talk about emergencies and disaster drills, this often relieves fears for preschoolers. Also try to:

- Restore classroom stability and routine.

- Encourage imaginative play where children can re-enact the event and express their feelings.[19]

- Read books to children about community helpers.

- Practice disaster drills with children regularly and provide parents with your center's emergency plans.

Abuse Prevention

All teachers in your child care program should receive training in recognizing, reporting, and responding to child abuse. Your director also should provide staff members and parents with written policies covering such areas as:[20]

- precautions for providing a safe environment;

- teacher/staff conduct guidelines in relating to children, especially regarding discipline;

- reporting requirements and the center's responses when child abuse or neglect is suspected;

- procedures in screening, hiring, and training staff.

State agencies for child protective services, human resources, or child care licensing provide specific guidelines and training courses in child abuse prevention. In addition, the federal Office on Child Abuse and Neglect,[21] the National Committee to Prevent Child Abuse,[22] and the Child Welfare League of America[23] provide helpful resources.

Precautions for a Safe Environment

An ideal environment protects children, safeguards good teachers, and reduces the legal liability risk for the child care center and host church. Appropriate procedures for screening, hiring, and training all staff members will be covered later in this chapter. In addition, these precautions are needed:

- careful supervision of anyone who works with the children, including volunteers and guest "speakers";

- frequent visits to classrooms by supervisors during various times each day, including nap time;

- an "open door" policy for parents to visit unannounced — but supervised — at any time;

- adequate staff so that children are never left alone at transition times, in the rest room, at nap time, etc;

- one-way windows in doors to classrooms so that all activities can be observed at any time;

- well-planned field trips with good supervision;

- security measures during children's arrival and departure times which also prevent "unscreened" persons from having access to children at any time.

Teacher/Staff Conduct Code

The director at your center should provide all staff members with the center's philosophy regarding conduct toward children. The conduct code should provide guidelines on methods of positive guidance, redirection, and consistent communication which is understandable to the children. Discipline should be educationally-constructive and developmentally-appropriate for each child and each circumstance. Teachers should receive training in positive guidance and seek help from child development specialists when approved strategies for behavior management are not effective.

The guidelines should state that teachers and staff members are not allowed to punish children physically through hitting, spanking, swatting, yanking, shoving, shaking, thumping, pinching, biting, pulling hair, or any excessive treatment that causes physical or emotional pain.

Other disciplinary prohibitions include putting anything in a child's mouth, putting a child in a dark place, isolating a child without adult supervision, allowing other children to discipline a child, or punishment which involves food, rest, or toileting. Also prohibited is a teacher's use of language which is threatening, humiliating, derogatory, or profane.

Recognizing, Reporting, and Responding to Abuse

The training that you and all staff members at your child care center receive should be based on the child abuse statutes in your state. The state law will define child abuse specifically and probably will state that the harm or threatened harm to a child's welfare includes non-accidental physical injury, mental injury, sexual abuse, and neglect. Your training also should include a list of signs that can alert you to possible child abuse. Some of these signs include:

- unexplained or repeated occurrence of bruises, welts, abrasions, lacerations, burns, or fractures;

- fear of physical contact;

- withdrawal or hesitancy to talk or participate;

- excessive timidity or clinging behavior;

- fear of parents or going home;

- excessive demand for affection;

- aggressiveness or self-destructive behavior;

- extreme anti-social behavior or cruelty to other children or pets;

- neglected appearance; or, over-neatness;

- unusual sleeping problems and nightmares;

- sexual knowledge beyond appropriate age;

- pain or difficulty in walking or sitting.

All 50 states have laws regarding mandatory reporting of child abuse. Most states require that private citizens as well as teachers, child care workers, and other professionals promptly report suspected abuse. In most states, persons making reports can request confidentiality, and "good faith" reports are protected from civil or criminal liability. "Failure to report, when required to do so, is punishable by a fine and/or imprisonment."[24]

The authors of *Healthy Young Children: A Manual for Programs* state: "No state requires that the reporter have proof that abuse or neglect has occurred before reporting. The law may specify reporting of suspected incidents or include the phrase *reason to believe*. Incidents must be reported as soon as they are noticed, since waiting for proof may involve grave risk to the child.

"Each state specifies one or more agencies to receive reports of suspected child abuse and neglect. Usually this agency is the department of social services, human resources, or public welfare . . . . Some states maintain a 24-hour hot line just for reports of suspected child abuse or neglect."[25]

In the child abuse prevention training you receive, the director of your center should provide you with the child care center's procedures for reporting suspected child abuse. These response procedures must be consistent with state statutes, but the director may instruct you to work through administrators in making the report.

The process may involve additional contacts with an administrator from the host church, an attorney representing the church and child care center, and the liability insurance company. If a child care center employee is suspected of possible abuse, further steps may involve suspension of the employee until an investigation is completed by the state agency which received the report.

In addition, your center's response guidelines probably will include procedures regarding further communication with the child and parents, counseling possibilities, cooperation with state investigators, protective confidentiality for innocent parties, and inquiries from the media. The response guidelines also should reflect the spirit of Christian love consistent with the center's ministry goals.

Security Safeguards

Clearly-stated policies which thoroughly cover the various concerns previously outlined in this chapter will go a long way toward providing security safeguards for children, teachers, child care centers, and host churches. An additional aspect of the security measures includes the appropriate screening of all employees before they are hired, along with ongoing and consistent training and supervision. Security precautions during the arrival and departure of children each day also are vital. Such precautions are in the best interests of the teacher, as well as for the protection of the children.

Screening and Hiring Procedures

Properly-prepared employee application and screening forms are imperative for child care centers. These forms should be reviewed by a local legal authority and the center's liability insurance company. Such forms are the source for basic information which may include the following (upon the approval of your legal authority):

- full legal name, current address, phone number, and prior addresses over the past five years;

- names and addresses of present and past employers and dates of employment;

- previous experience with children, including employed and volunteer positions;

- high school and colleges attended, degrees or certifications received, and other special training;

- church membership, prior church membership and dates, and volunteer positions held in churches;

- civic and professional organizations.

In another section of the form which requests a signed consent release for conducting reference and background checks, you may be asked to provide additional information, such as:

- social security number, driver's license number, photo identification, and fingerprints;

- statement of guilty pleas or convictions related to drugs, child abuse or molestation, crimes against minors, or felony charges of any kind;

- names, addresses, and phone numbers of personal and employment references.

Applicants generally are asked to sign a statement verifying the accuracy of all information they provide; authorizing the investigation of all statements provided; releasing persons and organizations from legal liability in providing information; agreeing to submit to drug, tuberculosis, or other medical tests; substantiating that they have read and understood the job description; and agreeing to conform to lifestyle and conduct codes consistent with the child care center mission.

An increasing number of states require child care workers to provide fingerprints so that background checks can be processed through the FBI's national criminal history record system. Several commercial organizations provide information and services which assist child care centers in screening and background check procedures.[26] Child care centers may check with the local police or state authorities for information and advice on conducting background checks.

The screening process also should involve a personal interview with the program director or other administrator. Job-related questions should be the focus of the interview. State and federal employment laws protect certain areas of inquiry including race, age (must be 18 years old, or older), marital status, and so forth. However, a church child care program has the right to hire persons who hold religious views consistent with the beliefs of the church. Therefore, hiring decisions can be based on consistently-applied religious criteria.[27]

As another area of inquiry in the interview, a teacher or staff member may be asked, "Were you a victim of abuse or molestation while a minor?" Applicants may refuse to answer the question. In most cases, leaving the question unanswered will not automatically disqualify an applicant from a position in working with children if all other job and personal qualifications are positive.

Teachers and staff members being considered for child care positions should seek and be granted full assurance that *all information* received by the child care center during the application and screening process remains confidential. Administrators must develop procedures for keeping all employee records confidential and filed in a secure area.

Orientation and Training of Staff Members

Child care programs must provide documentation regarding adequate orientation and training procedures if they are to demonstrate diligence in the care of children. Training might include on-site instruction, self-directed study, workshops, and other courses. The state child care licensing agency will indicate a minimum number of hours required annually for training of individual staff members. Child care directors should

provide training for teachers which exceeds these minimum requirements, with a goal of providing 24 to 30 hours of annual training.[28]

Training should include orientation and supervision for all employed and volunteer staff members, including substitutes. Orientation and ongoing training should cover the program mission and goals, developmental characteristics and needs of children, and written policies on the following:

- employees' assigned duties and responsibilities;

- daily schedule and planned program of activities;

- acceptable methods of positive guidance and discipline as well as methods teachers should avoid;

- hand washing and disinfecting procedures;

- diapering and toileting procedures;

- food handling and preparation;

- infection control and symptoms of illness;

- first aid and emergency response procedures;

- child abuse prevention and reporting;

- facility, supply, toy, and equipment safety;

- playground, field trip, and transportation safety;

- occupational health hazards;

- security during arrival and departure of children;

• confidentiality of information regarding families.

Arrival and Departure Procedures

Another security precaution to protect the children is a clear procedure for accepting and releasing children each day. All staff members must abide by written policies in this area, and these procedures must be communicated to parents and other individuals responsible for bringing and picking up children.

Children must be released only to parents or authorized adults which parents have listed on a signed consent form on file with the child care center. Any individual dropping off or picking up a child should sign a check-in/out sheet in the presence of a staff member and use other security measures required by the center.

Specialized security identification issued by the center which also must be presented at departure time might include a personalized card or badge; a claim-check or ticket; or the second of matched tags (one tag is kept for the child and the matching tag is given to the parent to use in picking up the child).[29]

If someone other than the regular caregiver comes for a child at departure time, teachers should check the name against the parents' consent form listing approved persons and also should ask to see a driver's license for identity verification. If a question arises, the director should call the parent for clarification. Special complications may arise when parental custody concerns exist. Always call on your director when in doubt about such situations.

Protection in Today's Legal Climate

Church-sponsored child care programs have become more vulnerable in recent years. Our society has become increasingly litigious, with millions of suits filed in state courts each year.[30] Most states no longer recognize the doctrine of "charitable immunity," and churches and church-sponsored child care programs now face the same liability as private businesses.[31]

The courts have ruled that churches are not "insurers" of the safety of children and are not automatically legally liable when a child suffers injury.[32] However, the courts have found churches liable and awarded damages when teachers or staff members have been negligent.[33] In fact, churches and other organizations entrusted with the care of children often are held to a higher standard of care. Diligence in caring for young children has been a longtime hallmark of church-sponsored child care centers. Today's child care centers and their host churches must continue to follow appropriate procedures and then *document* their diligence regarding the children in their care. They also must stay in compliance with all laws and seek the advice of their attorney and liability insurance company.

When loving, informed, well-trained child care teachers and staff members carefully plan and implement developmentally-appropriate programs for young children, this is the best possible safeguard for all parties. And this diligence, in turn, reflects the very best of Christian commitment and ministry as child care programs serve children and their families.

"May he [God] give you the desire of your heart and make all your plans succeed" (Ps. 20:4, NIV).

Chapter 17

Developing and Implementing Your Plan

The preschool teacher is a facilitator and enabler. A teacher does more than just "show up." Young children require us to share our presence emotionally as well as physically. By sharing our enthusiasm with children and displaying a positive attitude, children will feel welcome and loved in the classroom. The goal for every teacher is to create a classroom environment that makes learning enjoyable for every child. A well-prepared teacher has a plan and a purpose for the time she will be in the classroom.

Before You Plan

Consider the Children — To refresh your understanding of the children you teach and how they learn best, review chapters five through eleven which relate to understanding children.

Seek God's Guidance — Planning is an awesome responsibility, not to be undertaken lightly. Pray about what God would have you to accomplish.

Set Major Goals — Good plans benefit both children and teachers. To establish a positive learning environment a teacher needs to establish goals for herself professionally, the class as a whole, and each child. Learning goals as well as personal goals for each child are necessary to provide the best learning experience. A letter to parents will demonstrate that you are interested in establishing open communication and will set a positive tone as annual goals are stated. Our best intentions and goals hinge on the atmosphere in which children learn. The way a seemingly-small routine that arises during the learning activity is handled can either have a positive or negative impact on the developing child. Learning experiences do not happen only during a preplanned activity but anywhere or anytime a child is encouraged to explore. A teaching plan that benefits the children should:

- Provide firsthand experiences
- Stimulate language development
- Develop social skills
- Stimulate a thirst for knowledge
- Provide opportunities to make choices
- Build self-confidence
- Stimulate problem solving
- Lay the foundation for moral and spiritual development

A teaching plan helps teachers:

- Be more organized
- Feel more secure
- Plan more varied experiences
- Organize their thoughts and procedures
- Evaluate each activity

THE CURRICULUM

WEE Learn Curriculum Guides provide complete units for teaching preschoolers in a Christian weekday early education program. There is a guide for each preschool year from ages two through five plus an infant/toddler guide. For closely age-graded classes, you may choose the guide for the age of the children in your classroom. For children in multi-age groupings, determine the "middle age-range of the children" and adapt the curriculum upward and downward to meet the needs of all the children.

Each guide and the accompanying *Teaching Picture Set* make up the complete curriculum. Each guide contains 24 units for preschoolers. Each unit includes age-appropriate activities for each Learning Center (Art, Blocks, Books and Listening, Homeliving, Music, Nature and Science, and Puzzles/Manipulatives) which help develop the unit purpose. Each unit includes a Bible story and Bible thoughts. Large-group suggestions are included for older preschoolers. Activities are also suggested for outdoor time, snack time, and rest time. *WEE Learn Curriculum* is designed to be used in a variety of schedules from a half-day to a full-day program.

Planning as a Team

Teachers in weekday early childhood education need to work together as a team. Many weekday programs operate for ten or more hours per day. As a result a child may have two or more teachers in the course of a typical day. To enable teachers to meet the needs of the children, teamwork is a necessity. To effectively use materials, space, and resources teachers need to cooperate with one another in planning and implementing common goals, creating a learning environment that not only meets the needs of the teachers but the needs of each child as well.

Finding quality time for a planning meeting can be difficult, yet it is the key to quality. Some teachers plan for fifteen to twenty minutes each day after the children leave; others have a specific time each week designated for teacher planning. But teachers who work without adequate relief personnel have a harder time finding a time when teachers can plan together.

Planning meetings provide teachers an opportunity to:

- Select unit topics
- Write goals and objectives
- Plan curriculum activities
- Decide which materials and supplies are needed
- Decide who will do each task
- Evaluate past experiences

Grouping Children

Teachers communicate, plan, motivate, and organize not only the physical classroom but the students as well. Teachers may have an opportunity to group preschoolers. Often grouping is done on the basis of age.

For example, all two-year-olds are in one class while all three-year-olds are in another class. This type of age grading allows the teacher to plan and provide learning activities that are developmentally-appropriate for a specific age group.

An alternative to age grading is multi-age grouping. In multi-age grouping children of various ages are taught in one class. Preschoolers may spend two or more years with the same classmates and the same teacher. Multi-age grouping can assist in the bonding process. This type of grouping develops a sense of leadership among the older students as they model more mature skills and behaviors. In multi-age grouping the teacher adapts learning activities to the various ages of children.

CReatinG the LeaRninG EnviRonMent

Emotional Environment

Environments can foster the child's social development. An environment that encourages flexibility and spontaneity for preschoolers is essential. A good environment encourages learning and assists teachers in accomplishing learning objectives.

As a teacher, determine for yourself the kind of classroom environment that will lead to the most learning on the part of your students. The classroom environment a teacher establishes will be a result of her teaching style, experience, and understanding of how preschoolers learn and develop. The teacher creates an environment to facilitate the development of skills and stimulates the interest of the preschoolers, allowing them to feel comfortable exploring their world.

When children feel comfortable and successful in their environment, they will attempt new skills that will lead to independence. Preschoolers need warm, caring, knowledgeable adults who will take time to talk and listen to them and who will prepare a learning environment that meets their needs.

Treat each child as an individual, providing guidance and limits without humiliation. Begin by establishing procedures that will make the classroom run smoothly, developing routines for handling every situation.

Careful structuring of the environment is required to allow learning to take place despite interruptions of daily routine. One of the most important responsibilities of teaching is to create and maintain a learning environment that encourages play and exploration. Evaluation is an important aspect of planning. Evaluating the use of the space used for preschoolers will allow the teacher to determine the best use of space and materials.

(Use the checklist at the end of the chapter to evaluate the use of preschool space.)

Physical Environment

The preschooler encounters two significant learning environments — the classroom and outdoors. Classroom space needs to be well organized with good traffic patterns and materials that are accessible. While good room arrangement is not a guarantee of good behavior, poor planning in this area can create conditions that lead to problems. A room painted with neutral or pastel colors will help preschoolers feel secure and restful. While bright colors can be overly-stimulating to a child when used in large areas, these colors can be put to good use in the classroom in temporary teaching materials.

Space in a preschool classroom enables a child to participate actively, independently, and successfully. Adequate furnishings and supplies enhance the teaching and learning experience. Frequently-used areas of the room and traffic lanes should be unobstructed and easily accessible. Everything in the classroom should be child-oriented. Toys,

equipment, and furniture should be geared for the particular developmental level of the children in the class. The classroom should be arranged to enhance learning experiences while meeting the needs of the children.

Preschoolers need space to practice their developing small and large motor skills. Do not overcrowd the room with too much furniture or clutter. Leave floor space for children to sit on the floor to build with blocks or work with manipulatives. Sometimes it is easier for preschoolers to do activities on the floor than on a table.

Learning Centers should be set up in the classroom to facilitate learning. Centers that encourage or require children to sit on the floor, such as the book or library center, should be placed away from the door so that children are not accidentally hit when someone enters the room. Allow plenty of room for block building, avoiding walkways, doors, and traffic paths.

If the classroom requires cribs, place the cribs with the head against the wall. When placing cribs, leave enough space between them to enable teachers and staff to move and work with a child in a crib. Materials should be accessible and on open shelves to encourage children to explore.

Adequate light and ventilation are necessary. There should be a variety of quiet and active areas to accommodate preschoolers' temperaments, moods and learning styles. Children also need opportunities to participate in learning activities and Learning Centers both indoors and outdoors. Arrange the classroom in defined areas that contain equipment and materials that encourage learning.

Arranging Learning Centers

Preschoolers are active learners; they learn through their senses. Allowing them to make choices and explore a variety of activities facilitates the learning process. Teachers set up Learning Centers which contain activities that teach the theme for the week or month. Preschoolers are not required to participate in every activity but are encouraged to choose activities that are of interest. As children choose and experience success in the activities, their sense of worth is enhanced.

The first step in creating a learning environment is to divide the learning space into easily identifiable areas or "Learning Centers." The boundaries of the Learning Centers can be made by using furniture, walls, shelves, different flooring patterns or carpets. Even something as simple as masking tape can be used to define particular boundaries of a

Learning Center. Furniture can be pulled away from walls and placed at right angles providing barriers to define space. By providing boundaries to separate Learning Centers, children are able to stay focused on activities better because they are not distracted by other activities visible in the room. This arrangement also breaks up large space. Smaller, open areas discourage children from running.

The most complex part of planning the physical learning environment is coordinating the Learning Centers. The placement of Learning Centers is important to the overall atmosphere of the learning environment. Noisy or more active Learning Centers should be placed near each other, and quiet areas such as the Book Center or Puzzles should be placed near each other. Messy areas such as the Art Center or a sand/water table should be separate from dry areas and close to a water source.

Be creative and imaginative in designing Learning Centers and materials for each Center. Learning Centers should create interest and invite children to explore. Materials in the Learning Centers should change according to the unit theme. When designing learning environments, keep in mind the age of the children that will be in the classroom, and arrange the class space and furniture to meet their needs.

(At the end of this chapter you will find suggested floor plans for various age groups.)

Suggested Learning Centers to include in the classroom are:

- **Homeliving/Housekeeping** – Activities in this Center provide preschoolers opportunities to participate in dramatic role play. Homeliving allows children to play out social behaviors such as sharing and interacting as a family.

- **Books /Library** – Preschoolers love to read books. Books provide a quiet activity for children and enhance a child's development as she looks at pictures or has a book read to her.

- **Nature/Science** – Children have an opportunity to learn more about the world around them as they explore nature items.

- **Music** – Giving preschoolers an opportunity to play musical instruments or listen to music allows them to express themselves.

- **Blocks** – Cardboard or wooden blocks along with transportation vehicles and other materials provide children an opportunity to cooperate with one another and to develop  decision-making skills as they build.

- **Puzzles/Manipulatives** – Small motor skills are developed as preschoolers work puzzles and put together manipulatives. Thinking and problem solving are also encouraged through the use of puzzles and manipulatives.

- **Art** – Through art activities preschoolers can express their thoughts and feelings. Preschoolers need open-ended art activities. Open-ended activities allow them to use art materials in creative ways by not prescribing exactly what colors or paper to use. Open-ended art experiences allow preschoolers the freedom to create on their own level; they are not merely coloring in a color sheet.

Materials and Equipment

Providing children with appropriate supplies, tools, and toys will enable them to be creative and to implement creative ideas. Children need materials that they may observe, touch, and manipulate. For preschoolers, learning is experiencing with all five senses. Providing a variety of learning materials and methods invites investigation and imagination. When a preschooler is allowed to spontaneously investigate the world around him, he learns about the world. When choosing toys and teaching materials, keep the following in mind:

- Test all materials before giving them to preschoolers. If an adult can pull or break off small parts of the toy, it may be dangerous for preschoolers.

- Do not use materials with small parts.

- Teaching materials should be durable and washable.

- Toys should not have sharp edges or points.

- Teaching materials with glass or easily-broken plastic should not be used in the classroom.

- Avoid toys with long pieces of string or elastic, especially with younger preschoolers.

- Use age-appropriate labels on toys and products. Many toys and games provide an age-appropriate label warning consumers that the product may not be safe for children under a certain age.

- Watch for small pieces or mechanisms that could pinch a child's fingers.

Classroom toys and equipment can be labeled with picture symbols and later paired with printed words so that children naturally begin recognizing letters, thereby extending learning. Keeping an inventory of classroom items will assist teachers in maintaining class materials and in knowing when new items need to be purchased.

(NOTE: See additional safety information for equipment and teaching materials in Chapter 16, "Guidelines for Hygiene, Safety, and Security.")

(Use the inventory checklist at the end of the chapter to keep a record of classroom materials.)

Props, teaching materials, and toys placed in the Learning Centers should be changed to reflect the unit theme. Teaching materials should be kept simple. Too much clutter can be over-stimulating and distracting for some preschoolers. Shelves should be kept neat, clean, and organized. Baskets or other containers can be used to hold small manipulatives and toys.

Only a few toys should be placed on the shelf so that preschoolers learn that everything has a place. Provide duplicates of a few favorite toys so that preschoolers will be more willing to share and take turns. If a child has to wait half the day to have her turn with a favorite toy, she will be less likely to share once she does get the toy. By providing more than one toy, the amount of time a child must wait will be decreased to an amount of time that is more compatible with a preschooler's attention span.

Place as many open-ended materials in Learning Centers as possible — materials that can be used in more than one way. Allow children to use their creativity in using the item. Adding new items into Learning Centers can stimulate interest. New props will be used more constructively if they are introduced by the teacher. A teacher can, during group time, introduce a new item by showing it and discussing the following:

- What is this new item used for?

- Ask children how they have seen the item used.

- Ask the children to think of other ways to use the item.

- Discuss using the item safely.

Have Materials and Equipment Prepared

Having necessary teaching materials on hand to help the children learn and grow is a necessity. Classrooms that are developmentally-appropriate are active classrooms. Structuring a predictable, daily routine and interesting learning activities provides an orderly framework for the classroom. Each day prepare the materials you will need to teach the learning experiences planned. Check for the safety of the items the preschoolers will be using.

The Outdoor Classroom

Depending on weather conditions, many Learning Center activities can be experienced outside. During outside time children not only have an opportunity to exercise their large motor skills, they also observe, explore, and experiment with the world around them.

The playground should be thought of as the outdoor classroom. The playground should be specifically designed and equipped to support a wide range of activities. The outdoor classroom provides preschoolers with opportunities to explore a variety of elements and settings they would not be able to fully explore indoors.

A playground should offer more than large stationary structures such as slides and swings. The outdoor classroom should also offer equipment and structures allowing for exploration and creativity.

Outside time is not a break from teaching or a time for adults to socialize and relax. Teachers should interact with children outdoors the same way they do indoors. Teachers can talk with children about what they are going to do on the playground.

Allow children to set their own course. Observe and listen to the child's play and then support and extend the child's learning experience by asking open-ended questions, thus helping children to expand their observations and experiences on the playground. Teachers should be active participants in play, not play leaders.

Evaluate materials and equipment for safety and guide children in using them safely. Arrange playground areas or Centers with adequate space to allow preschoolers to move freely between the areas safely. Within each area space and equip-  ment should be arranged so that adults can observe children at all times and get to them quickly.

Provide toys for sand and water play as well as for dramatic role play for use in the outdoor classroom. Children should also be encouraged to participate in art activities while outside. Vehicle pathways for tricycles and other wheeled vehicles should be included in the play area. Climbing structures with safety material such as sand, pea gravel, rubber mats, or wood chips can provide large-motor activity for preschoolers.

Check with your state guidelines for safety regulations regarding outdoor playgrounds and equipment.

Providing Economical Equipment

Choosing materials and equipment requires careful thought. Teaching materials can be costly. When choosing materials, keep in mind many children will be using the materials on a daily basis. It may be less expensive in the long run to purchase commercial items that are made to withstand more use than a less-expensive item. Look for easily-cleaned, plastic surfaces. Buy high-quality furniture. Put casters on furniture whenever possible to aid movement and allow for greater variety of use. Teachers can make games, activities, and visuals for the classroom that are less expensive than many pre-made visuals available at teacher supply stores. Protect teacher-made materials with acrylic spray or lamination for longer use.

Computers

Computer activities can be available in a Learning Center. Once a quality software

program has been selected, be sure to provide non-intrusive adult support. Given appropriate software, preschoolers can become quite adept at using computers without extensive adult help.

Sharing Space and Equipment

Several other groups may use the preschool classroom you use during the week. All teachers and staff using the classrooms need to realize that any one room does not belong to any one group or organization, but the classrooms are for all preschoolers involved in learning. Teachers who use the same room need to work together, leaving the room ready for the next group.

The important thing to focus on is to act in a Christlike manner when sharing, being a good example to the preschoolers. How can we expect two-year-olds or three-year-olds to learn how to share with their "friends" if we do not model sharing with our "friends." Any artwork or teaching materials should be removed and placed in a storage area so that the room is clean for the next group. We should **find it clean, keep it clean,** and **leave it clean** as we share space.

Schedule a time when all teachers that use the room can get together and work out room arrangements and details that will make sharing space a positive experience. Meeting together can provide valuable insight into the unique purposes God has for each ministry. Discussing common goals as well as room arrangement and shared supplies can assist everyone involved in keeping the focus on the reason we are teaching preschoolers. Teachers and volunteers working together demonstrate a Christlike love to the preschoolers and their parents.

Planning the Schedule

Teachers must plan in all facets of the child's development for learning to occur. A well-planned schedule enhances quality learning experiences for children. Planning must center around the child. After preliminary planning, choices need to be made about unit themes and activities to build a total curriculum. Plan and prepare activities that encourage the development of the child physically, mentally, emotionally, socially, and spiritually.

Developing a workable schedule can be challenging. Follow a schedule that meets a young child's need for routine but is flexible enough to meet each child where he is. Though curriculum has certain basic elements, teachers must decide how much time to allot for each activity and how to order the various time segments of the day.

Despite this flexibility, developing a daily routine is difficult for staff because there are so many care-giving tasks to complete. Yet teachers can find creative ways to meet all these scheduling needs within the framework of the chosen curriculum. The key is to think through each part of the routine, consider the task that must be accomplished, and allow enough time for routine tasks to be handled in a calm, unhurried manner.

For example, arrival and departure times can be especially difficult because there are so many distractions. Arrange activities so that children are involved in self-directed learning experiences during the most hectic times, arranging routines so that the needs of the children are being met. Plan overlapping activities for transition times. Always have extra activities planned so that if unseen interruptions or distractions occur, you can be flexible with learning opportunities for the children.

Operate according to planned routines, breaking the day into segments that carry out the planned curriculum. By having a predictable routine, the children feel more comfortable with what happens in the classroom, even the unexpected. Schedules can be made to meet the need of the children, teachers, and the school as a whole. Regular times such as outdoor play and snack time must be scheduled to allow each classroom to participate. Experiment with schedules to find one that best fits your class.

Whether you are teaching in a half-day program or a full-day program, several factors influence your schedule:

- Age of the children

- Developmental level of the children

- Experiential backgrounds of children

- Length of day children are in weekday

- Weather conditions

- Transportation variations

- Physical facilities — amount of space, location of bathroom, proximity of playground to building

- Number of children in a room

- Staff-child ratio

(Sample schedules for half- and full-day programs are given at the end of this chapter.)

Develop the Lesson Plan

Teachers must plan for learning to occur in all facets of the child's development. Quality learning experiences for children are enhanced by a detailed lesson plan. Planning should center on the child. Planning is the *thinking* that takes place before the *action* occurs. Prepare and plan activities that encourage the development of the whole child — physically, mentally, emotionally, socially, and spiritually.

Lesson plans are written by teachers to determine the activities for each Learning Center related to the unit theme. Lesson plans are a thinking-and-planning process which includes determining materials needed, assessment, objectives, and evaluation. By thinking carefully about what the lesson is meant to accomplish, a teacher can choose, and guide children through, appropriate learning activities.

The purpose of a lesson plan is to communicate. Through lesson plans, parents, supervisors, and the teacher can see the purpose and objective in the learning experiences and can guide the teacher in helping students achieve intended learning outcomes. Each part of the lesson plan should fulfill the purpose in communicating the specific content, the objective, learning prerequisites, and materials required. Lesson planning is a skill. It takes practice to acquire this skill, and it will not happen overnight, but it is a skill that will help the teacher to be organized and to develop as a professional.

Planning both individual and group learning experiences is an integral part of the classroom experience. During group time or circle time, children come together to sing songs, do finger plays, or participate in other activities as a group. More complex group activities can be planned as more familiarity with the group occurs. Always be prepared to capture those teachable moments.

Activities are specific strategies planned to achieve learning and developmental goals. Activities are supported by materials available in the Learning Centers. Activities may be repeated or may be used only one time. Provide developmentally-appropriate, content-rich, and challenging activities, projects, and themes suited to the age and individual needs of the children in the class.

Instructional Methods

When planning, consider:

- The learning styles of the children

- Resources available

- Location of the learning experience

- Time available for the learning experience

Lesson plans are an integral part of carrying out instructional methods in the classroom. A well thought-out lesson plan will give direction and structure to learning experiences. Lesson plans can be made daily, weekly, or monthly, depending on the needs and characteristics of the curriculum and program used. Lesson plans also allow for advance planning in the use of materials and shared equipment. Lesson plans provide:

- Goals for the group

- Goals for individual children

- Activities as methods to achieve goals

- Materials needed

- Developmentally-appropriate learning activities

- Objectives

- Skills to develop

Teachers determine objectives in the lesson plan to clarify the expectation and learning changes that will occur. The objective will focus more on the child than what is being taught and more on what the child will do than what the teacher will do. Objectives are not descriptions of teaching but indicators of what the child/children will learn. A good objective is written from the learner's point of view and states how students will demonstrate the achievement of the goal. For example: The child will be able to: _____

_____

_____.

Lesson plan forms are available in each *WEE Learn Curriculum Guide*.

Choosing and Guiding Activities

A quality preschool program will provide activities that are stimulating and challenging to young children. Choosing appropriate learning activities for the classroom is an important part of implementing the plan outlined in the curriculum and lesson plan.

Choosing — When choosing activities consider the following:

- Provide a balance of noisy and quiet activities.

- Provide group and individual learning experiences.

- Provide a balance of active and sedentary activities.

- Provide daily opportunity for both outdoor and indoor gross-motor activities.

- Provide daily opportunity for small-motor skill practice.

- Integrate language-development skills into the activity.

Guiding — A quality preschool program will provide activities that are stimulating and challenging to young children. Offer a variety of activities using the Center suggestions described in the unit plans. Your role is to observe, help girls and boys learn to control their behavior, extend learning through questions, and enrich work with conversation and materials. The child's role is to select his own activities, stay constructively busy, and respect other people and property.

To manage Learning Center time:

- Plan activities that relate to the unit theme.

- Prepare materials and put them in the Centers before the first child arrives.

- Move around the room so you are facing as many children as possible. Try to keep your back toward the wall.

- Talk with a child about his work. Ask questions that require multiple-word answers and that have more than one correct answer. You might say, "Tell me about that."

- Give children time to solve problems themselves when they have difficulty with materials or with one another. However, if a child is in danger, intervene quickly.

- About five minutes before time to clean up, move around the room quietly and tell children they need to finish the activities.

Planning for Group Time

Group time (usually recommended for three, four, and five-year-olds) is a time when teachers and children gather in one area of the room for learning experiences. The length of group time may vary from ten to fifteen minutes depending on the developmental level of the preschoolers involved. In a weekday setting, two or more brief group times per day may be scheduled. Group time is usually more effective when scheduled after children have had free time in activities or Learning Centers.

The purpose of group time is to give children opportunities to develop language, social, thinking, and listening skills. It also provides good opportunities for children to express themselves and to learn to work and cooperate in a group setting.

Scheduling Field Trips

Taking a class to visit locations that are related to the theme or unit of study can enrich and extend the learning opportunity. As the children visit a farm or dental office, they will be able to see "real life" examples of what is being taught in the classroom. Children also have an opportunity to interact with community helpers.

When planning a field trip, be sure to make arrangements well in advance including permission slips and transportation for the children. When taking a group of preschoolers away from the school, be sure to abide by any local or state regulations that may apply to off-campus excursions. Each child should easily be identified with your group through the use of similar name tags or school shirts.

When leaving the school, bring a first aid kit and emergency numbers. Always have parents or volunteers go with the class to provide additional supervision.

SAMPLE SCHEDULE OPTIONS

FULL-DAY SCHEDULE (With Nap)	**FULL-DAY SCHEDULE** (Without Nap)	**HALF-DAY SCHEDULE**
6:30 Free Play/ Learning Centers	*6:30* Free Play/Learning Centers	*9:00* Group/Circle Time
8:30 Outside Time	*8:30* Group/Circle Time	*9:15* Planning
9:00 Group/Circle Time	*8:45* Planning	*9:30* Learning Centers
9:15 Planning	*9:00* Learning Centers	*10:15* Clean Up
9:30 Learning Centers	*10:00* Clean Up	*10:30* Snack
10:15 Clean Up	*10:15* Outside Time	*11:00* Outside Time
10:30 Snack	*10:45* Snack	*11:30* Learning Centers
11:00 Outside Time	*11:00* Learning Centers	*12:00* Dismissal
11:30 Learning Centers	*12:00* Group Time	
12:00 Lunch	*12:30* Lunch	
12:30 Outside Time	*1:00* Outside Time	
1:00 Nap/Rest Time	*1:30* Quiet Activities/ Centers	
3:00 Wake Up/Clean Up	*2:30* Group Time	
3:15 Snack	*3:00* Snack	
3:30 Group Time	*3:30* Outside Centers/ Activities	
4:00 Outside Time	*4:30-6:00* Free Play/Learning Centers	
4:30-6:00 Free Play/Learning Centers		

CHECKLIST FOR EVALUATING THE USE OF PRESCHOOL SPACE

SELDOM	USUALLY	ALWAYS	
			The environment is orderly, clean, and neat.
			Use of space supports cooperative and safe behavior.
			Children are able to choose their own activities.
			Equipment, materials, and toys are age-appropriate.
			Learning materials are carefully selected and maintained.
			Space is provided so that parents are obviously welcome in the class.
			Clear boundaries divide the Learning Centers.
			Walkways allow for smooth traffic flow between Centers.
			Learning activities reflect variety for individual learning styles.
			There are both quiet and active learning experiences.
			Preschoolers are able to use and take care of materials successfully.
			Local and state safety regulations are followed.
			Displayed teaching materials are current.
			Visuals are placed at the preschoolers' eye level.
			The schedule includes group and individual activities.
			The teacher can visually observe all activity areas.
			Emergency procedures and exits are clearly marked.
			Dangerous products and materials are out of the children's reach.
			Equipment is free from sharp edges or broken parts.

SUGGESTED PRESCHOOL FLOOR PLANS

Infants
(0 to 8 months)

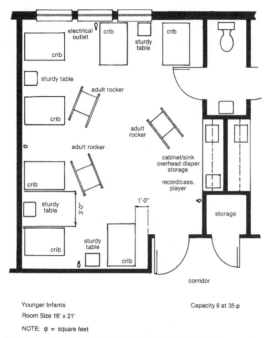

Younger Infants

Room Size 16' x 21'

NOTE: ⌀ = square feet

Capacity 9 at 35 ⌀

Infants
(9 to 14 months)

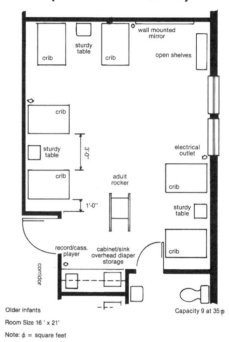

Older infants

Room Size 16 ' x 21'

Note: ⌀ = square feet

Capacity 9 at 35 ⌀

Toddlers
(15 to 24 months)

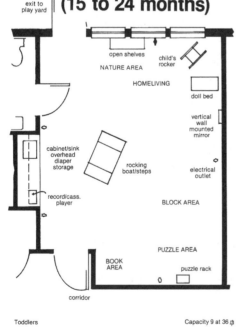

Toddlers

Room Size 16' x 20'

NOTE: ⌀ = square feet

Capacity 9 at 36 ⌀

Twos Through Threes

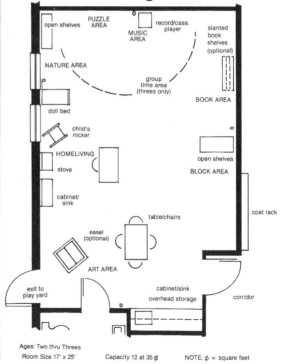

Ages: Two thru Threes

Room Size 17' x 25'

Capacity 12 at 35 ⌀

NOTE: ⌀ = square feet

SUGGESTED PRESCHOOL FLOOR PLANS

Fours Through Fives

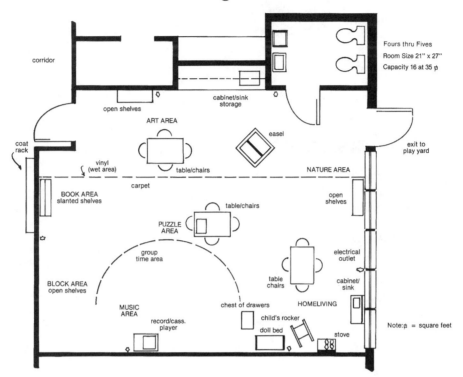

Fours thru Fives
Room Size 21" x 27"
Capacity 16 at 35 ꝑ

corridor

open shelves

cabinet/sink
storage

ART AREA

easel

exit to
play yard

coat
rack

vinyl
(wet area)

table/chairs

NATURE AREA

carpet

BOOK AREA
slanted shelves

open
shelves

table/chairs

PUZZLE
AREA

group
time area

electrical
outlet

table
chairs

cabinet/
sink

BLOCK AREA
open shelves

MUSIC
AREA

chest of drawers

HOMELIVING

child's rocker

Note: ꝑ = square feet

record/cass.
player

doll bed

stove

Infant/Toddler Equipment Inventory

# ITEMS	FURNITURE	MAINTENANCE NOTES
	Cribs	
	Changing Tables	
	Strollers	
	Infant Swings	
	Diaper Pail	
	Toy Shelves	
	High Chairs	
	Food Service	
	Sterilizing Equipment	
	Spoons	
	Baby Food/Bottle Warmers	
	Linens	
	Sheets	
	Blankets	
	Washcloths	
	Towels	
	Bibs	
	Music	
	Record/Tape/CD Player	
	Music Boxes	
	Drums	
	Manipulatives & Toys	
	Nesting Toys	
	Stacking Toys	
	Soft/Cardboard Blocks	
	Snap Beads	
	Books	
	Mobiles	
	Balls	
	Pull Toys	
	Riding Toys	
	Dolls	
	Mirrors	
	Teethers	
	Rattles	

PRESCHOOL EQUIPMENT INVENTORY

# ITEMS	FURNITURE	MAINTENANCE NOTES
	Mats/Cots	
	Changing Tables	
	Strollers	
	Potty Chair	
	Diaper Pail	
	Step Stool	
	Tables	
	Chairs	
	Floor Pillows	
	Bookshelf	
	Toy Shelves	
	Easels	
	Sensory Table	
	Child-Sized Kitchen	
	FOOD SERVICE	
	Cups	
	Spoons	
	Forks	
	Bowls	
	Plates	
	LINENS	
	Sheets	
	Blankets	
	Washcloths	
	Towels	
	MUSIC	
	Record/Tape/CD Player	
	Rhythm Instruments	
	Piano/Keyboard	
	MANIPULATIVES & TOYS	
	Blocks	
	Beads with Strings	
	Play Dough	
	Sewing Cards	
	Peg Boards	

PRESCHOOL EQUIPMENT INVENTORY *continued...*

# ITEMS	MANIPULATIVES & TOYS *continued . . .*	MAINTENANCE NOTES
	Puzzles	
	Board Games	
	TOYS	
	Dress-Up Clothes	
	Dolls	
	Books	
	Puppets	
	Transportation Toys	
	Tools	
	Mirrors	
	Telephone	
	LARGE MOTOR EQUIPMENT	
	Riding Toys	
	Large Blocks	
	Large Transportation Toys	
	Climber	
	Rocking Boat	
	Tunnel	
	Sports Equipment	
	SCIENCE & MATH	
	Magnifying Glass	
	Sensory Alphabet Letters	
	Magnets	
	Globe	
	Computer	
	Software	
	Prism	
	Color Wheel	

"Pay attention and gain understanding"
(Prov. 4:1, NIV).

Chapter 18

Observing Children's Play

Many theories that are widely accepted today resulted from experiences of individuals who observed the lives of people around them. Jean Piaget's observations of his own children led to his theory of cognitive development. Sigmund Freud's observations of his clinical patients led to his theory of personality development. Ignaz Semmelweis' observations of women dying of childbirth fever led to his discovery that infectious material was being spread from the doctor's contaminated hands to women during childbirth.

We owe it to the children in our weekday early education programs to become sensitive observers and perceptive interpreters of what we observe. We are told in Proverbs 4:1 (NIV) to, "Pay attention and gain understanding." The ability to really "see" each child is a learned skill of an effective teacher.

Observing and reflecting on what is seen accomplishes at least four important purposes.

WHY OBSERVE?

1. As an Aid in Curriculum Planning

Since curriculum in a weekday early education classroom builds upon what children already know and are able to do, an accurate, periodic assessment of every child is essential. Observations provide valuable information about children's capabilities, interests, and ways of learning. This information enables the teacher to plan appropriate activities and experiences to help children continue to make progress. Teachers must be willing to adjust curriculum to be not only age-appropriate but also individually-appropriate.

"Teachers cannot decide what, how, and when to teach without knowing what is happening with the children."[1]

2. For More Effective Parent Communication

"Parents are a primary audience for what is learned from assessment of their own children. They need to know that their children are well cared for and that they are making progress. Parents want to understand the program and feel confident about it. They want concrete evidence about what is happening and what their children are experiencing."[2]

Observations supply precise and graphic examples of a child's behavior and developmental progress. Selected observation records, work samples that show the difference in quality of work over time, photographs of work products in the classroom, and artwork samples allow parents to get a realistic picture of their child at school. An even more complete understanding of a child emerges when parental observation is added to such a portfolio of information.

3. To Identify Special Needs

Each child has needs, and it is the responsibility of the teacher in the Christian weekday early education classroom to meet those needs. From time to time, however, there is a child who has a unique need — one that the teacher cannot effectively meet.

Observing and recording at regular intervals can assess all domains of young children's learning — physical, social, emotional, cognitive, and spiritual. Multiple unbiased observations and accurate recordings will help identify areas of special need. Your training as an early childhood teacher has given you a background of information about children. You see a child many hours of the week in a variety of situations, and you have a classroom of children with which to make comparison. You even have some innate observational skills. And, because you organize information according to past experiences, what you know, and what you believe, you may tend to think that you know what is going on with the child. CAUTION: Don't draw conclusions without a great deal of evidence.

Do not go into an observation with a predetermined outcome. Be open to learning something new about the situation and to the possibility that you can do something to help the child. If it appears that a referral to another professional is necessary, consider all factors in the "Referrals" section that appears in this chapter.

4. To Assess the Program's Effectiveness

It is important to evaluate the Christian weekday early education program regularly to ensure that it is meeting its goals and that children and families are benefiting from participation. Such an assessment would be based on established goals such as health and safety, administration, staff evaluation, parental involvement, the physical environment, children's progressive development, and success in fulfilling the mission statement.

Parents, staff, members of the Christian Weekday Early Education Committee, and church staff members may be among the groups qualified to assess the program.

Assessment is the basis for curriculum planning, effective parent communication, identifying special needs, and determining the program's effectiveness.

Many commercially-prepared tests are available that claim to provide assessment of children. There are very few such instruments developed for young children, however. These tests are stressful to boys and girls with short attention spans for activities they do not choose, who lack auditory memory to follow directions as required, who are easily distracted, and who cannot use abstract symbols that are required. (Puckett and Black, 1994).[3] These tests do not measure a child's ability to problem-solve, to respond to open-ended questions, to demonstrate creativity and other important components of intelligence. Such tests are unrelated to the child's real life in the classroom. Furthermore, test scores can be misused, resulting in labels and comparisons that follow the child and negatively affect progress.

A more accurate assessment of young children is possible when more than one source of information is used — a portfolio-based assessment. Reflection on a collection of data provides the teacher with a more descriptive picture of the whole child.

Portfolios may include:

• A collection of children's work that illustrates progress over time (drawings, emergent writing samples, cutting samples, draw-a-person picture, a story told by the child and written down by the teacher, etc.).

• Photographs providing evidence of accomplished tasks (beads strung according to pattern, three-dimensional manipulative projects, block structures, collaborative projects, and beginning and end-of-year photos of the child).

• Documentation of parent and teacher observations of children interacting with others and their environment (stage of social play, language skills, attention span, small and large motor skills, etc.).

Portfolios take various forms, depending upon the teacher's preference. Accordion file folders, notebook binders, boxes, albums, and various combinations of these items can be used to organize information about each child.

Observation and Recording Methods

A number of effective observation strategies involve the use of narrative. The observer writes down, as accurately as possible, everything a child says and does, including nonverbal body language. Wright, in *Recording and Analyzing Child Behavior*, provides guidelines regarding the use of the narrative.

1. Describe the setting where the behavior occurs.

2. Describe the behavior of the child and the behavior of anyone who interacts with the child.

3. Record events separately and in chronological order.[4]

In a narrative recording, the observer must be objective, writing down all facts of what is seen and heard. Events must be recorded in the sequence they occur. To do otherwise may lead to faulty conclusions and misinterpretation. Recordings of this nature yield open-ended information that may allow unexpected or unreliable findings.

Cumulative narrative records may show evidence of achievement of a milestone. Likewise, they may reveal a pattern of behaviors, provide insight into the cause of a child's response to certain situations, and lead the teacher to institute changes in the environment or teaching/guidance methods. Two frequently-used narrative methods of observation are the Specimen Description (also know as a Running Record) and the Anecdotal Record.

• A **Specimen Description** or a **Running Record** is a continuous observation and narrative recording of unselected, ongoing behavior in natural settings over an extended period of time. Teachers will use this type of recording as they can arrange extended periods of time to observe.

• An **Anecdotal Observation** is a written narrative description of events that seem to be important. It is descriptive enough that the reader can get a visual picture. It differs from the specimen description in that the recording is of a single, relatively brief event. It can be recorded after the fact although it may not contain the same detail as if the observer had recorded while the event was taking place. The anecdotal method of observation is a realistic strategy for busy teachers. (An Anecdotal Record form is at the end of this chapter.)

Discuss the anecdotal method of observation in staff meeting. Arrange to have two or three staff members interact about some adult issue where different opinions are expressed. Ask remaining staff members to make an anecdotal recording of the interaction. As the recordings are read, encourage all staff members to provide feedback to increase effective use of this observation method. Analyze recording differences. Now, practice using the anecdotal method in your classroom. Bring your recordings to the next staff meeting to once again share with your colleagues.

• Rather than writing descriptive narratives, as in the anecdotal and specimen description or running-record methods, observers can simply check the occurrence of behaviors with a **Checklist.** This structure allows the observer's attention to focus only on the occurrence of pre-selected behaviors. Recording can be made after-the-fact. The checklist method of observation may include anything the teacher believes is important and is simple to use.

To prepare a checklist, the teacher must:

1. Determine the purpose of the observation.

2. Identify the behaviors to be observed (written in positive terms).

3. Design the actual checklist. (See sample "Checklist to Assess Certain Pre-Writing Skills" at the end of this chapter.)

Checklists can be developed on any particular aspect of child development or behavior. They can be used to observe an individual child or a group of children. Checklists are often used to identify a child's acquisition of skills and concepts, play preferences, use of materials, etc.

- **Rating Scales** look at the frequency or degree of behaviors. They often use numerical ranking such as 1 through 5 or words such as *always, never, sometimes,* or *usually.* Ratings are based on cumulative direct observation. Gordon and Browne, in *Beginnings and Beyond: Foundations in Early Childhood Education,* used the following categories on a rating scale to measure group-time attention:

  - Never Attentive (wiggles, distracts others, wanders away).

  - Seldom Attentive (eyes wander, never follows fingerplays or songs, occasionally watches leader).

  - Sometimes Attentive (can be seen imitating hand gestures, appears to be watching leader about half the time, watches others imitating leader).

- Usually Attentive (often follows leader, rarely leaves group, occasionally volunteers, usually follows leader's gestures and imitations).

- Always Attentive (regularly volunteers, enthusiastically enters into each group activity, eagerly imitates leader, almost always tries new songs).[5]

Rating scales, like checklists, may be used for an extended period of time or a brief time. They may be used as a method for observing individual children, groups of children, or the total program. (See rating scales samples at the end of this chapter. Example: "Progress Form for Infants and Toddlers.")

- **Event Sampling** is the process of trying to better understand why and when a particular behavior occurs. The observer waits for the selected behavior to occur and then records it as well as what occurred before and after the event. Event sampling requires on-the-spot coding or narration or both. Event sampling is an effective way for teachers to look at just about every aspect of child behavior.

Guidelines for using event sampling include:

1. Identify and define the behavior you want to study.

2. Know enough about the behavior to know when and where to observe.

3. Determine what kind of information you want to record.

4. Prepare a written system for describing and recording. To make it as easy to use as possible, you may use coding or narration or a combination of these. You can precode categories of behaviors you expect to see, using abbreviations or letters. You can prepare a checklist to aid in quick recording. Allow ample room for narrative.

Looking at particular situations objectively through event sampling usually causes some change to be implemented. (See a sample Event Sampling form at the end of this chapter.)

• While event sampling looks at a particular behavior, **Time Sampling** looks at the number of times a behavior occurs. Use of this method is limited to frequently or regularly-occurring behaviors that are easy to observe. Time sampling requires on-the-spot recording. To create a time sampling chart:

1. Identify the behavior to be observed.

2. Decide on specific time intervals to observe (the length, spacing, and number of intervals).

3. Determine categories for recording.

4. Develop a code for recording behavior.

The final printed format for recording the behavior will look like a tally sheet. Time sampling is an effective way to gather information about a group of children or an individual and can be used to observe either positive or negative behavior.

Time sampling is useful for determining the frequency of occurrences of behaviors or events. This method is limited in that:

◆ There is no information about the environment or situation.

◆ It seldom reveals cause-and-effect relationships.

◆ It can be biased due to the predetermined categories. (See a sample Time Sampling form at end of this chapter.)

• We have many **Electronic Resources** available today that permit the recording of classroom activities. On the one hand, an audio or videotape could be seen as an effective aid in observation, permitting the classroom teacher to record observations when free from classroom responsibilities.

On the other hand, use of such equipment is seen by some parents to be an invasion of their child's privacy. Parents must be notified when taping is to occur in their child's room, informed of how it will be used, and must sign a release form giving permission for their child to be present when taping occurs. Do not overlook this procedure as there are currently court cases involving this very matter.

Parents are more likely to be receptive if a tape of only their child is made and then given to the parents at the end of the year.

There are other problems to be considered in using electronic equipment for observation. Such devices can be distracting to the children's routine activities and the natural setting. Furthermore, it is almost impossible to catch the emotional aspects of child behavior through mechanical methods. Do not depend on this method alone to support your assessment of a child.

Methods of observation will vary depending upon the information being sought and the observer's comfort with the method's design. There are, however, a few basic principles that apply to all valid observation efforts.

OBSERVATION BASICS

- Observe during natural play activities rather than in a contrived environment. Your goal in observing is to better understand how a child or group of children responds and interacts in everyday situations. Observation is most effective when children are doing what they would normally be doing. Furthermore, they are more likely to be themselves when being observed by a familiar adult, one with whom they have an established relationship.

- Manage time to make observations of all children. It is important that parents understand that you are observing so you can better understand *all* children in your classroom. They would be uncomfortable thinking you were focusing on their child unless you agreed in advance to use observation as a means of understanding a mutual concern.

Regularly-planned observations will help you observe more objectively. Because observation and recording is time consuming, you may choose to record information on one third of the group on Monday, another third on Wednesday, and the remaining third on Friday. You may choose to observe two or three children each day. Decide on a schedule that seems workable to you and be flexible, knowing that things don't always go as planned in an early childhood classroom.

Rest time can be a good time for recording either after-the-fact observations or assessing the skill and concept development of individual children as they awake. Your director or teaching assistant may take responsibility for classroom management occasionally so that you can step aside and do sustained observing. In observing, you are a teacher-researcher.

- Record observations on 3-by-5-inch cards, on sticky pads, on notepads, or in spiral notebooks — whatever works for you and permits you to file the notes in each child's respective portfolio later. Record as inconspicuously as possible. At first, children may ask, "What are you doing?" Your reply may be, "I am writing myself a note."

As children become accustomed to seeing you record, they will pay less and less attention. Preplanned, printed forms such as those required for some observation methods may be kept on a clipboard that is close at hand in an area that is not easily noticed.

- Define the purpose for your observation. Observation is a means of answering specific questions. What is your question or purpose in observing? What do you want to know? Do you want to:

  . . . Understand individual personalities in order to develop rapport?

  . . . Learn about interests so that you can incorporate them into the curriculum or stimulate learning in other areas?

  . . . Assess individual progress toward center-selected goals?

  . . . Identify causes of unacceptable behavior?

  . . . Provide parents with evidence of a child's involvement?

  It is important to have a purpose in mind when you begin an observation, even though the observation records can be used in multiple ways. You are collecting data, asking the question, observing and recording to find the answer, reflecting on the findings, and perhaps generating a new question to explore.

- Select the method of observation that is most effective in meeting the stated purpose of your observation, the one that yields the most meaningful and useful information. Observations can be designed to consider various aspects of the child's behavior and development.

  The format for recording observations will vary, but the purpose is always the same — to learn more about a child and his environment. Teachers must observe children over time in order to get an accurate picture.

  Each observation note should include the child's name, age, and date of birth as well as the observer's name, date and time of observation. (See samples at the end of this chapter.)

- There must be a clear separation of objective (what was seen and heard) and subjective (observer's interpretation and/or comments) data. Interpretations are ways of trying to explain the cause or causes of the observed behavior. Accurate interpretations are impossible from single observations and should always be tentative. Draw no conclusions which cannot be positively justified by actual observations.

  Interpretations or comments by the observer are to be written separately from the actual observation, either in a side column or at the end of the observation. Try to interpret what you observe from the child's viewpoint rather than imposing adult perceptions on the information.

  The goal of your observation will determine if an interpretation should be made.

  The knowledge gained from unbiased observation will be valuable to the child, parent, and staff. "Your ability to be a good observer — to see what's happening — can make a critical difference to what you do. And what you do about what you see can make a critical difference to the child."[6]

Identify each of the following statements as either observations (O) or interpretations (I)

___ George is talking loudly.

___ Mary is an affectionate child.

___ Alice squints her eyes and shouts to Betty, "Don't touch me!"

___ Allen was angry at Edward and hit him.

___ Henry is a mean boy.

___ Hayden marked on Claire's picture.

___ Bill has a learning problem.

(Answers on page 254.)

Referrals

The decision to refer a child for screening or diagnostic evaluation is a difficult one and not to be taken lightly. Consider what is at stake: the child's future, the parent-teacher relationship, the reputation of both the teacher and the center, perhaps even separation of the child from the watch-care of the center. Therefore, careful consideration is necessary. The decision comes down to "What is in the best interest of the child?"

Joanne Hendrick, in *The Whole Child,* listed four criteria that teachers should consider when trying to make a decision about referring a child for further evaluation and testing. She said that behavior should arouse feelings of concern in the staff when: (1) it is too extreme, (2) it happens too often, (3) it persists too long, and (4) the number of symptoms manifested by the child is excessive at any one period of time.[7]

To assist in making a decision about referrals, each weekday early education program should have an organized **Referral Plan**. It should include at least the following three steps.

STEP 1: Evaluation of the School Setting

Is it possible that the problem the child is having is due to something that is going on, or not going on, in the classroom? Is the problem due to something you are doing or not doing? Is the school environment a source of the child's problem? These things need to be looked into, because these are easy to change.

Ysseldyke, Pianta, Christesnson, Wang & Algozzine (1983)[8], asked teachers to list alternatives they had tried in the classroom prior to referral. The results are divided into the following six categories to which have been added applicable activities for the early childhood classroom:

1. **Methods** — Changes in teaching, including varying curriculum and teacher expectations

2. **Behavioral** — Altered guidance practices and different interpersonal interactions

3. **Structural** — Change in room arrangement that physically discourages inap-

propriate behavior or alterations in the daily schedule that more nearly meet the needs of young children

4. **Specialized Help** — Observation by another experienced teacher or director; the help of a teaching assistant

5. **Materials** — Provision of age-appropriate games and multiple toys of the same type that are interesting to children

6. **Informational** — Collecting information from parents and multiple classroom observations

Teachers should make their director aware early on of any "hunches" about a child that might lead to a referral. The director's input and support will prove most valuable.

STEP 2: Home-School Cooperation and Communication

Communication with parents should begin long before a referral is made. Teachers should work hard at getting to know each child's family as soon as possible after enrollment. Families must know of the teacher's interest and appreciation of their child in order to develop a trusting relationship that will be vital if a referral becomes necessary. Make written and verbal acknowledgement of positive aspects of each individual child even while you are trying to figure out what is behind the behavior that concerns you. Every child has God-given qualities that can be seen by the wise and caring teacher.

Ongoing communication and getting-to-know-you conferences can help you under-stand a child's cultural and experiential background. This, and information about the child's behaviors away from the school setting, are a necessary part of understanding a child. Parental input is essential to making a decision about referral.

Parents are more accepting of referrals when they are given information on a gradual basis. Bring parents into the process by asking them to observe at school and to share their observations of the child at home. Make time away from children to share information with one another. Keep the parent informed about your attempts to understand what is going on and efforts you are taking to help with the issue. Ask for ideas from the parent. Agree on a plan of action. Implement that plan and get back together to see how it is going. If that plan is not successful, agree on another strategy.

Ideally, you and parents work as a team to do what is best for the child. The reality is, however, that parents feel great pain in being told that their child needs to be seen by a therapist, psychologist, or other specialist. Parents may be in denial due to well-meaning relatives and pediatricians who advise that their child will "grow out of it."

STEP 3: Making the Referral

After Evaluation of the School Setting (Step 1) and Home-School Cooperation and Communication (Step 2) have failed to influence a change in the child, referral to another professional may become necessary. This must be done in conference at a time when all parties can be present.

It is recommended that the director, classroom teacher(s), and all adults with decision-making powers for the child meet together. Include divorced spouses. It is important that everyone has input, everyone hears the same information, and that a plan of action is agreed upon. It is imperative that discussions with parents be balanced by noting the child's strengths as well as the area of concern. Never use language that indicates something is "wrong" with a child.

Be prepared at the referral conference to give specific information to parents about agencies that provide needed services. The names, services, and contact information of all agencies within the community that provide services to children should be maintained as a part of your program referral plan. *(This information may be compiled as a group activity listed under "Prompt Treatment" under the section "Health Care Providers" in Chapter 22.)*

It may well be that the parent's insurance will determine whom the child will see. Your guidance will still be needed to see that the appropriate type of services is received.

Few parents become really concerned that their child is affecting staff or other children. They may be more inclined to respond to conversation about their child's "happiness" and the child's "future success." Parents want their child to be happy and successful.

You may admit that you are not expert enough to know how to work with their child and state that you need professional support.

At the conference, obtain written permission to contact the professional that will be seeing the child. Write a letter and mail it directly to this person, with a copy to the parents. The letter should describe the child's developmental accomplishments (what he/she can do), personality traits, and social skills. The area of concern can be supported with examples from observations and examples of the child's work, if relevant. It is important that this letter be professional, unbiased, and make no diagnosis. You may already have a consent form on file allowing you to contact healthcare professionals. But, a release form, such as the one at the end of this chapter, giving permission to transfer information to a specific physician or agency, will provide additional legal protection.

Follow up after making a referral. Have parents been successful in securing an appointment? If parents have failed to follow through, try to determine the reason. They may need more encouragement from you. If contact with the professional was made, what was the outcome of the visit? What can staff do to implement recommendations? Provide support as needed and continue feedback on the child's progress in the classroom.

Because the needs of all enrolled children must be considered, the director may have to make a decision about continuing enrollment of a child who poses danger to others, creates continuous disruption, or needs services that the program cannot provide. The director would be wise to inform and seek support from appropriate church staff members and weekday committee members before telling parents of such a decision. This may prevent parents from attempting to circumvent the director's decision in the matter.

PROFESSIONAL ETHICS

Adults who work with children should always behave in a professional manner. This is ever so important in matters of assessment. Parent-teacher discussions about a child should be held at a time that neither the child nor other children or parents can hear. Teachers must respect the privacy rights of each family, sharing information about a child with only those adults who have a right to know.

Observational information must be kept confidential. Materials must never be left lying around where others can read them.

Parental written permission must be obtained before transmitting any information in a child's records to an individual other than the child's teachers and appropriate supervisory personnel of the program.

SAMPLES

The following samples are provided to increase your understanding of what you have read. The formats are by no means the only correct ones, but they do adhere to the guidelines established by researchers. As you practice and become comfortable with using the various observation methods, you will be able to design your own formats.

Included also are sample forms for recording children's mastery of developmental milestones.

Read *7 Kinds of Smart*[9] by Thomas Armstrong and discuss with your colleagues the multiple intelligence theory. This will strengthen your appreciation of each boy and girl in the program.

Answers to observation (O) and interpretation (I) statements posed earlier in this chapter:

O   George is talking loudly.

I   Mary is an affectionate child.

O   Alice squints her eyes and shouts to Betty, "Don't touch me!"

I   Allen was angry at Edward and hit him.

I   Henry is a mean boy.

O   Hayden marked on Claire's picture.

I   Bill has a learning problem.

ANECDOTAL RECORD

Child _____ Date of Birth _____ Age _____

Observer _____ Time _____ - _____ Date _____

Area _____

CHECKLIST

Purpose: TO ASSESS CERTAIN PRE-WRITING SKILLS   **Observer:** _____ **Date:** _____

Behaviors Being Observed	Names	Children Being Observed											
Uses art materials with hand in writing position													
Identifies first name by sight													
Names letters in first name													
Prints first name using upper case letters													
Prints first name using upper and lower case letters													
Draws a person with six details													

Event Sampling

Child _____   Date of Birth_____   Age (yr./mo.) _____

Observer _____   Date of Observation _____   Place _____

Recurring Event to Be Observed: *John's Aggressive Behavior*

Aggressive Behaviors Are: *Actions that Injure Others or Make Them Feel Bad*

Event	Clock Time of Occurrence			What happened before and after the event?
	1st	2nd	3rd	
HITTING				
PUSHING				
BITING				
WORDS				
OTHER				

Teaching in Christian Weekday Early Education

TIME SAMPLING

Behavior to Be Observed: Social Participation
To be observed and recorded every 15 minutes for 1 hour during Centers

Categories:

UNOCCUPIED: Child wanders and watches, follows teacher.

ONLOOKER: Child watches others play, asks questions, and makes suggestions but does not participate; sits or stands within speaking/hearing distance.

SOLITARY: Child selects toys with which to play but is not interested in other children's activities.

PARALLEL: Child plays near another child and may play with the same objects, but does not interact.

ASSOCIATIVE: Child plays with others in common activity, but there is no division of labor or organization of the activity. Each child acts as he wishes and may exclude some children.

COOPERATIVE: Child plays in a group that has a goal of organizing activity by a division of labor, taking of different roles, and negotiating turns. The efforts of one child are supplemented by those of another.

Observer _____ Date of Observation _____

CHILD	UNOCCUPIED	ONLOOKER	SOLITARY	PARALLEL	ASSOCIATIVE	COOPERATIVE

THREE-DIMENSIONAL ART

Child _____   Date of Birth _____

Instructions: Circle and date level of child's current achievement. Update as competency increases.

Stage 1.   RANDOM MANIPULATION

Play dough is squeezed through the fingers in a very uncontrolled way. Child beats and pounds for no special purpose. There is no attempt to make anything definite. Child merely enjoys the feel of the material.

Stage 2.   PATTING AND ROLLING

Play dough is patted and rolled into thin ropes or balls. Child finds that he/she can use hand movements to make play dough go in desired direction.

Stage 3.   CIRCLES AND RECTANGLES

Play dough is rolled to make balls and basic forms: circles first, then rectangles (boxes).

Stage 4.   SYNTHETIC MANIPULATION

Objects are made by putting together separate pieces of clay to make a whole.

ANALYTIC MANIPULATION
Objects are shaped from one whole piece of clay.

Stage 5.   FORMING FIGURES

Basic forms are put together to make up figures.

DRAWING

Child _____ Date of Birth _____

Drawing Stage	Date Milestone Observed
RANDOM/DISORDERED SCRIBBLING ✎ Lacks direction or purposeful marks ✎ Does not mentally connect own movement with marks on page	
CONTROLLED SCRIBBLING ✎ Explores and manipulates materials ✎ Often repeats action ✎ Makes marks with intention and not by chance	
BASIC FORMS ✎ Makes circle, oval, lines, rectangle and square ✎ Discovers connection between own movements and marks on page	
PICTORIAL ✎ Combines basic forms to create first symbols ✎ Names drawings	
Attach Child's Drawings	

TEACHER-MADE
PLAY MAP

Child _____ Time Observed _____ to _____

Observer _____ Date of Observation _____

DIRECTIONS: Identify the places the child plays during Learning Center time (45 min.) by recording the child's pathways.

ReLease FoRM

_____
(Name)

has permission to transfer records and information regarding

my child _____ to
(Child's Name)

_____
(Agency or Individual's Name)

_____   _____
(Signature of Parent or Guardian)   Date

_____   _____
(Signature of Program Director)   Date

SPIRITUAL CONCEPT ACQUISITION

The chart that follows demonstrates the progressive nature (across ages) of the acquisition of spiritual concepts. One concept is built upon the other. Also shown are approximate ages (in columns) when certain behaviors can often be observed. The actual age will vary depending upon a child's experiences and relationships associated with the concept. This chart is offered as a guide for teachers in planning for children's spiritual growth and can be used to document that growth. A suggested format for recording a child's progress in spiritual development is to list those concepts appropriate to the children being observed in one column titled "Concept." In a second column titled "Evidence" write the actual observed behavior that demonstrates the child's understanding or application of that concept.

INFANTS AND TODDLERS	2 AND 3-YEAR-OLDS	4 AND 5-YEAR-OLDS
SELF Demonstrates understanding that she is special. (Anticipates and responds positively to warm greetings and attention from caregiver.) Demonstrates trust that caregivers will meet his needs. (Can be calmed by prompt verbal response, encouraged by eye or physical contact, looks toward or goes to caregiver with concerns.) Expresses pleasure in accomplishment of many things.	SELF Demonstrates understanding that he is important to God and to others. Relates growth and increasing abilities to God's special plan for him. Is able to choose between two options, either of which is acceptable to the adult.	SELF Acknowledges that God gave her abilities to think, work, and play. Displays feelings of happiness when obeying God's teachings. Displays feelings of sadness after doing things that are wrong. Demonstrates the ability to make good choices.
FAMILY Acknowledges that God gave parents to love and care for him/her. (Responds positively to pictures of and conversation about her family.)	FAMILY Talks about his family. Demonstrates cooperation with the adults in his family.	FAMILY Accepts and obeys family rules. Assumes responsibilities by helping at home.
OTHERS Demonstrates interest in others by watching and playing alongside. Demonstrates affection toward others.	OTHERS Demonstrates helpfulness to others. Is a friend to others. Accepts contributions of others to the group.	OTHERS Is considerate of the rights and feelings of others. Demonstrates empathy to others. Willingly shares with others.

INFANTS AND TODDLERS *continued . . .*	2 AND 3-YEAR-OLDS *continued . . .*	4 AND 5-YEAR-OLDS *continued . . .*
CREATION Experiences a sense of awe as adults share in experiences with God's creation. (Child expresses surprise, wonder, contemplation, and/or excitement.)	CREATION Verbalizes that • God made him. • God made people, plants and animals. • God made the earth, sky, and the seasons. Beginning to demonstrate helpfulness in caring for the things God has made.	CREATION Verbalizes that God is the creator of people, plants, animals, and things in the natural world. Demonstrates acceptance of differences in people. Demonstrates acceptance of role in helping to take care of the things God made.
JESUS Is receptive to conversation with caregiver that "Jesus was a baby, too", "Jesus was a boy," and "Jesus grew just as you are growing!" Expresses happiness in hearing, "Jesus loves you."	JESUS Talks about things Jesus did. Acknowledges that Jesus did things that people cannot do. Handles the Bible with respect.	JESUS Asks questions or tells about Jesus dying on the cross and being buried. Demonstrates acceptance of the fact that Jesus is alive. Demonstrates understanding that the Bible contains rules that are to be applied to life.
GOD Attends to statements by adults that "God made (child's name)" and "God loves (child's name)." Demonstrates thankfulness to God by watching as adults say, "Thank You, God," vocalizes and/or assumes prayerful body posture.	GOD Listens attentively to short Bible stories. Participates in group prayer time with a quiet body, folded hands, and/or verbalization. Verbalizes Bible truths.	GOD Recalls portions of Bible stories heard in class. Independently expresses thanks to God. Verbalizes that God has a plan for his/her life. Verbalizes that God is ruler of the world. Accepts that God loves him despite the wrong things he may do.

INSIDE ACTIVITY CHECKLIST

	Children's Names																				
ART																					
BLOCKS																					
BOOKS																					
HOMELIVING																					
NATURE/SCIENCE																					
MUSIC																					
PUZZLES/MANIPULATIVES																					

LEARNING-CENTER AREAS

DATE_____ TIME_____ TEACHER_____

This type of checklist helps a teacher know the specific Learning Centers where each child works during a particular period of time. A teacher checks the block underneath the child's name that corresponds with the Learning Center where the child is working.

PROGRESS FORM FOR INFANTS AND TODDLERS

Child _____   Date of Birth _____

Date of Enrollment _____   Date of Rating _____
                                                                    (Month   Day   Year)

Observer _____   Position _____

BIRTH TO THREE MONTHS	ALWAYS	SOMETIMES	NEVER
1. Lifts head when held at shoulder.			
2. Smiles spontaneously.			
3. Responds to bell or rattle.			
4. Follows moving person with eyes.			
5. Follows object 180°			
6. Vocalizes sounds such as *ah* and *eh* or coos.			

THREE TO FIVE MONTHS	ALWAYS	SOMETIMES	NEVER
7. Returns smile.			
8. Laughs aloud.			
9. Rolls over.			
10. Holds head erect and steady in sitting position with slight support.			
11. Reacts at mirror image.			
12. Approaches offered object (ball or rattle) with both hands.			
13. Shows beginning crawling movements.			

FIVE TO NINE MONTHS	ALWAYS	SOMETIMES	NEVER
14. Transfers object, hand-to-hand.			
15. Sits without support.			
16. Squeals with joy or pleasure.			
17. Reaches and grasps toy.			
18. Holds two toys or two objects, one in each hand.			

SIX TO TWELVE MONTHS	ALWAYS	SOMETIMES	NEVER
19. Crawls or progresses on stomach or hitches in sitting position. Progresses without walking.			
20. Gets to sitting position alone.			
21. Exhibits thumb-finger grasp or feeds self cracker.			
22. Imitates speech sounds.			
23. Says *Mama* and *Dada* specifically.			
24. Vocalizes four different syllables.			
25. Stands, holding on.			

NINE TO FIFTEEN MONTHS	ALWAYS	SOMETIMES	NEVER
26. Cooperates in playing pat-a-cake.			
27. Walks, holding on to furniture.			
28. Stands alone for one minute.			
29. Looks at pictures in baby picture book.			

PROGRESS FORM FOR INFANTS AND TODDLERS *continued . . .*

ELEVEN TO FIFTEEN MONTHS	ALWAYS	SOMETIMES	NEVER
30. Walks alone, toddling.			
31. Uses pincer grasp, as picking up raisin.			
32. Indicates or gestures wants without crying.			
33. Initiates words. (Record which words are used.)			
34. Drinks from cup.			

TWELVE TO EIGHTEEN MONTHS	ALWAYS	SOMETIMES	NEVER
30. Turns pages of a book.			
30. Has three words other than *Mama* and *Dada*.			
30. Stacks blocks, two high.			
30. Scribbles spontaneously with pencil or crayon.			

FIFTEEN TO TWENTY-TWO MONTHS	ALWAYS	SOMETIMES	NEVER
30. Removes simple garment (shoes, socks, pants, etc.).			
30. Walks backward.			
30. Stacks blocks, three high.			
30. Walks up steps with help.			
30. Carries, hugs doll or stuffed animals.			

PROGRESS FORM FOR TWO-YEAR-OLDS

Child _____ Date of Birth _____

Date of Enrollment _____ Date of Rating _____

(Month   Day   Year)

Observer _____ Position _____

COGNITIVE	ALWAYS	SOMETIMES	NEVER
1. Uses words to express wants.			
2. Talks — Names 10-15 objects and a few familiar people or pets. Has a small non-verb vocabulary.			
3. Uses pronouns *me* and *my*. Shows possessive spirit.			
4. Names three familiar pictures in picture book.			
5. Points to parts of a doll or body (hair, mouth, eyes, etc.).			
6. Makes two- or three-word sentences.			
7. Complies with simple commands such as retrieving; carries or goes.			
8. Listens with interest to short rhymes.			
9. Matches, compares familiar objects as to color, form, or size. Groups similar objects such as blocks.			
10. Counts to two. Aware of "one more," knows "how many," up to "two."			

SOCIAL AND EMOTIONAL	ALWAYS	SOMETIMES	NEVER
11. Shows affection—carries or hugs dolls, shows regard for people or possessions			
12. Occupies self, initiates own play activities or on simple suggestion initiates own play.			
13. Explores, investigates surroundings; adventures in new ways.			

MOTOR SKILLS	ALWAYS	SOMETIMES	NEVER
14. Walks backward			
15. Climbs furniture and obstacles.			
16. Walks up steps with help of banister or wall, rather than on all fours.			
17 Kicks ball forward			
18 Throws ball aimlessly overhand.			
19. Runs.			
20. Stacks blocks, three high.			
21. Unwraps, removes covers from objects or peels bananas.			
22 Disassembles — takes simple objects apart with minimal difficulty; unfastens clothing.			

HYGIENE AND SELF-HELP	ALWAYS	SOMETIMES	NEVER
23. Drinks from cup or glass unassisted, but spills occasionally.			
24. Removes simple garment.			
25. Uses spoon, spills a lot.			
26. Begins toilet training, asks for toilet.			
27. Shows pride in toilet achievement and concern about failures.			

PROGRESS FORM FOR THREE-YEAR-OLDS

Child _____ Date of Birth _____

Date of Enrollment _____ Date of Rating _____
(Month   Day   Year)

Observer _____ Position _____

COGNITIVE	ALWAYS	SOMETIMES	NEVER
1. Compares sizes. Extends matching concept to size, as big or little. "Show" me the little block, the big block.			
2. Counts to three. Extends concept or counting to three. "Hand me three beads from the bowl." May count beyond this.			
3. Dramatizes. Acts out singly or with others simple stories, rhymes, characters, and scenes.			
4. Uses plurals.			
5. Converses. In short sentences answers questions, gives information, repeats, uses language to convey simple ideas.			
6. Sings. Short snatches of songs.			
7. Knows name. Gives first and last name.			
8. Names pictures and tells actions. Names pictures, and on request tells the action ("Baby is sleeping."). Can identify the usage of objects in the pictures ("Show me the one you wear.").			

SOCIAL AND EMOTIONAL	ALWAYS	SOMETIMES	NEVER
9. Plays beside. Plays singly with sustained interest alongside or among other children, adults, pets, or belongings, with little disturbance or disturbing.			
10. Plays with. Interacts with another child or children. Interpersonal play with other children, pets, or adults.			
11. Helps. Helps with cleanup, table setting, etc.			
12. Knows and relates to own sex. Can respond correctly to "Are you a boy or girl?" Relates and acts accordingly.			

MOTOR SKILLS	ALWAYS	SOMETIMES	NEVER
13. Assembles. Puts simple parts together requiring minimal mechanical skills (puzzles, toys).			
14. Builds. Uses simple building blocks, color blocks, construction toys. Shows imagination.			
15. Copies circle. Draws a circle, usually from copy.			
16. Builds towers. Stacks blocks, eight high in imitation of one you do.			
17. Jumps in place. Does so on command or in imitation. Jumps on both feet.			
18. Walks down stairs. One step per tread.			
19. Balances. On one foot for one second.			
20. Throws ball purposely overhand. Distance, direction, and accuracy unessential but should be more than grossly random.			

HYGIENE AND SELF-HELP	ALWAYS	SOMETIMES	NEVER
21. Is toilet trained. Exercises bladder and bowel control.			
22. Uses toilet alone without help. Cares for self at toilet (Knows papering.) Pulls up and pulls down own clothes, but may require help.			
23. Dresses. Puts on coat with help on hard parts, may need help buttoning.			
24. Puts on shoes. Verbal directions permitted. Many need help tying.			
25. Feeds alone. Uses drinking utensil and spoon or fork appropriately.			
26. Washes hands. Washes and dries hands acceptably, unaided.			

PROGRESS FORM FOR FOUR- AND FIVE-YEAR-OLDS

Child _____ Date of Birth _____

Date of Enrollment _____ Date of Rating _____

(Month   Day   Year)

Observer _____ Position _____

COGNITIVE	ALWAYS	SOMETIMES	NEVER
1. Knows parts of body. Can identify by pointing to, or matching, all major, visible parts of the body.			
2. Counts to four. Counts four objects and knows what he is doing (more than rote counting). Associates one-to-one correspondence.			
3. Draws square. Can draw a square design (angle corners and about equal side) with crayon, pencil, or pen on paper or suitable surface. Design may be drawn with or without copy as part of other drawing.			
4. Uses connected sentences. Tells experiences or simple events in sequence (beginning, middle, end). Uses sentence combinations.			
5. Draws one (1). Draws human figure with head, body, arms, and legs.			
6. Names coins. Names correctly three of four: penny, nickel, dime, or quarter. Unnecessary to know their numerical value or relative worth.			
7. Recites. Reproduces short verses, rhymes, little songs from memory — or makes them up.			
8. Speaks clearly. Speaks clearly enough for a stranger to understand.			
9. Knows age. Tells age to last, or nearest, birthday in whole years. Must be more than rote memory. Ask, "How old were you last year?" "How old will you be next year?"			
10. Names colors. Tells and selects names of primary colors (red, yellow, blue) when pointing out an object.			
11. Draws triangle. Same as drawing square except for difference in design.			
12. Knows address. Can give address (street and number) correctly.			
13. Knows simple, relative concepts. Can relate concept of weight (heavy and light).			
14. Knows simple, relative concepts. Understands concept of temperature (hot and cold).			
15. Knows simple relative concepts. Understands concept of size (large and small).			
16. Knows simple relative concepts. Understands concept of distance (far and near).			
17. Uses prepositions correctly. Knows the meaning of prepositions such as up and down, in and out, over and under. (Use "Simon Says" to see if child knows these.)			
18. Prints. Prints first name when requested or for self-satisfaction.			
19. Knows seasons. Knows seasons of the year and how they relate to events (School starts in the fall; Christmas comes in the winter.).			
20. Draws two (2). Draws human figure with head, body, arms, and legs. Indications of hands and feet and symbols for eyes and mouth.			

SOCIAL AND EMOTIONAL	ALWAYS	SOMETIMES	NEVER
21. Tells name. Identifies self by first and last name. Gives both when requested.			
22. Seems secure. Able to separate from parent without crying.			
23. Relates positively to adults. Talks positively to adults. Asks for help. Asks for approval.			
24. Relates positively to children. Seeks a child to play with or responds to overture from another child.			
25. Plays cooperatively. Plays in groups (two, three, or more children).			
26. Shares. Shares toys and materials with other children, usually.			
27. Takes turns. Asks for a turn; waits turns without too much impatience.			
28. Identifies others. Knows the name of and calls by name two adults on staff, or two other children.			
29. Helps. Helps or offers to do something, such as helping to set places at lunch or helping to clean up.			
30. Sings. Joins in song or group games with others — children's songs, action songs; memorizes words and melodies; shares in events when singing is desired.			
31. Persists. Sticks with problem-solving games (such as matching games, puzzles) and/or sits at a chosen task until completed (or at least fifteen minutes).			
32. Shows pride. Shows self-respect or is proud of accomplishments (such as paint, block building, making a sand castle).			
33. Protects self. Stands up for own rights; never permits other children to take advantage.			
34. Amuses self. Makes purposeful use of equipment or activity.			
35. Pays attention. Can sit through a complete story selected for the age group. Listens to a story the teacher is reading and looks at pictures to follow story.			

MOTOR SKILLS	ALWAYS	SOMETIMES	NEVER
36. Climbs. Is able to climb equipment provided for that purpose.			
37. Catches. Catches a twelve-inch ball or beach ball when it is thrown to him/her.			
38. Hops on one foot — four steps.			
39. Skips. Hops on one foot, then the other in continuous movement from place to place.			
40. Strings or threads. Can thread beads or spool on strings.			
41. Uses scissors. Understands the use of scissors and can cut a piece of paper.			
42. Hammers. Can hammer nails into a board until they are secure.			
43. Fastens. Buckles, laces, and zips on dressing frames with only minor help.			

HYGIENE AND SELF-HELP	ALWAYS	SOMETIMES	NEVER
44. Dresses self. Unfastens and removes and/or replaces and fastens most of own clothes without help or undue delay. Unnecessary to tie.			
45. Puts on socks and shoes. Limited assistance needed. Verbal direction permitted.			
46. Uses spoon. Can use spoon effectively.			
47. Uses fork. Can use fork effectively.			
48. Toilets self. Cares for ordinary toilet needs without undue assistance. Manages clothing, cleaning (papering), and bathroom facilities acceptably according to conventional routine.			
49. Washes hands and face. Wipes water on face and uses soap on hands and rinses hands; perfection not necessary.			
50. Samples food. Will try new foods when served.			

*"Those who plan what is good
find love and faithfulness"
(Prov. 14:22, NIV).*

Chapter 19

Managing Your Classroom

"Tyler, get over there and sit down and stop being so mean. You can't ever do anything right."

"Katie, don't throw those blocks. Someone might get hurt."

"Jason, give that back to Allison. Aren't you ashamed of yourself? Allison was using that spoon and bowl."

Do you ever hear any of these statements at your weekday program? How do you think they make children feel? How did they make you feel when you were a child?

Statements such as these help shape a child's self-image. Impressions children receive from teachers are powerful because teachers are an integral part of a young child's life.

SELF-IMAGE

Development of Self-Image

A person's self-image is composed of two parts: self-concept and self-esteem. Self-concept refers to how an individual feels about himself; self-esteem refers to how an individual evaluates himself in light of what others say about him or how he interprets what others think of him.

Developing self-image is a gradual process that begins at birth and continues throughout life. At the moment of birth, new impressions flood an infant's life. She learns about pain, comfort, hunger, love, affection, fear, trust, and acceptance. A child learns what it takes to get her basic needs met. The manner in which these needs are met leaves a marked impression on a child's mind. When the needs are met in a positive manner, a child feels good about herself.

During the first eight years of a child's life (defined by many researchers as the most crucial time of development), feeling like an important person is valuable for a young child. Coopersmith, in *The Antecedents of Self-esteem*, said that three conditions develop or mold a positive self-image: acceptance, limits, and respect.[1]

Acceptance — A young child needs to feel totally and unconditionally accepted. He needs to feel that an adult cares at *this* moment no matter what the circumstances. Children need to feel that they are of value. Dorothy Briggs, in *Your Child's Self-Esteem*, stated that "Children value themselves to the degree that they have been valued."[2] A child's future is built on how adults respond to him.

All children need to experience warmth and love. Often, the human part of us has difficulty accepting a child who pushes, pinches, and hits other children. For example, Mrs. Mitchell lives for the days that five-year-old Susan is home sick or visiting Grandma. When Susan comes to school, she pinches, hits, and kicks the other children. Just yesterday on the playground Susan wanted to ride a tricycle that Justin was riding. Rather than saying, "Justin, I want to ride that tricycle when you're finished," Susan pushed Justin off and hit him on the arms.

Often, wishing for a child to stop coming to the program is easier than becoming involved in helping him learn prosocial behaviors. The New Testament indicates that Jesus loved each child unconditionally. He did not single out one particular child. Jesus said, "Let the little children come to me." He probably was talking about more than just physical contact. Likely His focus was on the emotional well being of the children and His desires that they feel accepted.

Adult acceptance is most often communicated to the young child through nonverbal language. A soft touch and genuine smile tell the child that you care. Children are perceptive, and they often know how we feel toward them by the way we act rather than by what we say. The tone of voice conveys a great deal of meaning to a young child. How do you sound to the Susans in your room?

Limits — Parents and teachers set limitations on the behavior of the very young child to help her learn about safety and living with others. Our world has rules, and children must learn how to live in a world with others. These limitations should fit the development level of the child.

Providing limits and guidelines helps young children develop self-control. Helping children master the skill of self-control is one of the most, if not the most, time-consuming tasks teachers have, but it may be just as important as physical growth and development.

Classrooms need limits. They should be worded positively, stated simply, and be behaviorally related. Teachers should have as few limits or rules as possible but should consistently follow through with those established.

Teachers should be one step ahead of children and have limits clearly in mind so a response can be made when the need arises. For example, when a new climbing apparatus is added to the playground, the teacher is prepared with a safety limit that says, "We climb using both hands."

Reasonable limits give children an opportunity to choose appropriate behavior. Limits also discourage inappropriate behavior, such as destroying materials and disturbing or hurting others. Without limits, children feel insecure and unsure of themselves. Limits only become meaningful to children when they affect them directly.

Respect — Each child is an independent person and must be viewed in that light. God created each child with a special uniqueness. Each child has certain rights and privileges and should be treated as a worthwhile person. First Peter 2:17 says, "Show proper respect to everyone." When adults are unkind and disrespectful to children, children, in turn, are unkind and disrespectful to adults. Adults should model the behavior they expect children to use.

Teachers demonstrate basic respect for a child when they refrain from talking about a child in the presence of the child, unless the child is directly involved in the conversation. For example:

(Inappropriate): A child is standing beside her mom and the teacher says, "Mrs. Smith, I hate to tell you, but Helen was such a bad girl today. She hit Andy and then did clown stunts on her cot all during rest time. We just really had a horrible day."

(Appropriate): A child is standing beside her mom and the teacher says, (looking directly at the child) "Helen, let's tell Mommy about some of the things that happened today." The child should then be allowed to relate the day's experiences, either positive or negative.

Another way teachers show respect to children is pausing to listen as they share ideas and experiences. For example, a child comes into your room and says, "Mrs. Johnson, we went on a picnic, and I saw a great big rock. It was *this* big. *(Child demonstrates with his hands.)* My daddy and I couldn't carry it, or we would have brought it back for our Nature Center."

During the time the child is talking, the teacher should stoop to make eye contact with the child and focus on what the child is saying. When the child finishes, an appropriate response from the teacher might be, "I am happy that you thought about our Nature Center while you were on a picnic."

We demonstrate respect for children when we give them a choice about sharing what they have brought from home with the weekday program. For example, Jason walks into the room carrying a cuddly teddy bear, and Sarah rushes over to take it from Jason. Jason is becoming upset, and Mrs. Tanner walks over and says, "Sarah, that is Jason's bear. He will tell us when he's ready for other people to take turns holding him."

We also demonstrate respect when we offer choices relating to other learning experiences. These should be phrased according to each child's developmental level, and a teacher should be prepared to accept either choice the child makes. For example, "Kim, do you want to stack the blocks on the truck to get them to the shelf, or do you want to carry them?" When children are given choices, teachers are saying, "What you desire is important, and I have confidence in you."

According to Coopersmith in *The Antecedents of Self-esteem*, a child's self-image is influenced by four factors:

• The impressions a child receives from others

• A child's own accumulated experiences

• A child's ability to live up to and internalize the goals set for the child

• The capacity to evaluate a child's performance on the basis of the child's own standards.[3]

The first of these factors, *impressions from others*, is a strong force in a child's life. Experiences with others help the child form either pleasant or unpleasant attitudes or beliefs about herself. These attitudes actually determine who a child is and what a child may become. Young children form a picture of themselves from how others respond to them. Each response contributes to a child's developing self.

A child learns that he is shy, selfish, overactive, bad, lazy, neat, or good by the way others talk to and act with him. Sometimes children are talked about as though they were not present even though they are. When a child is in the room, he usually hears what is being said, even though he may be doing another activity.

Another factor that influences a child's self-image is *accumulated experiences*. A child who uses appropriate behavior and whose face and charm bring consistent positive comments and attention from adults certainly has a different self-image than a child who constantly uses inappropriate behavior and seldom gets positive comments and attention from adults.

A child who is told repeatedly that she is dumb and stupid will begin to believe that she is dumb and stupid. A child who consistently has difficulty working puzzles will begin to tell himself that he cannot work puzzles, especially when he gets adult reinforcement that says he cannot work puzzles. Memories of success and failure and of acceptance and nonacceptance are a real source of a child's self-image.

A third factor that influences a child's self-image is her *ability to live up to goals* that she has internalized. These goals have been set primarily by significant adults. If the goals are realistic and attainable for the child, then she will feel positive about herself and her accomplishments. However, if the goals are unrealistic, the child is likely to have a low self-image. Goals that are too high and unrealistic often cause a child to give up before trying. The child's frequent comment is, "I messed up. I didn't do it good enough."

Providing activities that bring success for young children is a valuable tool for enhancing self-image. Young children need experiences that bring success daily because these everyday experiences help young children set up their own evaluation standards. A child's *capacity to evaluate himself according to these standards* is the fourth factor that influences self-image. These standards will be based primarily on how significant others have responded to the child.

A child's belief about himself is a key to every part of his life. This belief affects his attitude about life as well as his behavior. The child who feels good about himself behaves more positively than the child who feels bad about himself. Children form ideas about themselves through direct experiences and observations. However, adults confuse and deceive children by telling them they are doing a good job when they actually are not.

One of the most important elements in developing a child's self-image is the confidence that significant others display in the child. When a teacher believes in a child, that child begins to believe in herself. The child who feels positive about herself is more receptive to guidance and to new ideas and growth experiences than the child who has been made to feel unworthy.

Your response to children influences their self-concept and self-esteem. You are a significant person in a child's life. Young children want to feel proud, big, and important; they are egocentric and tender, and they are beginners.

The following guide might help you recognize children in your classroom who have a low self-image and need extra attention. The child who consistently exhibits many of these signs may need professional help. All children will exhibit some of them at various times, depending on the circumstances surrounding the experience. All children need the secure feeling that their teacher loves and cares for them.

Possible signs of lack of a positive self-image:

- Is afraid to play games or try new activities because of fear of failure

- Exhibits negative behavior when he does not get his own way

- Complains, "They don't like me," or "They won't play with me."

- Seldom asks questions or is afraid to answer questions

- Brags or boasts by saying such things as, "I'm better than you are."

- Often asks, "Do you love me?"

- Is jealous when a parent or even a friend shows attention to others

- When asked to do something, immediately says, "I don't know how" or "I don't want to."

- Seeks attention by doing something prohibited or by acting silly or disturbing others

- Is critical and judgmental of others; tattles often

- Blames others for her own mistakes or finds excuses for her own behavior

- Calls others names, such as "baby" or "dummy" to make himself look better

- Deliberately disobeys

- Seldom wants to participate in group activities

- Seldom asks for things she needs

The Teacher's Role in Development of Self-Image

Are you helping children in your classroom to like themselves? Use the following situations to help you decide.

Situation:

Jenny is three and has taken a nose dive off the slide. She's crying because she is scared or may be injured.

Inappropriate Response: Mrs. Jackson runs over, sees that she has a tiny scratch on her knee and says, "Don't be such a cry baby; you're all right."

Appropriate Response: "Jenny, I'm sure that was really scary. Let's check for scrapes and bruises."

Situation:

Jonathan is four and afraid of thunder. At rest time a severe thunderstorm is raging outside. Jonathan sits on his cot sobbing.

Inappropriate Response: Mr. Davis says, "Jonathan, there's nothing to be afraid of. When it thunders like that, God is just moving His furniture around."

Appropriate Response: "Jonathan, are you afraid of the thunder? It's really loud today. I'll be in the room all during the thunder. I'll come by your cot every few minutes to check on you."

Situation:

Stacey is five. She urinates on herself during rest time.

Inappropriate Response: Mrs. Pearson is assisting the children as they get up and she says. "Oh, Stacey, I hope this isn't going to start again! See, I told you not to drink so much water before rest time."

Appropriate Response: "Oops, Stacey, I see signs of an accident. Let's go find you some dry clothes."

Discipline

When teachers of young children are asked to identify their most crucial needs, a frequent response is, "more positive discipline techniques." People have been trying to answer questions about guidance and discipline for centuries.

What do you visualize when you think of the word *discipline*? Do you see a child running in the classroom and a teacher yelling, "Tommy, don't run inside. I just told you that. Can't you ever remember what I say?" Or, do you see a child running in the classroom and a teacher saying, "Tommy, we run outside. When you run inside, I'm afraid you might get hurt."

What is discipline? For some teachers discipline means punishment. For others discipline means guidance in the form of helping children change undesirable behavior into more acceptable, satisfying behavior. Guidance is a process. Discipline is the slow, bit by bit, time-consuming task of helping children to see the sense in acting a certain way.[4] Stated another way, discipline is helping a child learn self-control and self-direction. Discipline is any attempt by an adult to influence, control, or change a child's behavior, either directly or indirectly. We should think of discipline as guidance that improves, strengthens, molds, and helps a young child control his own actions.

No magic formulas or easy solutions exist because each child is different and has a unique set of characteristics and traits.

Teachers and parents have to find a special guidance approach that works for each individual child. What works for one child may fail miserably with another child. Discipline is a never-ending process of teaching.

- *Discipline accentuates the positive.* — "Christine, the blocks are for building." "James, I like the way you are bathing the baby doll so gently."

- *Discipline provides choices.* — "Anthony, would you like to use the chalk, the crayons, or the felt-tip markers?" Alicia said, "Mrs. Moore, what should I do with these tiny pieces of paper?" Mrs. Moore said, "Alicia, you can leave them on the table with the collage materials, put them on the art shelf in the collage basket, or put them on your own collage."

- *Discipline sets realistic limits*. — "Kim, we use both hands to climb up the tree. I'll hold the baby doll for you." "Shane, we ride tricycles on the sidewalk."

- *Discipline encourages a child to express feelings.* — "Pat, you really seem upset about something. Tell Mrs. Gonzales what happened." "Jackson, you're really angry because you're having to wait a turn to build with the blocks."

- *Discipline uses consequences that are related to the behavior.* — "Jason, you need to come down the slide on your bottom, or you will have to find another place to play."

• *Discipline listens carefully to what the child is saying.* — Mr. Anderson stoops and looks directly into Paige's eyes as she says, "I don't want to feel those snails." Mr. Anderson says, "Sounds like you're afraid they might crawl on you." Paige says, "Yes." Mr. Anderson says, "That's all right. Some people like to feel the snails, others like to just watch the snails, and other people want to stay away from them." Paige says, "I just want to watch them." "Thank you, God, for making the snails so Paige can watch them," says Mr. Anderson.

Discipline is helping children change their uncontrolled or impulsive behavior into controlled or purposeful behavior. Discipline helps a child become a self-controlled individual.

Discipline is trying to prevent problems before they happen. It is reinforcing acceptable behavior. It is also letting children know what to expect. Another important part of discipline is modeling the behavior you want children to use and providing a structure in which they can function. Proper discipline provides security and reduces anxiety for a child. The goal of all discipline and guidance should be to help young children become happy, functioning individuals who are responsible for their own behavior.

Behavior

Behavior is the way a person acts and reacts. It is anything a person does or says. Behavior is motivated by a person's thoughts and feelings. Behavior may be positive, negative, or exceptional.

Positive behavior is defined as that which is good or acceptable. Negative behavior is that which is inappropriate or unacceptable. Exceptional behavior is that which is tolerated because of the circumstances. In most instances, an individual's beliefs or values influence how behavior is categorized. The time, place, and situation also determine if behavior is positive, negative, or exceptional.

For example, Curtis may run, jump, and yell to the top of his lungs on the playground, and that would be positive behavior. However, if he starts using this behavior inside during activity time, his behavior immediately will be categorized as negative.

An example of exceptional behavior follows: Mary, age three, arrives for her first day in your program. Mom leaves, and Mary begins crying. Talking, cuddling, singing, and redirecting seem futile. Mary cries incessantly until she goes to her cubby and gets her blanket. Your classroom rule says that blankets belong in the child's cubby until rest time, but you decide to let Mary keep hers because it prevents her crying. Also, this seems to be the best way for Mary to experience a sense of security on her first day.

Definitions of Behavior

Behavior of children can be explained in several ways. Some people believe that behavior is primarily the result of heredity. Others believe that it depends mainly on environmental influences, and still others say that children just go through stages which occur at certain ages. All of these explanations have validity.

Certain traits of temperament are hereditary, but research has not proved a direct inheritance of personality traits. If behavior is primarily the result of heredity, why do children of the same family behave so differently? If behavior is caused by environment, why do individuals with the same circumstances react so differently? The environment of a young child in your care is made up primarily of her home and the weekday program.

Many factors influence behavior; determining which factor is causing the behavior is often difficult. Sometimes behavior may be caused by a combination of factors.

Human behavior is complex and difficult to understand. To meet the needs of young children, those who work with them should have a basic understanding of their behavior. Some of the external factors that influence behavior are parents, family life, teachers, peers, television, the physical arrangement of the classroom at the weekday program, the child's level of maturity, and the weather.

Internal factors such as how a child feels both emotionally and physically, a child's previous experiences, and a child's expectations of herself also influence or cause behavior. Yet, other behavior occurs because a child may have allergic complications, inner-ear problems, visual disabilities, poor sensorimotor coordination, or problems of depth perception. All of these internal and external factors contribute to a child's behavior.

To get a glimpse of what might be causing a specific behavior, those who work with young children must look at the total child. We must remember that much of a child's behavior is learned from imitating and observing others. Whatever the cause of the behavior, our responsibility is providing children with an acceptable, caring, consistent environment.

Children need to be given opportunities to make decisions that are appropriate to their developmental level. For example, you might ask four-year-old Tiffany, "Do you want to use the yellow paper, the blue paper, or the red paper?" Toddlers and twos also can be given opportunities for making decisions, "Joshua, do you want to work the puzzle or read a book?"

Each person has a basic need to belong. Each child wants to feel a part of those around him. He wants to be accepted totally by the group. A child wants to feel that others like him. Being a participant in a group is important to a child.

To feel accepted in a group, a young child usually begins by using positive behavior; but positive behavior is often ignored in our culture. Therefore, a child's basic need of belonging goes unmet. When this happens, a child decides to exhibit negative behavior to see if anyone notices her or includes her in the group. To the child's surprise, someone does notice. So the child says to herself, "I feel better now; someone likes me." Because an adult reinforced the negative behavior, the child thinks, *This is what I must do now to get my needs met*. Only reinforced behavior tends to continue. Do you want to reinforce negative behavior or positive behavior?

People are social creatures, and many individuals will go to great lengths to be part of a group. As teachers, our responsibility is to help meet the needs of young children in a positive manner. God created each of us with basic needs, and we are dependent on one another to help meet these needs.

Goals of Behavior

The goal for all behavior is to meet the basic need of belonging. This basic need causes all of us to want to feel a part of a group — either a genetic family group, a church family group, or a peer group. We want to be included.

All behavior, including negative behavior, has its roots in a child's goal and inner motivation. Children do everything within their power to make sure their basic needs are met, whether by using positive or negative behavior. When adults ignore positive behavior, negative behavior is reinforced. Therefore, children get the message that negative behavior meets their needs better than positive behavior.

"A child who sees himself as worthwhile and useful has no need to develop destructive patterns. He does not turn to drugs and rebellion. He possesses a cooperative spirit, a sense of responsibility, and positive attitudes toward his family. His relationship with adults is one of mutual trust and respect."[5]

Effect of Traumatic Experiences on Behavior

Divorce, illness, and death are significant events that occur in the lives of many children today. Teachers of young children should be supportive during these traumatic times. Such events represent a difficult transition period for the entire family, but especially for a child.

Children's behavior during traumatic periods may be characterized by sadness, dependency, aggressiveness, restlessness, guilt, shame, depression, disobedience, whining, or disaffection. E. M. Hetherington and others have noted three areas of anxiety that often occur during these traumatic times: fear of abandonment, which often leads to an inability to be alone; loss of love; and bodily harm.[6] Other research indicates that signs of regression, immature behavior, or strong attachment to one parent may occur.

Initially, during most traumatic experiences, children go through five sequential stages. Elizabeth Kubler-Ross, in *On Death and Dying*, identified these stages:

• Denial of the reality of the event

• Anger because the event occurred

- Bargaining to try to change the event

- Depression because of the realization that the event is unchangeable

- Acceptance of the situation[7]

These are general stages, and each person will react differently. Each person's personality, experiences, and available support system will determine the response that occurs.

Teachers can determine how they can be supportive of children in crises by observing the child. Be a conscientious observer by looking for clues that help understand how the child is feeling. Pay attention to both verbal and nonverbal language. Listen to conversation the child uses as he moves from one Learning Center to another. Especially significant will be conversation in such areas as Homeliving, Puppetry, and Art.

Make observations at different times on several days rather than one segregated experience or one isolated day. Varied observations will provide a more realistic picture about what is happening in the child's life. Several observations also will help you be less judgmental and more objective in your responses.

Teachers can support children in crises by providing opportunities for expression of feelings. Help children learn to recognize and to express their feelings through varied curriculum materials such as creative art, puppetry, homeliving, carpentry, role playing, books, music, and movement.

Provide children with a quiet area where they can be alone when they feel the need. The area may be a soft pillow, an open barrel lined with carpet, a large cardboard box, or a folding table draped with a blanket.

Talk daily with children in your classroom about their feelings, but place special emphasis on feelings during crisis experiences. Use reflective listening and repeat to the child what you think she is feeling.

Make a special effort to let children know that they are worthwhile and important. Take advantage of every appropriate opportunity to give smiles, hugs, encouragement, and praise.

A consistent environment maintains stability. The environment in your classroom may be the only secure environment the child experiences during a crisis. Use the same positive guidance techniques you have always used. Avoid the temptation of overprotectiveness, even if the child reverts back to immature behavior. This may be the child's way of asking for security. Children should never be permitted to run wild. Reasonable limits are important to the child in trauma as well as to others in the class.

Each child reacts differently to traumatic events, and you should never assume that a child is going to behave a certain way just because there is a crisis in his family. The crisis may or may not be causing a specific behavior. The child may be reacting to an experience that occurred sometime earlier in the life of the family. With proper support, traumatic experiences can be a time of growth.

Guidance Techniques

Positive Statements

Positive statements simply tell children what you want them to do rather than what not to do. For example, "Billy, we run on the playground."

Look at the following statements and phrase them in a way that tells the child what to do. As you work, use a piece of paper to cover the suggested positive response.

- Don't climb on the table.

  (We climb outdoors.)

- Don't leave the puzzle like this.

  (The puzzle goes in the puzzle rack.)

- Don't fight over the truck.

  (Todd, Linda is using that truck. Here is one for you.)

- Don't bump the bench with the tricycle.

  (Ride the tricycle on the trail.)

- Don't drip the paint all over the floor.

  (The paint goes on the paper.)

Teachers should take advantage of every opportunity to be positive. For example,

when a child says, "Can we go outside?" The teacher can respond with, "Yes, we'll go outside after cleanup time."

I-Messages

In *Parent Effectiveness Training*, Thomas Gordon pioneered a technique called "I-messages." I-messages permit the teacher to focus on her own feelings.[8] For example, "When the blocks are thrown, I'm afraid someone may get hurt."

When you look carefully at the above statement, you will notice there are three basic parts to I-messages: the teacher's feelings, the behavior that caused the teacher to feel a particular way, and what makes the behavior upsetting to the teacher. The last part of the statement is what the teacher believes may happen if the behavior continues.

The following formula may help you remember this technique:

"When the, or **when you** __(the child's behavior)__ , **I feel** __(adult's feeling)__ , **because** __(what makes the behavior upsetting)__ ."

"When the or when you . . ." — Begin the statement with these words *("When the blocks are thrown . . . .")*

" . . . I feel . . ." — Substitute the real feeling *(". . . I'm afraid . . .")*

"Because . . . ." — Begin the last phrase with this word. *(This actually begins the part of the statement that tells what may* *happen if the behavior continues. After you learn how to use I-messages comfortably, this word may be changed or omitted.)*

The order given for phrasing I-messages is not essential, but beginners often find this order helpful. After you have acquired the skill of phrasing I-messages, you may put the statement together any way you desire. For example, "I'm afraid someone may get hurt when the blocks are thrown."

Using a partial I-message may be appropriate: "I'm afraid you might fall," or "I'm happy you're taking turns with the ball." This method is workable with toddlers and twos.

No communication technique is going to work all the time, and this is true with I-messages. On occasions you may state an I-message to a child, and he may give a "so-what" response. This means that the child will glance up, look at you, and continue doing whatever he was doing before you stated the I-message. When this occurs, simply send a stronger I-message. "Justin, I'm really afraid someone is going to get a big cut on the forehead when the blocks are thrown." A more explicit statement usually brings results.

Sometimes a child will send an I-message to you after you have sent one to him. For example, "I'm not afraid that someone is going to get hurt." This is the child's way of expressing his feelings about the situation. When the child does make such a statement, send a second I-message. Make sure that the second I-message is stronger than the first.

For example, "Justin, I just said that I am afraid someone is going to get hurt. When the blocks are thrown, I'm afraid someone is going to get a big cut that will really hurt and require a visit to the doctor." Occasionally an I-message like this needs to be followed by a positive statement: "The blocks must stay on the floor."

On some occasions when you send an I-message, a child may simply ignore you. When this occurs, touch the child, call her by name, and state the I-message again.

Most of the time I-messages bring positive results. Usually, children are simply unaware that their behavior is affecting others. Once they are made aware, unkindness may turn into kindness.

I-messages should not be delivered in anger. I-messages delivered in anger become you-messages that focus on the child's character. For example, "When the blocks are stacked so high, you scare me because you're going to cause someone to get hurt." This is a judgmental response that is phrased similar to an I-message but places the blame on the child rather than on the child's behavior. These kinds of responses destroy, rather than build up, the child's self-image. Teachers of young children should make statements that focus on the child's behavior rather than statements that attack and pass judgment.

I-messages enhance communication between teachers and children, and we should work hard at sending I-messages that match the intensity of inner feelings. Any difficulty that occurs with an I-message is usually because the sender forgot to use an honest inner feeling. Communicating an honest expression is important.

Imagine the following situations and phrase an I-message for each. Cover the suggested response with a piece of paper.

Situation:

• Sliding down the slide head first

("When you slide down this slide on your stomach, I'm afraid because you might get hurt.")

Situation:

• Screaming inside the building

("When someone screams indoors, it really hurts my ears because the room is so small.")

Situation:

• Throwing sand on another child

("When the sand is thrown, I'm unhappy because it might get in someone's eyes.")

Teachers should avoid overuse of I-messages that contain the phrase "I like." These words convey the teacher's personal approval or disapproval, and if used excessively, may cause children to strive only for adult approval and praise.

Natural Consequences

This technique lets the child accept the results of her own decision without any adult interference. For example, a child may decide to leave her coat inside on a cold, windy day, and she gets cold.

Look carefully at this example and discover the value of this technique. As the children are getting ready to go outside, the teacher says, "It's cold outside today, and we really need to bundle up." Most children put on their coats, but one child says, "No, it's not cold outside. I don't want to wear my coat." To avoid a power struggle, the teacher makes no further comment. She and the children go outside. After a brief period of time the child says, "I'm cold." Another teacher is on the playground so the teacher and the child go back inside to get the child's coat. The next time the children go outside this child might say, "It's cold outside. We'd better wear our coats." The child learned more about appropriate behavior from this experience than she would have from a power struggle with the teacher.

Another example of a natural consequence is when a child refuses to eat her food. The teacher encourages the child to eat by making several statements such as, "This really is good," or "Carrots are good for us. They give us Vitamin A. Let me see you take a bite." Even after comments such as these, the child still looks at the food. The teacher again lets the child experience the results of her decision and before afternoon snack time, the child is saying, "I'm hungry."

Logical Consequences

Logical consequences are prepared by the teacher but experienced by the child. This technique requires the teacher to provide two choices. For example, "Shane must ride the tricycle with this much space (demonstrate about fifteen to twenty inches with your hands) between his tricycle and Amye's, or Shane is going to have to get off the tricycle and find another place to play." After the choices are presented, the child then decides which choice he will accept. When the choices are stated, either decision the child makes should meet with the teacher's approval. Logical consequences help children develop self-control and responsibility.

Dinkmeyer and McKay have suggested the following guidelines for using logical consequences:

- *Try to understand the child's goal for the behavior.* — Keep in mind that all behavior is goal-directed.

- *Be both firm and kind.* — Kind refers to the tone of voice that the teacher uses, and firm refers to the follow-through approach. Learning to be both firm and kind is a difficult technique to master. Most individuals are usually kind but not firm or firm but not kind. For consequences to work effectively, both firmness and kindness should be used. Firmness relates to the teacher's ability to control her own behavior, and kindness considers both the verbal and nonverbal way the response is stated.

- *Be consistent in your actions.* — Let the children know what you expect. Mean what you say. Talk less and act more.

- *Respect the child even when the behavior is unacceptable.* — Your tone of voice and nonverbal language is the key. Failure to show respect often causes the child to see the consequence as punishment.

- *Avoid pity.* — Never do for a child what a child can do for himself. Pity is a form of over-protectiveness and can cause the child to feel incapable and unimportant. Children should be permitted to experience the consequences of their behavior.

- *Provide choices.* — Provide at least two choices from which the child can choose. Use as few words as possible to get the message across. For example: "Tammie, the block structure should be built only as high as your nose, or you will have to find another place to work." The two choices in this statement *are build the block structure as high as your nose*, or *find another place to work*. Choices help children learn to make decisions by assuming responsibility for their own behavior.

- *Provide assurance.* — As you follow through with a consequence, assure the child that she will have another opportunity to try again later. This particular step is crucial for making logical consequences work. After children are given a choice, they often decide to test the limits to see what will happen. When this occurs, let the child know that the decision still stands and that she can try again in a little while. Be realistic about how long a child has to wait before she can try again.

Consequences should relate to the behavior, be phrased positively, be realistic and reasonable, respect the child, and be specific.

Encouragement

Encouragement is the process of focusing on the strengths of children by describing to the child what he is doing that is appropriate. For example: "Johnny, you are doing a good job taking the puzzle pieces out one at a time." "I'm glad that you remembered to get the matching pictures ready for the next person to do." "Marsha, that's really a hard puzzle, and you almost have it finished." "You can do it. Let me see you try to put this piece over here" *(pointing to where the puzzle piece goes)*. "Thank you for asking Julie if you could play the step bells when she finished." "I'm happy about the way that you and Gloria are taking turns with the dress-up clothes."

Encouragement should be used frequently as individual children are working on specific tasks or as an entire group of children is doing an activity.

Teachers who want to provide an encouraging classroom environment should keep in mind that each child is different and should be accepted as such. They should separate the child's actions from the child's character. Children will not always perform as we would like, but we must let them know they are valued as persons no matter what they do. We should have a positive attitude and tell both adults and children what we like about them.

Praise

Praise is a response made to a child once a particular task is finished but should be used with care. Some children respond well to praise; others respond poorly. According to Jane Nelsen in *Positive Discipline*, children who respond best to praise are those whose self-concept is solely dependent on the evaluation or opinion of others. Nelsen also believes that those who respond poorly do so because they are afraid to compete with those who get so much praise or because they believe that they are unable to come up to the expectations of others.[9]

Haim Ginott, in *Between Parent and Child*, said that "Praise, like penicillin, must not be administered haphazardly."[10] Praise should be specific and deal with the child's accomplishments rather than with her personality and character. Praise has two parts: what the teacher says and what the child thinks the teacher said. For example: "Thank you for washing the snack table" *(teacher's statement)*. "I am important. I did something all by myself" *(child's conclusion)*.

What we say and how we say it are critical when dealing with children. Ginott said that "Our words should be like a magic canvas upon which a child cannot help but paint a positive picture of herself."[11] When praise is given properly, it is of unlimited value in the lives of young children. Encouragement, coupled with praise, is often the cornerstone that a child uses to build a positive self-image.

The key to effective praise is using descriptive words rather than abstract or judgmental words. An example of inappropriate praise is the statement, "You're a good boy." This is an abstract, judgmental response and can have a detrimental, long-range effect on the child. A much better response would be, "Terry, you did a great job of pulling up your clothes after you used the commode."

Active Listening

Active listening is a technique used to reflect on a child's feelings. Follow the example below, observing how the teacher reflects on the child's feelings.

For example, Mrs. Green is moving from one Learning Center to another. Just as she gets to the Block Center, Pat begins to cry. She stoops, puts her arm around Pat, and says, "Pat, you really seem upset. Tell Mrs. Green what happened." Pat says, "Eric isn't my friend anymore." Mrs. Green responds, "You feel left out because Eric is going to play with someone else." Pat says, "Yes, I want to play with him." Mrs. Green says, "Pat, I know it makes you feel really sad when Eric goes to play with someone else. Let's go read a book."

This technique helps the young child learn about his emotional composition. It elicits feelings and demonstrates understanding and acceptance.

Young children need to understand and accept what they are feeling. Children who learn to express feelings during childhood seem to develop effective communication skills when they reach adulthood.

Many children are taught that expressing a feeling is wrong. What do you believe about encouraging children to express their feelings? Are we teaching children to be dishonest when we tell them there is no pain when there is pain? Are we teaching children to be dishonest when they are afraid and we tell them they have nothing to fear? What kinds of feelings do statements like these stimulate?

A caring teacher will want to help children express feelings, either positive or negative. This is done best by rephrasing to the child what you think he is feeling. Your response to the child will need to be tentative, because discerning the right feeling every time is impossible. When a child makes a response, the teacher should think to himself, *What is the child feeling?* When you do reflect an incorrect feeling, try another response.

For example, you might have said, "Charlie, you're really upset because Catherine got to the tricycle before you did." The child might respond, "No, I'm mad." At that point, pick up on the word *mad* and ask, "You're really mad because Catherine got to the tricycle before you did?"

Another example of active listening or reflective response is: A child is walking across the playground with an intense frown. A teacher responds by saying, "Bobby, it looks like you're really upset." The child says, "I hate Brandon." The teacher says, "Sounds like you're really, really mad at Brandon because of something he did." The conversation will continue with the teacher using reflection until she has helped the child talk through his anger.

The child should never be told, "Oh, you don't hate Brandon. He's your friend." At this moment the child does hate Brandon, and telling him otherwise would be teaching dishonesty. When a teacher imposes her view ("Oh, you don't hate Brandon! He's your friend.") on a child, it suggests to the child that his view of the situation is totally wrong. Knowing that misbehaving children are often those with low self-images, responses such as this may make them feel worse about themselves.

When children become angry and express feelings of hatred, it only lasts for a short time. Children know about forgiveness. They can be angry with a child one minute and accepting the next.

Using a calm, nonthreatening tone of voice is always important with young children, but it is especially crucial with this technique. Listening is also an important part of this technique. The teacher should not make a statement after every response. Let the child's verbal and nonverbal language assist you with your responses.

Redirection

Redirection, also called distraction, is helping a child move to another activity when a disagreement or problem is about to occur in the area where the child wants to work. You are helping the child find a suitable replacement for something that he was about to do. This is especially effective with toddlers and twos.

When you need to redirect or offer a child an acceptable substitute, think: *What does the child need, or why is the child getting involved?* and respond accordingly. For example, James is painting with a paintbrush and water on the playground. Travis comes over to James and is about to take the brush and water away from him as you walk up. As you take Travis by the hand, an appropriate response would be, "Travis, over here is a paintbrush and a bucket of water for you." Go with the child to get the brush and water.

Acceptable substitutes usually can be found. In many instances, you may redirect to the same material that the other child is using, but in some instances you may have to redirect to another inviting activity. Try to be prepared when such instances occur.

Guidelines for Positive Behavior

Use the following guidelines to enhance positive behavior:

- *Model appropriate behavior for children.* When the teacher screams across the room, the children will scream, too.

- *Teach children what to do rather than what not to do.* "The blocks are for building. Balls are for throwing outside."

- *Avoid the question "Why . . . ?"* "Why can't you be good for a change?" "Why do you have to fight every day?" "Why are you so slow?" "Why are you crying?" This type of question is detrimental to children's self-image because children are unable to answer and may dwell on the question excessively.

- *Be aware of the tempos of children.* Some children eat more slowly than others; some require more adult interaction than others.

- *Always get a child's attention before you start talking to her.* State the child's name or touch the child appropriately. "Heather, we take the puzzle pieces out one at a time." Always be within touching distance before you start talking with the child.

- *Create a classroom environment that encourages pro-social behavior.* Arrange furniture and equipment into learning areas where three or four children can work together. Include several of the same toys to avoid disagreements.

- *Give positive reinforcement when you see a pro-social act.* Describe what the child has done that is positive. For example, "Thomas, I like the way you took one of the blocks from the structure and gave it to Rachel."

- *Understand developmental levels.* Young children are egocentric. They do things that have the appearance of misbehaving when actually they may be perspective taking. Perspective taking is when a child actually goes over to a specific situation and tries to participate. For example, two-year-old James is riding a rocking horse that is making noise. Susan hears the noise and goes over to check it out. She wants to see if she can cause the horse to make the noise and pushes James off the horse. What seems to be misbehavior is perspective taking.

- *Give children a definite time that you want something done.* "When all the sand runs down in the sand timer (a three-minute sand timer), it will be time for Jada to play the bells." "In five minutes, it will be cleanup time."

- *Provide choices only when you are willing to accept either choice the child makes.* Avoid questions such as "Do you want to put away the blocks?" or "Can we stop for a snack now?" These are directions that sound like questions and give children choices. When teachers use questions such as these, they actually expect the child to do what has been asked. When the child does not do what has been asked, the teacher becomes upset with the child. The teacher and the child usually end up in a power struggle, and the teacher is totally unaware that she caused the behavior. Questions such as, "Would you put the doll clothes in the drawer?" or "Can you bring me the storybook?" create the same problem. They give the child an option to say either *"Yes"* or *"No."* When you want the child to do a particular task, simply state, "Nathan, I want you to put the doll clothes in the drawer." or "Jessica, it's time to start putting the blocks on the shelf."

- **Nourish the roots.** Give love with warm eyes and a kind tone of voice. Build a trusting community between parents, staff, and children. Model caring behavior.

- **Use buffers to stop aggression.** Step in before an inappropriate act begins. For example, the veterinarian has brought a pet to your center, and two children are about to become upset over petting the dog. You could say, "Look, one can rub the head, and the other can rub the tail."

- **Be flexible when evaluating aggression.** Aggression may be the first step to prosocial behavior. People who are too strict may miss many learning opportunities with children.

- **Teach communication skills.** Say to Micah who goes over to take a dress-up shirt from Carla, "Micah I want you to ask Carla to let you wear the shirt when she's

finished." Suggest actual words, and have Micah ask Carla for the garment. Then involve Micah with another garment or another activity until Carla is finished. Encourage Micah until he gets a turn to wear the shirt.

- **Use clear statements.** "I want you to stop poking Alicia." Children feel more secure when teachers set reasonable limits and make the limits clear.

- **Be firm yet kind.** Firmness refers to your follow-through, and kindness refers to your tone of voice. "Vickie has a name, and I *expect* you to call her Vickie." Use serious eyes. "Hitting other people hurts. When you feel like hitting, I *expect* you to go over and hit the big pillow or the punching bag."

- **Ignore inappropriate behavior when possible.** When a child is having a temper tantrum, ignore it even though the natural tendency is to soothe and comfort. Reinforcing tantrums causes the behavior to reoccur.

Sometimes ignoring a child who hits another child is appropriate. If the hitter is using hitting to get attention, ignoring the behavior is a must. Give the victim lots of attention, and the hitter will see that hitting still leaves her basic need unmet. The child who does excessive hitting needs much attention when she is using appropriate behavior. "Nathan, I'm really proud of the way that you and Mandy are working together." On occasion, say to the hitter, "Nathan, hitting hurts

Mandy. I expect you to be kind to the other children."

Tattling is another behavior that should be ignored. Children know the difference between tattling and informing. When ignoring seems to be ineffective, try to determine why the child feels the need to tattle.

- **Create a caring classroom climate.** All classrooms need lots of CQ (caring quality). When children say, "We could beat him up," involve them in conversation about something they could do to make the child feel better.

- **Use appropriate hugs.** Appropriate hugs often work with the hitter. "Jacob, the next time you feel like hitting someone, come over and let me give you a hug."

- **Use active listening.** Listen to what the children are really saying and repeat to them what you hear. "Nathan, it looks like you're really upset because you're having to wait a turn."

- **Use activities that encourage using pro-social skills.** Blowing bubbles, moving with scarves, and bouncing a small ball encourage pro-social skills. Also use music and movement often.

- **Use problem solving.** Take advantage of every available opportunity to teach problem-solving skills. Problem solving teaches children to be responsible for their own behavior. Also, problem solving sharpens decision-making skills for children and helps them understand the

feelings of others. The more involved a child is in helping make decisions, the more likely she is to adhere to those decisions.

When you first start encouraging children to solve problems, they will need adult stimulation. Statements such as, "What could we do to . . . ?" "What could you do when Boyce hits you?" "How can you . . . ?" "What would happen if . . . ?" "What else can you do while you . . . (wait your turn)?" "What other way can you use . . . (the clay)?" Over a period of time children will learn to formulate their own solutions.

Children can cooperate. They can be responsible, caring, and creative; but their ability to be responsible, caring, and creative depends on us.[12]

Section 5:

The Foundational Relationships

Teaching in Christian Weekday Early Education

"Let us not love with words or tongue but with actions and in truth" (1 John 3:18, NIV).

Chapter 20

The Family Relationship

Family Dynamics: Yesterday and Today

What a great idea God had when he planned for families! In creating families, God made provision for a place of understanding, love, and companionship. God gave the highest priority to the husband-wife relationship. God's original design for families has not changed, but the family of today differs dramatically from His design. Statistics show that 50 percent of all marriages will dissolve and two out of three children born today will live with only one parent. "Researchers estimate that 30 percent of all children born today will live with a step-parent before reaching adulthood."[1] In a study of one urban area, a group of social scientists discovered over 80 different family living styles.[2]

Not only has the family undergone dramatic structural changes through the years, but its function has also been affected. According to Dolores Curran, an author and family consultant, the family traditionally had five major functions.

The first function of the family was to *achieve economic survival*. The father worked to provide food and shelter for the family while his "helpmate" stayed at home, nurtured the children, and cared for the household.

Another function of the family was to *provide protection* from an antagonistic world. As families explored and settled new territories, they united for protection and safety. The family's three other functions were to *pass on religious faith* from generation to generation, to *educate the young*, and to *confer family status*.

Over the years, these family functions began to change and disappear. Financially, both men and woman began to work and to live independently. By the year 2000, some researchers predict that two of three mothers will work outside the home. Family members have also become less reliant on each other. Contrary to God's plan, the church has assumed responsibility for children's religious instruction, while schools have assumed the education function.

Consequently, the family, ever changing and evolving, created new functions. Curran concludes that the primary function of today's family is relational.[3] These relational tasks have to do with loving and being loved, sharing and being shared with, and giving and being given to.

BUiLDiNG ReLaTioNSHiPS WiTH FaMiLieS

When a child is enrolled in a church's weekday ministry, a relationship begins. The parent and the center have a common point of interest, the child. Since their on-going relationship is inevitable, building a positive relationship is important. The parents and the weekday center are interdependent. The parents rely on the center to provide quality care, love, a safe and secure environment, and age-appropriate teaching, while the center depends on the parents to be partners in their child's development and to provide financial support.

Although the church and its weekday early education ministry is not a substitute for family, it can be a stabilizing force in a child's changing world and can at least foster family-like experiences.[4] It can be a model of healthy relationships and actively demonstrate caring, concern, and good communication.

The weekday education program should be perceived as an integral part of the church's total ministry. It can be a network of support and a presence in times of crisis. The weekday program can be the pivotal connecting point between families and the church. As an extension of the church, the weekday program can attract families to the church and be a source for understanding, loving, and caring relationships.

The Teacher's Relationship to Families

One of the most important relationships a child develops outside of his family is with his teacher. In the midst of change, a child needs familiarity. Seeing the same teacher each day, playing with the same friends, and being in the same classroom give the child a sense of security. The consistency of a daily routine in the weekday schedule provides an additional sense of stability and security. Schedules and routines offer comfort and reassurance while the family may be in turmoil.

Teachers can express their care and concern for children and families by being attentive to the child's physical needs, washing hands before snacks and meals and after rest room use, providing safe environments, labeling personal belongings, sending creations home for parents to treasure and enjoy, and relating amusing incidents. When this is done, the teacher demonstrates that she recognizes each child as an individual.

Each child's family is special to him and is essential to his growth and development. It is important for the weekday teacher to be aware of the members in each child's family. Knowing with whom the child lives, e.g., a foster parent, adoptive parent, a grandparent or other relative, will help the teacher to plan, develop unit themes, and prepare communication to parents. The teacher will make her language relevant and applicable to each family situation.

For instance, a letter may need to be addressed to a grandmother or aunt rather than a mother or father. Teachers can provide activities which acknowledge the diversities in families, especially on holidays and special occasions. Books, teaching pictures, and dolls in the Homeliving area should reflect cultural differences in families. Teachers can effectively use these as tools to expand a child's understanding and acceptance of those who are different.

Sociologists contend a child lives and grows within the context of his total environment. Therefore, the unique dynamics of his family will have a tremendous influence on the child's attitudes and behaviors. What occurs within his family impacts his behavior in the classroom or his interaction with friends.

Knowing the children's family environments, the teacher can respond appropriately, allowing the children to talk freely and openly about their feelings, while accepting and listening to their thoughts without making judgments. For example, when a child says, "I hate my stepbrother," the teacher could say, "Your brother must have made you very angry."

The Teacher's Ministry to Families

The weekday teacher will also be able to support in times of crisis. Moving to a new house, the death of a grandparent or pet, the serious illness of a parent, a divorce or separation, or the birth of a baby are some forms of crises a family may face. When families are caught in the midst of an emotionally-charged crisis, the parents often do not have the physical or emotional energy to help their child effectively. The caring teacher can be there to love and comfort the child. Preschoolers have a keen sense of the family's emotional climate. They realize when something is wrong and may feel they are responsible. The teacher can help the parent understand the importance of including the preschooler during a crisis and talking with her at her level of understanding.

Naming the crisis and encouraging the child to talk about it and to express his feelings through play will help the child deal with the situation. Preschoolers may fear, "What will happen to me?" The weekday teacher who is there everyday can reassure them that they are loved and will be cared for. The calm amidst an emotionally upsetting crisis can be a model for other adults.

If there is conflict among family members, the teacher can assure and comfort the child. Disagreements about visitation rights or custody battles may necessitate extra security measures to ensure the child's safety and protection. Respect the family's privacy and refuse to gossip or discuss the situation with others.

The weekday teachers and other preschool teachers at church can work together to coordinate efforts to reach and to minister to families.

Teachers Involving Families

Through family involvement, good communication, parent enrichment, and focusing on family relationships, the weekday program can be effective in reaching and strengthening families.

As teachers come to know families, they will discover that each family has unique attributes, gifts and insights. Involving mothers, fathers, stepparents, aunts, uncles, grandparents, foster parents, and other adults as resources and partners in the child's development will enhance the child's learning experience.

Parents may be involved in a weekday program's activities in countless ways. "The more the parents are involved in a preschool program, the greater the achievement of their child."[5] Reading books, playing musical instruments, giving assistance with bilingual programs, sewing dress-up clothes, demonstrating needlework, talking about jobs in the community, giving tours of workplaces, and participating with children in cooking experiences are some of the ways parents can become involved in their child's classroom or weekday center.

Tapping into parents' specialized talents, skills and interests can bring stimulating learning experiences to preschoolers. In addi-

tion to the valuable contribution of parental involvement, children benefit and enjoy seeing parents and teachers in cooperation.[6]

Acknowledge their participation by sending a thank you note to provide important recognition to these hard-working volunteers.

SUPPORTING FAMILIES

In her book, *Precious In His Sight*, author Diana Garland states that one of the most caring and loving ways the church can respond to the needs of children is to listen and respond to the needs of their parents. She adds, "to care for the parent is to care deeply and meaningfully for the parent's children."[7]

Diana Garland, like Dolores Curran, emphasizes that drastic changes in our style of living have affected families. Parents have become isolated and alienated from extended families. They miss the encouragement and the support of their own mothers and fathers. Families do not know their neighbors and often travel across town to school and work. Parents need friendship and support once provided by church and community.[8]

Inviting parents to serve as committee or task force members, room parents, or chaperones on field trips gives them opportunities to meet and spend time with other adults who have preschoolers.

Support for families may also include sponsoring parent groups or support groups formed around common interests and concerns. The sharing of ideas and concerns can provide a network of support for adults. *ParentLife* (a monthly magazine available from LifeWay) and William Mitchell's *Building Strong Families* (Broadman & Holman, 1997) are good resources to make available to parent support groups.

The ministry of the weekday education program can be further strengthened by designing parent education programs to encourage parents in developing better parenting skills. Different families have different needs. A single father's needs and interests may be different than those of a father in a blended family. Thus, content must reflect the interests, educational levels, cultural and socioeconomic background of the parents. Such topics as nutrition, stress and time management, and how to improve parenting skills are some options.

Workshops, seminars, lectures, videotapes, discussion groups, and films are all useful and informational tools for parent enrichment. Training modules such as *Love, Laughter, and Learning* or *The Five Love Languages* (available from LifeWay Christian Resources) can provide helpful content for group study. These modules can also be studied independently to help parents better understand a preschooler's growth and development and to strengthen their parenting skills.

Periodically conduct a survey to assess the needs of families. The results of the survey can help identify areas of strength, as well as areas of weakness.

HELPING PARENTS UNDERSTAND KINGDOM EDUCATION

Contact with a child's parents gives the weekday teacher a tremendous opportunity to help parents understand important principles that apply to this foundational stage of their child's education. These contacts also allow teachers to help parents understand the importance of their future educational decisions. Children should have a Bible-based, Christ-centered education not only in the preschool years but also in the years that follow.

A resource to put in the hands of parents is *Kingdom Education: God's Plan for Educating Future Generations* (LifeWay, 1998). Kingdom Education is defined as the life-long, Bible-based, Christ-centered process of leading a child to Christ, building the child up in Christ and equipping that child to serve Christ. When a child's formal educational process is complete, the child will have developed either a man-centered or a God-centered world view. Teachers play a significant role in shaping this world view. The home, the church, and the school should be partners in providing opportunities for children to grow and develop according to God's plan.

Other resources that may be provided for parents are *The ABCs of Selecting a School for Your Child* (Convention Press, 1997) and *A Parent's Greatest Joy* (Convention Press, 1997).

WORKING WITH PARENTS

Teachers will encounter all types of parents. It is important to create an exciting learning environment, giving attention to each child to make each day special. The teacher must not allow the parent's lack of support to be detrimental to the child.

Other parents may wish to be involved and help in the classroom. The teacher can assign tasks like mixing paint, cleaning and organizing book shelves, and cutting out pictures.

Some parents may be over-committed and find it difficult to help. Accept whatever assistance they can give. Even small contributions can make a big difference. Teachers must be sensitive to the time limitations of parents. Seek opportunities to involve parents with the weekday center in ways which will not infringe on family time.[9]

Some parents are overly protective. They have concerns about their children's new experiences. Be patient. Over a period of time, they can gradually give the child freedom and encouragement to experience new things.

Teachers must learn to work with all parents. Treat parents with respect and consistently convey genuine love and concern for their children.

Teams of church members and representatives from the weekday program can cooperatively sponsor an event, such as a fall festival or spring carnival, which can build positive relationships.

REACHING FAMILIES

Include families of children enrolled in the Christian Weekday Early Education Program when planning church-wide events. Add unchurched families to the church's mailing list to receive newsletters and correspondence from the church.

The church and the weekday program play a significant role in the lives of preschoolers. Teachers must make every effort to build and strengthen relationships with preschoolers and their families.

Invite the pastor to visit the classroom to read a Bible story, play a game, or share a snack with the boys and girls. Be sensitive to his schedule when planning his visit.

His presence and involvement are meaningful in informal settings which give him an opportunity to meet parents and begin building relationships with them.

COMMUNICATING WITH FAMILIES

Communication is the key to developing, strengthening, and building relationships. Some communications specialists suggest that to effectively communicate an idea, one should give the message in at least five different ways. Teachers must use a variety of communication methods to establish, foster, and maintain relationships with parents.

The family's relationship to the weekday center and its teachers begins with their first visit. First impressions are lasting impressions. The way parents and children are greeted is of utmost importance. Positive experiences promote good public relations and are the best form of advertising. Parents tell other parents about their satisfaction with the weekday ministry.

A Family Room — A room near the entrance of the facility can supply information, articles on parenting, books, and other items which can present a feeling of warmth and hospitality as parents enter the building. Coffee and magazines plus racks of information on safety, health and nutrition, child development, and community services may be made available along with information about the church's worship services, family ministries, and programs.[10] An attractive bulletin board is another good way to communicate with parents.

Open House — An open house affords an excellent opportunity for parents to become acquainted with the center, visit classrooms, ask questions, and meet teachers and other parents. Smiling faces, warm greetings, and a well-kept, clean building send positive messages. Parents want the best weekday program and learning environment for their child.

Enrollment — Enrollment provides a time for discussing school policy, explaining the educational philosophy of the center and answering questions. Packets of material,

which will give thorough and complete information, can be furnished. These packets may include:

- Enrollment Forms
- Parent-Center Agreements
- Health Forms
- Parent-Involvement Survey Forms
- The Center's Handbook
- Policies
- Field Trip Permission Slips

Parents can also be given an overview of the upcoming year and told what to expect from the program and its staff. You may wish to give an opportunity to sign up for parent-teacher conferences, field trips, and other classroom needs.

Newsletters — A classroom or program newsletter is another effective communication tool. Volunteers may produce, edit, and duplicate each issue, monthly or quarterly to relay pertinent information. The newsletter could include:

- Special Events and Projects
- Overview of Unit Themes
- Important Dates, Parties, or Field Trips
- Favorite Class Recipe
- Artwork or Stories Written by the Children.
- Tips on Parenting
- Ideas for Reinforcing Unit Themes at Home
- Nutritious Snack Recipes
- Monthly Menus
- Recognition to Parent Helpers

Class Scrapbook and Videotape — A class or center scrapbook or videotape is another way to share information. Photographs, artwork and mementos capture memorable moments throughout the year.

Journals and Erasable Boards — Two other tools which may enhance parent-teacher communication is the use of a journal or a white dry-erase board. The journal can be a spiral bound notebook placed outside the classroom door. As parents sign the child in or out, they can "log" information about the child. Statements like: "Conner may be irritable today. He did not sleep well last night," can help a teacher better respond to a child's needs.

A small, white erasable board can be used to catch a parent's attention and remind him or her of upcoming events. "Remember: Field trip to the farm on Thursday."

OtHeR Communication Opportunities

Communication is essential and is a part of everything we do. Teachers must use a variety of ways to communicate and to communicate clearly. No matter how brief, teachers must take advantage of every opportunity to have daily contact with parents. When the child is leaving, build conversation around the child's positive experiences that day. As the teacher identifies needs of families, they should be brought to the attention of the church's ministerial staff.

"The communication between parent and teacher is easy for they have the child in common. Each has feelings for the child and these feelings serve as the foundation for solid communication."[11]

There is no better way to get to know a child and his or her family than through a home visit. An informal, scheduled visit can be enlightening. Richard Shahan, a minister to preschoolers, says, "Visiting a child's home communicates caring and concern."[12] In the book *Good News for Preschoolers & Their Families*, we find seven benefits the teacher receives from home visits:

1. Learning: The teacher learns about the child's home environment.

2. Discovering: The teacher discovers the interests of the child.

3. Increasing security and trust: The time a teacher spends with the child and his family helps the family feel more comfortable with the teacher.

4. Identifying needs: Through personal observation, the teacher may see ways in which the weekday center and the church could minister to the family.

5. Sharing a Christian witness: The teacher may have opportunity to personally share her faith. *Share Jesus Without Fear* (Fay and Hodge, LifeWay, 1997) is an excellent resource to guide non-believers to the Word of God through casual conversation.

6. Explaining information: The center's parent handbook, a classroom scrapbook, a

videotape of a school program, or a sample newsletter may be taken on the visit.

7. Extending an open invitation: Encourage parents to participate in other church-wide events, programs, and ministries.[13]

Teachers demonstrate the depth of their care and concern when they make the extra effort to meet each family in their home.

Telephone Calls — A telephone call is one of the quickest ways to reach parents. A telephone call to introduce yourself, welcome a child to your classroom, send birthday greetings or get-well messages, inform a parent of a special achievement, express concern, or report a child's progress can lead to positive relationships. Both parent and child experience affirmation and encouragement. If the family is not at home, leave a message for the child on their answering machine.

Afterward, document your call, keeping copies of all communication with parents, both written and verbal. These notations may be helpful when providing assistance to families.

Personal Notes — In addition to the telephone calls, mail a note or a "Happygram" to the parent. This one or two sentence message is designed to share something a child did that day and is a tangible way to reinforce positive attitudes and keep lines of communication open.

E-Mail — Many families own personal computers and have access to the Internet.

In these situations, the teacher and parent can exchange e-mail addresses for quick and easy correspondence. The center could also use this technology to build a Web site to advertise or to promote the weekday program. Each class could have its own page to overview a unit of study, promote an upcoming field trip, or distribute newsletter information.

Parent Conferences — Regularly-scheduled parent conferences are excellent communication tools. The purpose is to enable the parent and teacher to exchange information about the child's progress, to understand the child and family better, and to develop a partnership to enhance the child's development. Two conferences per year are helpful — one in the fall and another in the spring.

Good conferences keep lines of communication open between the weekday program and the family. They must be well-planned. Teachers should adjust the schedule to accommodate parents and offer a variety of times for parent participation. Once the conference is scheduled, a confirmation or reminder should be sent stating the time, place and date of the conference. A few days prior to the conference, a questionnaire requesting parental feedback may be sent home to help identify parental concerns.

Before the conference the teacher should outline what will be covered and plan to specifically address the issues raised by parents. Samples of creative art and anecdotal records provide important information to share with parents.

Locate an area which provides complete privacy, free of interruptions or disturbances from other adults or children. Begin the conference on time with positive statements about the child. Motivational sentences like, "Did Michael tell you about _____?" or "How did Amber like _____?" stimulate conversation. Encourage parents to make comments, ask questions, and make suggestions.

Improving Communication — Be a good listener. Effective listening is one of the most important skills a teacher can develop. It is a skill which improves with practice. Effective listening requires effort, discipline, and concentration to comprehend the message being sent. A teacher who is preoccupied with what she must do later or begins thinking of how she is going to respond, fails to communicate effectively. Full attention to what is being said shows sincere interest.

To set the stage for listening, remove any physical barriers between you and the parent. Placing a table, chair, desk or other obstacle between you and the parent sends a nonverbal message. Those barriers may convey, "I don't want to get involved. Let's keep our distance."

Proxemics, the study of how people use gestures, posture, and speaking distance, tell us that each distance communicates a message.

The illustration below shows various distances in which interaction occurs.

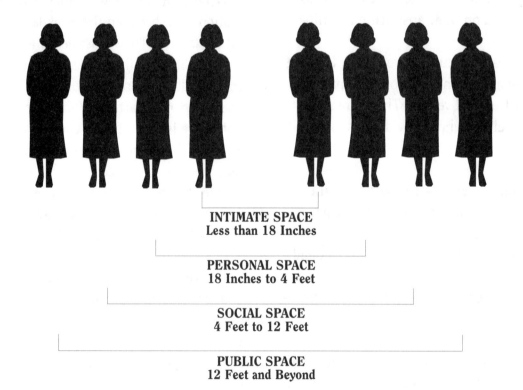

INTIMATE SPACE
Less than 18 Inches

PERSONAL SPACE
18 Inches to 4 Feet

SOCIAL SPACE
4 Feet to 12 Feet

PUBLIC SPACE
12 Feet and Beyond

When the distance between two individuals is great, verbal and nonverbal details are lost and effective communication is jeopardized. When talking with parents, the teacher will want to be close enough, approximately four feet away, to communicate without making the parent uncomfortable. Sitting side by side at a table is one of the best seating arrangements for a conference.

Smiling, nodding encouragement or approval, using words like "Uh-huh" and "I understand," leaning forward, and maintaining eye contact are techniques which enhance communication and indicate that you are listening. An open body posture (leaning forward slightly with unfolded arms) shows open-mindedness and willingness to listen. In contrast, a sagging posture, downcast eyes, or a far-away gaze may communicate disinterest and unconcern.

The teacher's tone of voice, volume and intensity also communicate. When parents are upset, the teacher should not raise her voice to match other adults but should reflect concern by saying something like "I hear how upset you are."

COMMUNICATION CHALLENGES

When a teacher must talk with parents, she should first let the parents know that she is genuinely interested in the child. She should clearly state the reason for the conference.

Remain calm even when emotional issues are discussed. Ask the parents to tell you why they are upset. Listen carefully to parents' exact words. Ask for clarification and repeat back to them exactly what you heard. Ask for suggestions for finding a solution. Make notes on the parents' ideas working cooperatively to determine a plan of action. After a few days, follow-up with the parent on what has occurred since your meeting.

SEEKING PROFESSIONAL ASSISTANCE

When additional professional help is required, refer parents to appropriate community resources. Keep a list of referral agencies from which families can choose. This might include health clinics, hospitals, local pediatricians, and public health nurses.

Help parents leave the conference with a positive feeling of partnership. They can understand areas in which the child is making progress, where the child is still developing, steps that can be taken to help the child grow, and when the next communication can be expected.

CONFIDENTIALITY

A professional weekday teacher maintains confidentiality following a conference. Parents must feel confident and secure in sharing information. The only time confidential information should be shared is when permission has been granted or the well-being or safety of the child may be in question.

Abraham Lincoln said, "The strength of the nation lies in its families. As goes the family so goes the American society." To build a better society, we must build better families. We will build better families by investing time and resources in individual lives. It all begins with the preschool years as we provide positive learning environments which help them grow and develop at their own pace. It comes through laying spiritual foundations by setting Christ-like examples in all relationships.

The weekday early education ministry can be a real opportunity to minister to young children and their families.

Personal Learning Activities

1. List five things a teacher can do to involve parents:

    (1) _____
    _____
    _____

    (2) _____
    _____
    _____

    (3) _____
    _____
    _____

    (4) _____
    _____
    _____

    (5) _____
    _____
    _____

2. Match the distances to their corresponding labels:

Intimate Space	**12 Feet and Beyond**
Social Space	**18 Inches or Less**
Public Space	**4 Feet to 12 Feet**
Personal Space	**18 Inches to 4 Feet**

3. Which space is recommended for conducting parent teacher conferences?

    _____

4. What are some ways you can improve communication with the parents of the preschoolers you teach?

    _____
    _____
    _____
    _____
    _____
    _____
    _____
    _____

"Be kind and compassionate to one another, forgiving each other, just as in Christ God forgave you" (Eph. 4:32, NIV).

Chapter 21

The Staff Relationship

What is it that is causing the greatest stress in your life right now and in the recent past? The root cause of most stress is discordant relationships. Conflicting opinions, clashing values, unfriendly responses, and overbearing personalities consume our minds and fill our bodies with tension. Focus on such matters limits our effectiveness in the many roles we attempt to fill.

People working in Christian weekday early education programs are not immune to relationship problems. To the contrary, ours is a profession where daily interactions occur with coworkers, supervisors, and parents, as well as children. Why does a coworker insist on doing it *her* way? Why does my supervisor expect me to do that? Why can't that parent see things as I do? Why is that child so headstrong?

CONFLICT

Conflict is a natural consequence of human interaction. Any two groups, two persons, or two ideas pose the potential for conflict. "Conflict is inevitable. For as long as people care about themselves and others, conflict will emerge."[1]

Most people would like to avoid dealing with conflict. However, failing to deal with conflict will only intensify feelings and "sabotage every facet of our personality and infiltrate each dimension of our being."[2]

- **Physical** — Conflict creates stress, which puts a strain on physical health.
- **Social** — Conflict causes fragmentation and social isolation.
- **Emotional** — Conflict causes feelings to run rampant, activating unacceptable behaviors.
- **Psychological** — Conflict infiltrates the thinking process and lowers one's self-worth.
- **Ethical** — Conflict usually involves attacks on character.
- **Intellectual** — Conflict causes fixation on one's own point of view and retards growth.
- **Spiritual** — Conflict feeds our carnal nature at the expense of spiritual growth.

Personal Learning Activity

Recall times when you were involved in conflict. Which areas of your life can you identify from the previous list that were affected?

_____

_____

_____

_____

_____

Resolved conflict can have positive benefits that include:

- Personal growth as our beliefs and attitudes are reexamined in light of another person's perspective

- Unity as we come to see our mutual reliance on one another to provide a quality weekday program

- Strengthened communication and relationships as we learn to listen to others and understand them

- Greater interest in work-related issues and involvement in problem solving and decision making

- Program improvement created by positive change

Because of the positive benefits of resolved conflict, we conclude that conflict in and of itself is not bad. Experts tell us that it is the *way* that conflict is dealt with that determines whether it is positive or negative.

An important step in conflict management is recognizing the cause for conflict. Norris Smith has identified six root causes for conflict.[3]

PRIMARY CAUSES for Conflict:

1. *Intrapersonal* — Conflict within a person

2. *Interpersonal* — Conflict between people

3. *Substantive* — Conflict over methods, values, ideas, goals

SECONDARY CAUSES for Conflict:

1. *Perception* — A person's perception is his/her reality

2. *Tacit* — A person discovers unwritten rules within the organization when he breaks them

3. *Authoritarian* — A person ignores the rules, defies established processes

Things to Consider in Dealing with These Conflicts:

A person with an **intrapersonal** conflict may be experiencing a self-worth issue. His behavior may be an attempt to meet a perceived need, perhaps a feeling of importance, control, and even inadequacy. This person behaves in a certain way because it has been effective for him.

Sometimes the behavior is manipulative. Manipulative behavior is selfish. It seeks rewards for oneself. Cooperation and interdependence is the most effective model for working together in a Christian weekday early education program. "There are six things the Lord hates, seven that are detestable to him: haughty eyes, a lying tongue, hands that shed innocent blood, a heart that devises wicked schemes, feet that are quick to rush into evil, a false witness who pours out lies and a man who stirs up dissension among brothers" (Proverbs 6:16-19, NIV).

You cannot change another person's behavior. You can, however, change your *response* to the person, which may result in the person changing his or her own behavior. For example, recognizing that the person may be experiencing feelings of low self-worth, you can provide genuine, appropriate feedback that will help to meet her perceived needs.

You can acknowledge positive characteristics and provide opportunities for her to use her strengths in endeavors that contribute to the overall program. You can learn more about her so that you can better understand the life experiences that may be causing certain behavior. You can accept her for who she is and for who she can become in Christ.

Interpersonal conflicts are based on feelings, personality, culture, and other differences between people. These conflicts may be the most prevalent type of conflict occurring in a weekday early education program. Committed to the children in our care, we give little time and thought to the way we communicate with other teachers during our busy day.

Some of the conflicts are simply misunderstandings that could be eliminated if we took time to clarify what we thought was said. Sometimes we offend someone with words that come out of our mouths before they are processed through our brains!

Some conflicts occur because parties disagree and fail to listen to one another's perspective in order to find common points of agreement. These conflicts can turn into resentment. Actions that result from such an attitude make life unpleasant for the parties involved and for other colleagues, as well. Sides may be taken among staff members, creating a spirit of discord. But, the one who really gets hurt in this situation is the one harboring the ill feelings. Distrust, bitterness, and negative thinking stagnates growth and affects mental health. The joy of a positive relationship is missed.

"Do not let any unwholesome talk come out of your mouths, but only what is helpful for building others up according to their needs, that it may benefit those who listen. And do not grieve the Holy Spirit of God, with whom you were sealed for the day of redemption. Get rid of all bitterness, rage and anger, brawling and slander, along with every form of malice. Be kind and compassionate to one another, forgiving each other, just as in Christ God forgave you" (Ephesians 4:29-32, NIV).

This Scripture provides us with what we need to know about interpersonal conflict. First of all, avoid acting and speaking in a manner that would offend anyone. Secondly, refuse to let hurtful emotions take hold in your mind. And finally, respond to others in the manner that Christ has modeled.

Perhaps a relationship is in disrepair because you have not followed the principles expressed in these Bible verses. Go to the person you have offended. Admit any wrong in provoking hurt. Ask for forgiveness and wait for a response. Then, interact with that person in a manner that will restore trust.

Perhaps you are the offended party. You may need to take the first step in reestablishing this relationship. Go to the one who has offended you ". . . show him his fault, just between the two of you" (Matt. 18:15, NIV). Your goal is reconciliation; therefore, avoid blaming. Use good communication skills and make it clear that you want to do what you can to restore the relationship. Be prepared to apologize for anything you have done or said that provoked the other. Be soft and tender. Practice forgiveness.

A **substantive** conflict occurs when there is disagreement over how things should be done. Everyone has an opinion. This is healthy and offers great potential for Christian weekday education program improvement. A forum for expression of all ideas, identification of common goals, evaluation of possible solutions, and collective commitment to an agreed-upon plan is important to the resolution of such conflicts.

This means that everyone involved must really *listen* to the ideas expressed by others with the attitude that there are points of agreement and the possibility that they might learn something from one another. It is possible and desirable to have a win-win situation whereby the resolution results from collective ideas of the parties involved. Such a goal would not apply, of course, if morals or professional ethics are compromised.

When a person's **perception** is the cause of conflict, you can help by providing information that will influence his or her viewpoint. No one likes to be wrong. So, be gentle. Try, "Have you considered . . . ?" or "Let me share with you an article that changed my thinking about that" or "Were you aware that . . . ?"

No doubt the one involved in a **tacit** (implied but not actually expressed) conflict is experiencing some emotions. Acknowledge those feelings and provide an explanation for the unwritten rule that is consistent with the philosophy, the organization, or other written policies. Such reasoning may enable the person to generalize the information in future situations. Or, if the person continues to feel strongly that the *rule* is inappropriate, encourage him/her to pursue appropriate administrative channels for review of the matter. Refuse to *take sides* or be drawn into *gossip*.

Someone involved in an **authoritarian** conflict can create great dissention in the Christian weekday early education program. "Everyone must submit himself to the governing authorities, for there is no authority except that which God has established . . . . Consequently, he who rebels against the authority is rebelling against what God has instituted, and those who do so will bring judgment on themselves" (Romans 13: 1-2, NIV). The person who has a *better way* of doing things should take his/her idea to the director for consideration. Good leaders will be receptive to the review of established rules and procedures and will seek feedback from the staff. You must report willful non-compliance to established leadership. Without a central authority there is chaos.

Practice the following in conflict resolution:

- Respond to conflict in a timely manner.

- Practice good communication skills.

- Focus on the issues involved at the root of the conflict.

- Accept and acknowledge the opinions and feelings expressed by each party.

- Jointly create a list of possible solutions.

- Evaluate desirability of each proposed solution.

- Agree on one solution to implement.

- Check back with each other to assess effectiveness of the chosen solution.

- Practice forgiveness.

By now you are probably thinking, "Yeah, but you just don't know the difficult person I work with." The bottom line is you choose your own responses to people. Erase the scripts played out before. Choose to be pro-active instead of reactive. Change the things you can change. Instead of blaming others, admit your mistakes, correct them, and learn from them. Instead of judging others, be compassionate. Instead of being part of the problem, be part of the solution. Even if the difficult person remains the same, see yourself responding to that person differently.

Personal Learning Activity

Name and define the six causes for conflict:

1. _____
   _____
   _____

2. _____
   _____
   _____

3. _____
   _____
   _____

4. _____
   _____
   _____

5. _____
   _____
   _____

6. _____
   _____
   _____

The Bible has much to say about relationships. It contains principles for building successful relationships with others, affirmation of personal worth, and a plan for restoring individuals to a permanent relationship with God.

Love God

Your relationship with God, in Jesus Christ, is foundational to all other relationships. You cannot love others as you should until you experience the love that God has for you personally. You cannot forgive others until you experience the forgiveness that God provides. You cannot live in peace with others until you have peace within.

"In the beginning God created . . . ." (Gen. 1:1, NIV). God genetically designed each of us to be unique. Yet, within each of us is a void that only God can fill. The emptiness exists because of man's ability to make choices.

Man made a choice when Adam sinned against God in the Garden of Eden. This bad choice resulted in separation from God. But, God yearned to reestablish a relationship with those He created. Still, the consequences of sin had to be paid. In order that man would not have to die (a spiritual death separated from God for eternity), God accepted the blood sacrifice of an animal as payment.

You and I no longer have to sacrifice animals to achieve absolution of our sins. God provided the final blood sacrifice when Jesus died on the cross (John 3:16). To fill that God-shaped void in our lives, we must only confess our sinful nature, receive Jesus Christ as our Savior, and accept God's forgiveness (Romans 10:9). This single act establishes a permanent relationship with God, which includes abundant life in the present and eternal life in the future.

Through prayer, Bible study, worship, and service, you will learn a lot about everyday life. With God's resources, you will be able to do things you cannot do by yourself. One of them is to live in peace with others. Study and practice the relationship principles found in the Bible.

Personal Learning Activities

1. **Recall the time when you accepted God's gift of salvation:**

   • Where were you? _____
   _____

   • Approximately what age were you?
   _____

   • Did your response follow a sermon, leading by an individual, or another source?
   _____
   _____
   _____

2. **If you are unsure about your salvation, stop now and pray this prayer:**

   "Dear God, I am aware of my sinful nature. I have sinned against You and my fellow man. Please forgive me. I believe it is Your plan that through the death of Jesus my sins are forgiven and I will enjoy eternal life in Your presence. Come into my life right now and guide my way. In the name of Jesus I ask these things. Amen."

Love Yourself

The Bible instructs us to "Love your neighbor as yourself" (Gal. 5:14, NIV). We cannot possibly have the appropriate concern for another's welfare until we feel that we, ourselves, are valuable and worthwhile.

This feeling of worth and value is called self-esteem, self-acceptance, or high personal regard. It is basic to our mental health and affects relationships with all others. This self-love is not self-serving or selfish. In fact, we are taught, "Do not think of yourself more highly than you ought" (Roman 12:3, NIV).

According to C. Sybil Waldrop, when you love yourself as God would have you 4

1. You know your value and worth. You know who you are and why you are here.

2. You respect yourself as one made in God's Image (likeness).

3. You are aware of your gifts and cultivate them.

4. You do not have to compete or compare yourself with anyone.

5. You discipline yourself.

6. You expect the best.

7. You are free to forget yourself so you can see and meet the needs of others.

8. You accept responsibility for your actions, accepting blame when you are at fault.

9. Your conversations are positive, uplifting, and enhancing.

10. You do not criticize. You know that all people, including you, make mistakes.

11. You know that others are valuable and worthwhile. You are not better than anyone else, but you are different from everyone else.

12. Your mission is to help others know that they are valuable and worthwhile and that they, too, are worthy of love.

13. You need praise less and less. You do not need attention for your good works. What you do for others is solely to meet a need.

14. You are humble. You do not think more highly of yourself than you ought.

15. Love wants the best for every person, and that includes you.

Sometimes, the words of parents, teachers, and siblings resonate in our minds, reminding us that we are not worthy. We must put these opinions behind us for God has found us worthy! We are created in His likeness. "So God created man in His own image, in the image of God created he him; male and female created he them" (Gen. 1:27).

He knows us, "For you created my in-most being; you knit me together in my mother's womb" (Psalm 139:13, NIV). And He can enable us to become the person He intends us to be. "I can do all things through Christ which strengtheneth me" (Phil. 4:13). God loves us so much, "He that spared not his own Son" (Romans 8:32). God knows us intimately and loves us completely. Each of us is a special creation of God. We are valuable and worthy. "I will praise thee, for I am fearfully and wonderfully made" (Psalms 139:14).

Sometimes, we devalue ourselves by our destructive self-talk. Have you told yourself something like: "Wouldn't you know I would mess that up?" "Boy, what a dumb thing to do!" or "That's just like me to blow an opportunity!" The next time you find that you are putting yourself down, deliberately switch to encouraging, affirming statements. Say aloud to yourself: "That's not like me to act that way," "I can do better than that!" and "Next time I will . . . ." Self-acceptance allows room for mistakes.

"Your self image — who you think you are — is literally a package you put together from how others have seen and treated you and from your conclusions as you compared yourself to others."[5] You can choose to change your belief system. You must free yourself of past experiences and programming in order to become who you were born to be.

The *real you* resides in inner qualities given you by God. He has made you a unique being. He has implanted a spirit of energy and power within you. This spirit is a connection to God. Tapping into this spirit awakens sleeping potential for the development of characteristics that will allow you to contribute to others. There is a need for what you have to offer.

When you reposition your belief system from that which you think others think you are to that which God plans for you to be, you will begin to experience the real you. An inner quietness and acceptance of His unconditional love will permit you to see yourself and others from a different vantage point.

Self-acceptance is essential to building enduring relationships. You can't have a sturdy house without a solid foundation. The foundation of meaningful relationships comes from what we *are* more than what we *do*.

Know yourself, control yourself, and conduct your life around established moral and ethical principles. Establish roots of honesty, kindness, consideration of others, and commitment.

Personal Learning Activities

The Self-Esteem House[6]
By C. Sybil Waldrop

WHAT ROOM DO YOU LIVE IN?

I am valuable and worthwhile.

Room 4 Low self-esteem masked by Superiority I am important. You are not important.	**Room 1** High self-esteem I am important. You are important.
Room 3 Low self-esteem You are not important. I am not important.	**Room 2** Low self-esteem You are important. I am not important.

I am not valuable and worthwhile.

1. **Assess your self-esteem.** Consider each rectangle a room in the house. Which room do you live in most of the time? Remember, each room has doors, and you may move from one to another. You can choose your favorite room.

2. **Answer the following questions.** If your answer to any question is "yes," decide which room you live in. *(Possible answers are at the end of this chapter.)*

   _____ (1) Are you overly concerned about what others think of you?

   _____ (2) Are you primarily interested in others for what they can do for you?

   _____ (3) Would you hurt someone and risk hurting yourself to get even?

   _____ (4) Are you always telling others what to do, taking charge?

   _____ (5) Do you accept another person's feelings and options?

   _____ (6) Are you willing to do unto others, as you would have others do unto you?

3. **Each column below contains the description of one of the rooms in the house. Match the identifying traits with its room.** *(Answers are at the end of this chapter.)*

COLUMN A. ROOM _____	COLUMN B. ROOM _____	COLUMN C. ROOM _____	COLUMN D. ROOM _____
• Parenting Style: Overly Permissive	• Parenting Style: Authoritarian	• Parenting Style: Authoritative Approach (Protector and Guide)	• Parenting Style: Inconsistent
• Indulgent	• Controlling (Uses Power over Others)	• Gets On with Life	• Chip on the Shoulder
• Slave	• Domineering — Do as I say	• Friendly	• Abusive
• Helpless	• Big "I," Little "You"	• Winner	• Hostile
• Indecisive	• Egotistical	• Can See from Viewpoint of Another	• Hopeless
• Does Not Value Uniqueness	• Self-Centered (Has Difficulty Seeing from Viewpoint of Another)	• Feels Safe, Secure	• Negligent
• Patterns After Others		• Lets Others Be Themselves	• Gets Nowhere
• Little or No Self-Respect		• No Need to Control	• Little Respect for Self or Others
• Afraid		• Caring	• Hurts Others
• Insecure		• A Feeling of *Us*-ness (We Are in This Together)	
• "Help me."		• Can Be a Leader or Follower As Needed	
• "Tell me what to do."		• Democratic	
• Little "I," Low Self-Esteem		• Servant Attitude	
• Little "I," Big "You"			

4. **What is it that has limited your feelings of self-worth? What actions will you take to free yourself from these limitations?** _____

_____

_____

_____

_____

Love Others

"Love must be sincere . . . . Be devoted to one another in brotherly love" (Romans 12:9-10, NIV). The love being spoken of here is active. This kind of love identifies with others in their happiness and sorrow, meets needs, and shows hospitality.

It's easy to love some people in this manner and difficult to show this kind of love to others. So, how is it possible to really love everyone you work with?

Think for a moment about a person that you find easy to love. What similarities exist between this person and you? What shared values, experiences, opinions, and interests permit clear communication? Now think of a person that you find difficult to love. You can probably list many differences between the two of you.

The fact is that people are different. And, it is the differences between people that usually cause stress in relationships. However, being different does not mean that someone is wrong. Other people are a creation of God, too; they are valuable and worthy.

Consider what the world would be if everyone were alike. What if everyone could tell really good stories but no one could sing? What if we all sang beautifully but no one could write a poem? What if we all could write inspirational poems but no one could paint a beautiful picture? Remove any of these talents and the world would be less wonderful. What if, in your Christian week-day early education program, there were no creative thinkers, problem solvers, organizers, or anyone with a sense of humor? What if everyone was a follower and there were no leaders, if all were socializers and no one task-oriented? The workplace would be incomplete and ineffective.

Despite the sharing of similar goals, teachers in a Christian weekday early education program will differ. Still, each person has a contribution to make. Each brings certain characteristics, strengths, and skills to the program. There is much that can be learned from one another.

Accepting others as they are is an important first step in being able to really love others. Learning to understand them will help you know how to best relate to them and meet their needs.

- Everyone needs to feel important!
- Everyone likes and needs affirmation!
- Everyone needs to experience forgiveness!

Personal Learning Activities

1. Identify one person with whom you wish to develop a more positive relationship. Write down positive characteristics and attributes of that person.

2. Group Activity: Distribute sheets of paper listing the names of all staff members. Ask each person present to write positive characteristics and attributes of each staff member listed. Designate a separate sheet of paper for each staff

member. On this paper, combine all the nice things everyone has written about that person. Deliver these words of affirmation to the individual staff member.

Understanding Our Differences

"Do unto others as you would have others do unto you" is a relationship rule that fails us unless we recognize that others may prefer having things done for them that differ from what we would like done for ourselves. It is important that we deeply understand people so we can know how to best meet their needs.

Differences can be attributed to genetics, environmental factors, generational characteristics, birth order, and family atmosphere. Other factors contributing to differences include personality, spiritual gifts, level of professional development, life stages, and interpersonal intelligence.

Many authorities in these fields have detailed their findings in resources that are available today. To entice your interest in understanding more about yourself and others, a discussion of some of these factors follows.

You may have heard someone refer to himself as being a "sanguine," a "feeler," an "expressive," or another descriptive type. These are but a few of the many names that are used to identify **personality types**. This concept has endured for many years.

Hippocrates (c 460 B.C.) and Carl Jung (1875-1961) are credited with early efforts to explain personality differences in people.

Florence Littauer made popular the study of sanguine, choleric, melancholy, and phlegmatic[7] personalities in the Christian community.

John Trent and Gary Smalley have used animal categories (Lion, Otter, Golden Retriever, and Beaver) to guide parents in understanding and appreciating their children's personalities.[8] This concept has been translated into an adult personality survey, as well.[9]

Paul, Peter, Thomas, and Moses are biblical examples of the Four-Temperament Model of Human Behavior,[10] a study that includes identification of spiritual gifts as well as personality.

The common thread among the various instruments used to identify personalities is the grouping into four categories and the various characteristics that go with that category. For example, Littauer's descriptions of her four categories are:

Choleric: Take Charge, Leader
Sanquine: Outgoing, Fun-Loving
Melancholy: Detail-Oriented, Pessimistic
Phlegmatic: Easy Going, Peacemaker

"So, what is the purpose for all of this?" you ask. It is an attempt to explain the differences in people.

You bring certain personality strengths to relationships with others. However, because of those strengths you have tendencies that may be irritating to others. For instance, along with many other traits, the Phlegmatic or Golden Retriever or Moses is generally peaceful, agreeable, sympathetic, kind, and a good listener. These are all very positive characteristics. However, this same person may not like change, is indecisive, and would rather watch than get involved. These traits can be a source of irritation to other members of a team who are into problem solving and goal setting.

Therefore, a study of personalities provides information that enables you to take action to adjust aspects of your personality to interact more effectively with others.

A study of personalities enables you to grow in your appreciation of the strengths and weaknesses of your coworkers, as well. You can learn what you can do for others that will meet their unique needs. When people's needs are met, self-esteem increases, and they function in a more harmonious manner.

Identifying personalities provides interesting insight and is great fun! Participate in a study of personality types. This is most effective when members of a staff attend together. Excellent courses are offered by professional career seminar services.

In addition to a unique, God-given personality, each Christian has been given different **spiritual gifts** to exercise for the good of others. "And He gave some, apostles; and some, prophets; and some, evangelists; and some, pastors and teachers; For the perfecting of the saints, for the work of the ministry, for the edifying of the body of Christ" (Ephesians 4:11-12).

The gifts (abilities) that are practical today as identified by Dr. Mels Carbonell include:[11]

- *Evangelism:* the ability to communicate the gospel effectively;
- *Prophecy:* the ability to point the way, declare specific truth, or stand up for something significant as motivated by the Holy Spirit;
- *Teaching:* the ability to search for a deeper understanding and explain why things are true;
- *Exhortation:* the ability to encourage others, to counsel, give advice, comfort;
- *Pastor/Shepherd:* the ability to encourage others to work together, emphasize harmony, serve with a motivation to unite;
- *Showing Mercy:* the ability to focus on feelings of those who hurt, to perform acts of kindness, to be there when needed;
- *Ministry/Serving:* the ability to help others, to meet needs, to be involved;
- *Giving:* the ability to provide financial insight; a genuine interest in wise stewardship;
- *Administration:* leadership, the ability to see the big picture and work to keep everyone on track.

Everyone does not receive the same gift. Each believer must identify and cultivate his own gift and help others do the same. A Christian is not to envy another's gift but to enable others to exercise their gifts. The diversity of abilities is to be used to unify. "Just as each of us has one body with many members, and these members do not all have the same function, so in Christ we who are many form one body . . . . we have different gifts, according to the grace given us" (Romans 12:4-6, NIV).

Are you having difficulty identifying your gifts? Oswald Chambers has said, "God will never reveal more truth about Himself until you have obeyed what you know already."[12] Be obedient. As you exercise the abilities you have, God will increase your effectiveness and reveal other areas of service.

People who work with young children are at various stages in their **professional development**. Each person began with some excitement about teaching. Each has varying degrees of experience with children and understanding of the application of theory. Lilian Katz has identified at least four development sequences in the professional growth of preschool teachers.[13]

STAGE 1: Survival *(May last throughout the 1st full year)* — The teacher experiences discrepancies between anticipated successes and classroom realities — needs instruction in specific skills and insight into the complex causes of behavior. He or she requires guidance, support, understanding, encouragement, and reassurance.

STAGE 2: Consolidation *(Usually by the end of the 1st year)* — Teacher adapts successes of the first stage to learn new tasks and skills — needs information about individual children who pose problems and on troublesome situations. She will need to explore a range of resources and opportunities to exchange information and ideas with more experienced colleagues and to share feelings with teachers at the same level.

STAGE 3: Renewal *(Often in 3rd or 4th year)* — Teacher tires of doing same things; seeks understanding about new developments in the field — needs experiences that stimulate interest in the field. Visiting other classrooms/programs, exchanging ideas with colleagues, participating in regional and national workshops, reading magazine and journal articles, and membership in professional associations will provide that stimulation.

STAGE 4: Maturity *(3rd - 5th years)* — Teacher deepens understanding of complex environment in which he/she is trying to be effective — needs encouragement to continue to search for insight into field. Participating in introspective and challenging seminars, taking college courses, reading professional journals, and interacting with colleagues moves the teacher to maturity.

The amount of time spent in each stage varies but is generally linked to experience gained over time. With this information, you can see that your needs and those of the teachers you work with are particular to the stage in which they are in their work. Ask, "How can I succeed, and how can I help each team member succeed?" Then, make an appropriate, helpful response.

Are your professional needs consistent with the stages described by Katz? Ask your director for information or experiences that will meet your professional needs.

Think about a teacher with whom you work closely. Are you providing feedback and help that meets his/her professional development needs?

People differ in their characteristics and priorities depending upon their **Life Stage**.

Early childhood teachers participated in a study (Williston, 1993) that resulted in the following:[14]

LiFe CHaRaCteRistics anD Key conceRns

AGE GROUP	CHARACTERISTICS	KEY CONCERNS
17-20	Idealistic and optimistic Eager to get career started Social life important Learning about self needs	Getting away from family Finding a job Financial stress/trying to support self Want more respect from elders
21-25	Feel creative, productive, and satisfied Enjoy good times but can get serious when needed More responsible (than earlier) Impatient, motivated, busy, hurried	Want to feel sense of accomplishment Becoming one's own person Fitting into adult world Graduating and finding a job
26-30	Interpersonal relationships important Social life revolves around family Is job benefiting children? Balancing school/children	Am I really the best I can be? Want to demonstrate competence Job security Marriage and parenting
31-41	Time is limited Responsible, confident Busy, hurried, motivated, but tired Health and exercise are valued	Feel creative, productive, and satisfied Family obligations create stress Want to see children through college Financial stress now and in future
42-54	Social service-oriented values Time spent with family is priority Empty-nest syndrome Motivated to work hard; glad to be busy	Want to continue to demonstrate competence Use self-knowledge to help ease stress Energy level slightly less Financial security/retirement
55+	Enjoy leisure activities Sense of satisfaction Accept ending of career Accept self as part of older generation	Physical changes/health concerns Unknown qualities about later life

The typical Christian weekday early education program will have staff members in different life stages. Being aware of the goals and needs of individuals will enable you to demonstrate support through that stage of their lives. Recognize that not everyone fits the description attributed to his or her age group.

A **life stage** theory that is not age-related but rather associated with a person's needs at a given point in time has been defined by Abraham Maslow.

Maslow determined that human needs were in a hierarchical order. A lower need must be satisfied before the person would be motivated to consider the next higher need. The lower (most basic needs) are internal and physical. The higher needs are external and psychological.

A person can move back and forth between stages depending upon changing life circumstances. For example, loss of a job, a change in marital status, or a threat to physical security may cause focus on meeting a previously-satisfied need. Multiple needs can be active at any one time, but one will dominate.

Needs of teachers in the Christian weekday early education program that may correlate with those identified by Maslow include:

• *Physiological Needs:* Obtaining a job. Concerned with food and shelter. Needs a paycheck.

• *Safety Needs:* Learning a job. Concerned with job security and freedom from emotional harm. Needs feedback on job performance and accepting, affirming environment.

• *Social Needs:* Sense of belonging. Concerned with fitting in. Needs support, collaborative projects, and recognition.

• *Esteem Needs:* Increased self-awareness and control of own affairs. Concerned with achievement. Needs challenges and recognition of contributions.

• *Self-Actualization Needs:* Pursues knowledge on one's own. Concerned with making a contribution. Needs growth opportunities and outlets for sharing knowledge.

J. C. Bradley looked at the life and teachings of Jesus from the perspective of Maslow's hierarchy of needs.[15]

• *Physiological Needs:* Jesus met the needs of the hungry when He fed the thousands with the little boy's five loaves of bread and two fish (Matthew 14:13-21).

Maslow's Hierarchy of Needs

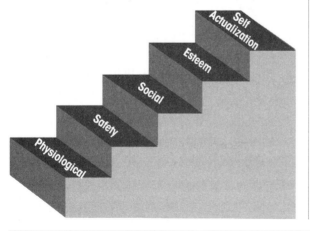

- *Safety Needs:* Jesus is the Savior and the Good Shepherd (Psalm 11:2-3, Psalm 23).

- *Social Needs:* Jesus set the example, "As I have loved you, so you must love one another" (John 13:34, NIV).

- *Esteem Needs:* Jesus taught the value of each person — the woman taken in adultery (John 8:1-11) and the reunion of the father with his prodigal son (Luke 15:11-32).

- *Self-Actualization:* Jesus came so that "they might have life, and that they might have it more abundantly" (John 10:10).

Maslow described self-actualization as man's continuous, never-ending process of becoming all that he has the potential to become. As Christians we believe that man can never become all that he has the potential of becoming except in Christ.

It is our responsibility as Christians to follow the example of Jesus: to recognize and meet the needs of those people with whom we come in contact.

People have unique capabilities. Some areas of intelligence are developed and recognizable, others are hidden due to neglect. Each area of intelligence can be developed. Thus, our capacity to perceive and be responsive to the moods, temperaments, intentions, and desires of others (interpersonal intelligence) can be improved.

Personal Learning Activity

How can understanding another person's needs and personality help you relate more effectively to him or her?

_____

_____

_____

_____

_____

_____

With the goal of achieving a better understanding of ourselves and others, we've looked at some of the ways people differ: personality types, spiritual gifts, levels of professional development, and life stages. Have you been able to identify yourself in the categories? Do you have an idea of the categories into which some of your colleagues fall?

Each individual brings to a Christian weekday early childhood program an accumulation of behaviors and experiences in her life. Collectively, the talents, dreams, knowledge, and skills of staff members can result in a quality weekday early education program and opportunities for personal growth for all.

Appreciate the fact that people are different. Use those differences to sustain and deepen personal and working relationships.

Understanding the Role of Leadership

When it is appropriate, we are to submit to the leadership of others.

Teachers in a Christian weekday early education program will assume a leadership role from time to time. Someone with organizational skills will coordinate the reorganization of the resource room. Someone at the maturity level of professional growth will lead discussion of fresh approaches to teaching preschoolers. Someone with the gift of ministry will coordinate arrangements to meet needs of a hospitalized coworker. Some sanguine personality will coordinate plans for the staff party. Support them in their tasks. Show your caring spirit. Ask, "How can I help you?" Work alongside them. Acknowledge their contribution. Be careful that rivalry and negativism do not find their way into your heart. Lead in your areas of strength and allow others to lead in theirs.

Relationships are enhanced when a spirit of teamwork exists. Such a spirit is possible only when teachers cooperate with their supervisor's efforts in leading.

"Obey your leaders and submit to their authority. They keep watch over you as men who must give an account. Obey them so that their work will be a joy, not a burden, for that would be of no advantage to you" (Hebrews 13:17, NIV).

The director of a Christian weekday early education program fills many areas of responsibility. The more you understand about the many roles he/she plays, the better you will be able to relate to this person.

As the coach of your team, the director will provide feedback on your job performance in order to motivate you. You will be encouraged by recognition of your areas of strength. You are to be receptive to suggestions for improvement. How you perceive feedback is your personal responsibility. The manner in which you receive coaching (feedback) may well set the tone for your entire relationship with your director.

- Listen objectively. What can you learn to improve your effectiveness?

- Avoid excuses. Offer explanation only if your director needs clarification about a matter.

- Keep emotions in check.

- Be sure you understand what the director is recommending. (Writing down recommendations will enable you to review and assess your own progress.)

- Express appreciation for feedback.

- Correct problems with a positive attitude and effective action.

Sometimes the director must play the role of an official. It is an official's responsibility to see that the game is played by the rules. All players (teachers) must know these basic rules. In fact, the rules should be made with input from the teachers. These rules are written in the employee handbook, job descriptions, policies, and procedures for the program's operation. When someone chooses not to play by the rules, it becomes necessary to call "time out" to focus again on these basics. When these established rules are followed, there is time to focus on acquiring skills and developing a game plan for attaining mutual goals.

The director must also be an astute business manager. This person is challenged with the task of balancing your salary, benefits, materials, and operating expenses with the income from tuition. Express your appreciation to the director for whatever benefit comes your way as a result of his/her efforts.

The director bears the final responsibility for the program's operations. Good administrators value the opinions of teachers, so you can be an advisor to your director. However, do not take offense if the director does not follow your counsel. The director must take into account perspectives that include those of other teachers, children, their parents and the church. In other words, there is a big picture that must be considered and one about which you may not have complete information.

Your director is every bit as human as you. Your relationship develops best when you mutually affirm and support one another. Demonstrate respect. Communicate directly with your concerns. Request what you need — materials, feedback, training, etc. Give suggestions for solutions to problems you see. Encourage and pray for your director.

Understanding the Role of Celebration

Time must be set aside to commemorate success. Look for opportunities to celebrate — even making it through the first week of a new school year is occasion to rejoice!

Most sports enthusiasts know how to celebrate! People of different ages, cultures, and professions come together to cheer their favorite team. Even opposing factions will cooperate by participating in "the wave" around the stadium. After the game there is yelling and horn honking between fans wearing colors of the winning team. And on the field or on the court, there is backslapping and high fives all around. It seems that in the sports arena, it is acceptable to have passion, excitement, and involvement.

How would you rate the passion, excitement and involvement in your Christian weekday early education program? Will not the work you do have longer lasting significance than the winning of a ballgame?

Staff members are to function as a team, to cheer each other on and to celebrate together. Such times of casual fellowship will give energy to staff and increase cooperation.

Communicating Our Message

Relationship implies interaction. At appropriate times, you share attitudes, ideas, and experiences. You extend yourself to others. Relating is risky for your openness may not be reciprocated. You may even be rejected. However, only by taking the risk of sharing yourself will you enjoy the understanding and trust of others.

Good communication is at the center of a good relationship. What do you think about when communication is mentioned? You probably think about talking, perhaps even writing. Yet, listening may be the most important part of communication.

Listening is time consuming and energy draining. We must put aside what we are doing to be available when someone wants to talk and to focus on what is being said, what is not being said, and what the speaker is feeling. We must clear our minds of what *we* are going to say and concentrate on what's going on inside the other person. We must see the world from his or her point of view. Henry Ford said, "If there is any one secret of success, it lies in the ability to get the other person's point of view and see things from his angle as well as your own."[16]

Effective listening involves:

- Body language that shows interest (give direct eye contact, lean body toward speaker)

- Feedback that encourages speaker to continue (nod head, smile, frown, use phrases such as "Mmm . . . I see.")

- Reflect feelings/attitudes that you sense from speaker's words and body language ("It sounds as if you're feeling . . . ." "You appear to be . . . .")

- Clarification, when needed to be sure you understand ("Did I understand you to say . . . ?")

- Paraphrase the essence of what you believe you have heard the speaker say. (You may not have read the speaker correctly. This will enable the speaker to clarify before further misunderstandings occur.)

Listening has a powerful and positive influence on a relationship. We open ourselves up to be influenced when we listen well. Through the efforts of a skilled listener, the one talking will often find solutions to his/her own problem. Good listening skills can also de-escalate conflict between people. Feelings are accepted. Facts are identified. Empathy and nonjudgmental attitudes enable parties to remain calm and to negotiate a solution to the problem. Listening is a *learned* communication technique. It requires patience and practice.

Personal Learning Activity

With a fellow teacher or in staff meeting, practice listening. Ask one person to tell something about which they feel strongly. Ask a second person to listen, using the elements previously listed.

Using "I" Messages

Effective **"I" messages** express your concern to others without placing blame. "I" messages focus on behavior, not a person. "I" messages show you accept responsibility for your feelings.

The components of "I" messages include:

- A non-blaming, non-judgmental description of **behavior** that is creating a problem

- **The effect** on the sender of the specific behavior described above

- Statement of **feelings** generated because of the effect of the identified behavior.

These components can be in any order. For instance:

1. "When I return after break and find toys broken, I feel discouraged because it is important to me that the children use toys appropriately" (behavior, feeling, effect) "Can we work together on boundaries for use of the toys?"

2. "I was embarrassed when Michael's mom asked me about his accident on the playground yesterday. I could not answer her questions because I had not been informed" (feeling, effect, behavior) "Is there a way we could communicate better about such matters?"

3. "Teaching opportunities are lost and I feel insecure when it is necessary for you to leave the room to gather supplies." (effect, feeling, behavior) "Please gather materials needed for tomorrow before you leave today."

The optimal outcome from using an "I" message is that the one receiving the message will want to alter his/her behavior in order to eliminate future problems in the relationship. However, even the best-constructed "I" message may cause the receiver to feel embarrassed, tearful, argumentative, or defensive. If so, you will want to avoid confrontation by employing your good listening skills. (Examples of using "I-Messages" with children are on page 282.)

Personal Learning Activities

Convert the following inappropriate statements with helpful, non-threatening "I" messages:

You are so irresponsible.

_____

_____

_____

_____

_____

You are always late to work.

_____

_____

_____

_____

_____

You never return my teaching materials.

_____

_____

_____

_____

_____

Nonverbal Communication

It has been said that we cannot *not* communicate. Everyday we send and receive **nonverbal messages**. Harriet Harral writes of three different ways that nonverbal communication functions.[17]

First, nonverbal communication enhances verbal communication. We use gestures and facial expressions to emphasize spoken words and direct eye contact to hold attention.

Secondly, nonverbal communication can be used instead of verbal communication. Teachers often employ this, giving a 'thumbs up' to signify a good job, winking and nodding to give approval, moving close to a group of children to prevent acceleration of behavior. Sign language, of course, is another example of communication without words.

Nonverbal communication is often unintentional. Body language — posture, speed of movement, and facial expression — give clues to inner feelings. The orderliness of the classroom, the time spent in planning, your personal hygiene and grooming, and the way you dress — all send a message about you, whether you intend it to or not. Nonverbal communication is a powerful means of communication.

What non-verbal behaviors do you have that may cause others to receive a less than positive message?

_____
_____
_____
_____
_____
_____
_____
_____
_____
_____

Dale Carnegie, author of the widely-read book, *How to Win Friends and Influence People*, offers this advice on relationships:[18]

Six Ways to Make People Like You

Rule 1: Become genuinely interested in other people.

Rule 2: Smile.

Rule 3: Remember that a man's name is to him the sweetest and most important sound in any language.

Rule 4: Be a good listener. Encourage others to talk about themselves.

Rule 5: Talk in terms of the other man's interest.

Rule 6: Make the other person feel important — and do it sincerely.

Dare to Care

"There should be no division in the body, but that its parts should have equal concern for each other. If one part suffers, every part suffers with it" (1 Cor.12:25-26, NIV).

God has given each member of the body of Christ an incredible resource. In almost unlimited capacity, you have the ability to care. In the Christian weekday early education setting it is a ministry responsibility to care for the everyday needs of the people with whom you come in contact.

Certainly you have your own needs to take care of; perhaps someone else could meet that other person's need. Excuses, reasons and logical perspectives aside, Jesus would say, "You do it!"

Study to understand people, communicate your message, practice caring and learn to really love others.

If you're going to play
together as a team,
you've got to care
for one another.
You've got to love each other.

Vince Lombardi
1913-1970

Possible Answers
to Self-Esteem Activities

Self-Esteem Activity #2, page 317:

Question 1: Room 2

Question 2: Room 4
                    Room 3
                    Room 2

Question 3: Room 3

Question 4: Room 4

Question 5: Room 1

Question 6: Room 1

Self-Esteem Activity #3, page 318:

Column A: Room 2

Column B: Room 4

Column C: Room 1

Column D: Room 3

"Love your neighbor as yourself"
(Gal. 5:14, NIV)

Chapter 22

The Neighborhood Relationship

A neighborhood extends beyond the immediate area of residence or location of a weekday early education program. Included in a "neighborhood" is a diver-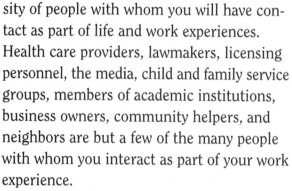sity of people with whom you will have contact as part of life and work experiences. Health care providers, lawmakers, licensing personnel, the media, child and family service groups, members of academic institutions, business owners, community helpers, and neighbors are but a few of the many people with whom you interact as part of your work experience.

In your personal life, there are grocers, cleaners, neighbors, friends, and many others with whom you interact. As you relate to these people, they will form an opinion about your Christian weekday early education program and the value you place on the work you do.

These people may not enroll children in your program but may influence those who

will. They can become an effective public relations tool for your program. Therefore, it is important that attention is given to the neighborhood relationship.

The staff of a Christian weekday early education program can positively influence the neighborhood relationship by practicing two fundamental principles:

1. Be proactive in educating the community about the services provided by the program; and

2. Be professional in interacting with all people.

Following are ideas for implementing these principles with specific groups of people in your neighborhood.

Health Care Providers

Christian weekday early education program staff members can be active partners with children's parents and health care providers in **prevention, early detection**, and **prompt treatment** of illness or developmental delays.

333

Prevention

The role of staff members in prevention of illness or disease is paramount as they practice appropriate routines of toileting, diapering, handwashing, the disinfecting of soiled surfaces and sanitary food-handling procedures. Parents must be informed as to why these procedures exist and encouraged to apply similar procedures in the home. (Obtain information on these subjects from your local health department, licensing agent, and from the book, *Caring for Our Children*.[1])

To reduce the introduction and transmission of communicable diseases, each Christian weekday early education program must develop and adhere to health policies. The policies will include a list of conditions for which exclusion and dismissal from care are required. Parents can be informed about the preventive purpose of these policies and be expected to comply.

Procedures must be in place for notifying parents about possible exposure of their children to communicable disease while in the weekday program. Likewise, parents are to be informed of their responsibility to notify the program after their child develops a suspected communicable disease. In addition, each program is responsible for reporting certain communicable diseases to public health agencies. These measures will permit better care for each child and prompt implementation of control measures.

Weekday early education staff members can encourage families to schedule routine checkups at recommended ages and can insist on up-to-date immunizations records for each child's file.

Weekday early education staff members play an influential role in the prevention of illness by helping children develop good habits of hygiene, safety, and diet. Staff members model healthy behaviors and attitudes and intentionally integrate age-appropriate health education as a daily component of curriculum.

Personal Learning Activity

List health concepts that can be understood by the children you teach and incorporated into the daily curriculum. *(Refer to Section 2 of this book to be sure that your planning is appropriate for the preschoolers you teach.)*

1. _____

_____

2. _____

_____

3. _____

_____

Early Detection

Teachers of children in weekday programs are often the first to detect developmental delays. This is due to the number of children they have opportunity to observe and through periodic evaluations against age-appropriate assessments. No evaluation is complete without a discussion with and input from the parents of the child. Parents must be included in the process of making decisions involving their child.

Likewise, teachers can often detect illness in its early stages. Symptoms of illness can be identified through daily health assessments and observed changes in a child's behavior or appearance. This information must be relayed to parents in a timely manner.

Prompt Treatment

Prompt treatment usually depends upon parents' willingness to seek health care. But, even in this matter, weekday early education staff members can encourage parents to be prompt in seeking treatment.

Most neighborhoods have resources for health services, developmental evaluations, family counseling, and child guidance. Knowing about these agencies enables staff members to refer parents to appropriate sources of assistance.

Personal Learning Activity

List the health care services available to families in your neighborhood. Check your telephone book for additional health agencies. Call or visit to inquire about the services provided. *(In a group study, individuals may select different agencies to call and report their findings back to the group.)*

_____

_____

_____

(continued in next column)

_____

_____

_____

Often a source of frustration for weekday early education staff is a parent's reluctance to seek health care services. This hesitance may be due to the fact that the parent does not have insurance coverage. If so, teachers can link families with free or subsidized sources of care.

Sometimes parents delay taking action because they hope the problem will go away or because they do not have a good understanding of the developmental expectations of children of a certain age. Sometimes when parents do seek assistance, they fail to provide the health care provider with the information necessary to determine treatment. In other words, communication that began with the teacher does not reach the pediatrician, psychologist, or counselor.

Any weekday early education teacher who has experienced such a situation will agree: "A major barrier to productive working relationships between child care and health care providers is inadequacy of communication channels."[2]

The American Public Health Association and the American Academy of Pediatrics make this statement in a joint effort to set national health and safety performance standards. In *Caring for Our Children*, they have recommended two steps to increase communication between weekday early education staff and health care providers.

1. At the time of enrollment, families identify the child's health care providers and provide written consent to enable caregivers to establish communication with those providers, and

2. Parents inform their health care provider that their child is enrolled in an early education program and request the provider's cooperation in consulting with the facility in the event of an illness that excludes the child from care.

Include consent for communication with health care providers in the enrollment form. Send a signed form showing the parent's permission for consultation between the health care provider and the child care provider with the health form that goes to the physician *(immunization and health history information). (See Chapter 16, "Guidelines for Hygiene, Safety, and Security.")*

Parents need to recognize this openness in communication as a team effort, working for their child's best interest. They need reassurance about the confidentiality of such communication.

Weekday early education staff members must be prudent in the use of such a communication channel. In most instances, it will be the program director who makes such a contact after consultation with the classroom teacher.

Ideally, any such communication comes after parents demonstrate that they are receptive to seeking additional input regarding a concern expressed by the teacher and

director. In these instances, you can explain your interest in obtaining greater understanding about an illness or in supplying the child's health care provider with the observations you have shared with the parents. With parent's verbal agreement, you can proceed to make the contact.

Telephone contact with the child's health care provider will provide a forum for two-way discussion. However, it is unlikely that your call will fit the health care provider's schedule. Be prepared to wait for a return call.

When the concern is a developmental delay or behavioral issue, a written letter may be the most effective means of contact. In a letter to the child's health care provider you can describe the difficulties a child is experiencing in the group setting and the effects on the child and/or others. Once again, in most instances it will be the director who corresponds with the health care provider after consultation with the parents and the child's classroom teachers. The letter must contain only accurate and pertinent information. Double check to be sure that you have *described* and not *diagnosed*. Mail the letter to the health care provider and give a copy to the parents. This way, everyone has the same information.

As a weekday early education staff member, you may be able to recognize development or behavior that is unusual. Be careful that you only *describe* the difficulties a child is experiencing and refer parents to appropriate sources of assistance. It is the health care specialist's role to *diagnose* and recommend treatment. Respect their expertise!

Additional ways of interacting with health care providers include:

- Review your center's policies which relate to health issues.

- Ask your director about networking with health consultants to provide hearing and vision screening in your program.

- Know the procedure for contacting emergency medical personnel in your neighborhood in case it becomes necessary for you to call them. You will need proper information for directing them to your center and to a specific entrance to the building.

- Invite health care providers and consultants to visit your classroom or speak to parents.

- Your director may arrange for qualified persons to provide staff training in CPR and First Aid.

- Find out what kinds of authorizations are required if it becomes necessary for you to take a child to a local hospital or emergency room.

Elected Officials

Be an advocate for laws and decisions that are good for children and families. Identify the elected officials in your neighborhood and communicate with them about issues affecting children — high quality child care, libraries, playgrounds, health, and education. Include these people on your mailing list for newsletters and invitations to special events. They are often interested in appearing at an event where the media will be present.

Personal Learning Activity

Who makes the laws that affect your neighborhood? Obtain contact information on your city mayor, council members, state representatives, senators, members of congress, and U. S. senator from your district.[3] Use this information to express your views on matters relating to young children and their families.

Name _____

Address _____

_____

Zip Code _____

Phone number (_____)_____

FAX number (_____)_____

CONTACTS MADE:

Date	Subject
_____	_____
_____	_____
_____	_____
_____	_____
_____	_____

LICENSING & ACCREDITATION REPRESENTATIVES

View representatives from regulatory agencies and voluntary accreditation programs as colleagues in your work. They want to help your program succeed! In addition to their regulatory role, most state and local agencies provide free training and resources. Many voluntary accreditation programs have mentors available by phone or in person to provide assistance.

Be familiar with established standards of operation and incorporate them everyday. By so doing, you will feel more confident when representatives do visit.

Go above and beyond *what is expected* to *what is best* for children and their families. Demonstrate eagerness to learn better ways of doing things. The job of assuring that standards are met is a difficult one, and experienced licensing and accreditation personnel appreciate a high-quality program.

Personal Learning Activity

Ask your director to review licensing requirements or accreditation standards for your program. Make note of issues that concern you directly as a classroom teacher. List ways you can help your center meet the highest standards.

_____
_____
_____
_____
_____
_____

BUSINESS OWNERS

Look for opportunities to involve local businesses with your Christian weekday early education program. Some businesses in your neighborhood may be appropriate sites for children to visit or to provide guest speakers for the classroom or parent meetings. Often, businesses will give away paper or other materials that can be used in the classroom and will donate items for fundraisers.

FIELD TRIP LOCATIONS

Thoughtfully-planned, neighborhood field trips can enrich curriculum for older pre-schoolers. Such activity can provide positive relationships for you, the children, and the program with the neighborhood. When you explore your neighborhood with preschoolers, consider:

- Visiting the site yourself and making plans with the person in charge. Agree on what the children will see and information they will be given, the arrival and departure times, ratio of adults to children, etc.

- Prompt arrival and departure. Call ahead if you are going to be delayed or must cancel.

- Appropriate behavior of children. Parents and teachers must work together to assure that children's behavior is safe and reflects positively on the program.

- Arrange for the children to give the host a certificate of appreciation bearing the program's name.

- Write a thank-you letter to express appreciation to the host for the learning opportunity provided for the children. Include words and drawings from the children about what they liked about the visit.

colleagues

Develop a cooperative-versus-competitive spirit among those who work in other centers. Join professional groups. Participate in salary and/or tuition surveys that will be shared with all participants. All programs benefit from knowing what is happening in programs in the neighborhood. Better budget decisions can be made when tuition and salaries are reviewed in comparison to services offered by other neighborhood programs.

Make yourself available to discuss common issues. Build a network of people you can call for information and ideas. Exchange visits among programs in the neighborhood. Plan joint training sessions.

Professional cooperation can result in a greater awareness of similarities and differences and a wider base of experience from which to make decisions. In addition, a cooperative relationship extends the ministry of a Christian weekday early education program.

Public Relations

Ongoing efforts are necessary to build and maintain a positive relationship within the neighborhood. Stay abreast of what is happening in the neighborhood. Read city newspapers and neighborhood newsletters. Walk through the neighborhood. Drive to and from work by different routes. You may discover a new construction site the children can safely view or a neighborhood activity in which you or the children can participate. Look for ways you can contribute to the neighborhood.

What other connections can you make in your neighborhood? Are there **senior citizen centers** or **retirement facilities** to team with to build friendships between generations? Is there a **hospital** that would allow your children to do something helpful, such as bringing books or painting pictures for distribution to the hospitalized children? How can you involve members of the neighborhood in your **parent education** programs and **fundraisers**? Who lives in your neighborhood — an **author**, an **artist**, a **gardener**, or a **carpenter**? People whose work is of interest to children are valuable resources.

Each neighborhood is different. Each offers a variety of sources for information, referral and education.

Linking with other groups strengthens the neighborhood and extends the effectiveness of the Christian early weekday education program and the ministry and influence of your church.

You are an integral part of the public relations team for relating your center to the neighborhood. Be proactive and plan for building a positive image of your program.

- Show a positive attitude toward your work in interactions with all people.

- Establish good relations with those in your neighborhood.

- Communicate weekday education program services with all people.

- Express appreciation of services others provide.

- Enjoy successful experiences dealing with people. Settle disagreements in a respectful manner.

- Respect the property rights of others by parking in appropriate places.

- Teach children to respect the property of others. For example, unless the owner gives permission, children are not to pick flowers growing in someone's yard or to walk on lawns.

- Keep commitments for field trips.

- Maintain positive relations within the Christian weekday education program and the church, as this also affects perception of the program.

As an employee of a Christian weekday early education program, you represent the program. Your positive attitude and conduct can foster trust and inspire confidence among those members of the neighborhood with whom you have contact. Ultimately, the reputation of the Christian weekday early education program is a reflection on the Church and its ability to love and minister. Be a part of the team that makes a positive impression on the neighborhood.

"Go . . . teaching them . . . I am with you always" (Matt. 28:19-20, NIV).

Conclusion

Dear Church Weekday Education Teacher:

Thank you for the commitment you have made to the lives of young children and their families. May you find strength to meet the challenges of teaching and joy in knowing that you are making a difference in our world.

It is our prayer that this book will provide inspiration, knowledge, and motivation to assist you in giving each child the very best learning experiences while in your classroom. Whether you are in the beginning stage of your journey as a teacher, whether you have taught several years, or whether you have given your entire life to teaching, may God bless you as you continue to grow and learn.

May this book give constant support and guidance to you as you minister to young children and families and as you become the teacher God wants you to be.

Sincerely,

Writers
Editorial Staff

Resources

Listed below are specific teaching resources suggested in this book. Additional lists of books, toys, and other resources are included in each unit of the *WEE Learn Curriculum Guides*.

BOOKS:

Book titles are listed with publisher's name. They should be available through most book stores that sell children's books:

- *Baby's First Picture Book*, George Ford (Random House)
- *Bein' with You This Way*, W. Nikola-Lisa (Lee & Low Books Inc.)
- *Big Friend, Little Friend*, Greenfield (Writers & Readers)
- *Busy Feet*, Elizabeth Elaine Watson (A Happy Day Book, Standard)
- *Carrot Seed*, Ruth Krauss (Harper and Row)
- *The Cat in the Hat*, Dr. Seuss (Random House)
- *The Good-Bye Book* Judith Viorst (Macmillan)
- *Goodnight Moon*, Margaret Wise Brown (Harper and Row)
- *I Have a Sister — My Sister is Deaf*, Jeanne Peterson (Reading Rainbow Book, Harper & Row)
- *I Touch*, Isadora (Greenwillow)
- *In a People House*, Theo LeSieg (Random House)
- *It's Fun to Be One*, Pragoff (Aladdin)
- *Let's Play*, Fujikawa (Grosset and Dunlap)
- *Look at Me*, Shott (Dutton Children's Books)
- *The Lunch Box Surprise*, Grace Maccarone (Hello Reader, Scholastic)
- *Read-to-Me Bible for Kids* (Holman Bible Publishers)
- *Shake My Sillies Out*, Raffi (Crown)
- *Shoes*, Elizabeth Winthrop (Reading Rainbow Book, Harper Collins)
- *Silly Tilly's Thanksgiving Dinner*, Hoban (Harper Collins)
- *Toilet Learning*, Alison Mack (Little, Brown and Company)
- *Trucks*, McNaught (Random House)

MUSIC:

- Instrument: Autoharp
- Cassettes: *Adventures in Sound* (Melody House)
  Quiet Time (Melody House)
- "In the Hall of the Mountain King," (recording or CD) *Peer Gynt*
- "Syncopated Clock," (recording or CD) Anderson
- "William Tell Overture," (recording or CD) Rossinni
- *'Specially Special Songs, Music for Early Childhood*, Billingsley, Purdy and McMahan-Wilson
  (Church Street Music, LifeWay Christian Resources)
  Song Book   0-7673-3488-4
  Double Cassette   0-7673-3482-5
  Double CD   0-7673-3481-7

PUZZLES

- "Easy Fruit," Judy (4 pcs.)
- "Vegetables," Judy (4pcs.)

TOYS

- Blockbusters (LifeWay Church Sales)
- Corn Popper (Fisher-Price)
- Stack 'm Up Cups (The First Years)
- Musical Mirror (Playskool)
- Rolling Bells (Battat)
- Wobbly Fun Ball (Fisher-Price)

WEE LEARN CURRICULUM GUIDES:

Each preschool curriculum guide provides a range of age-appropriate activities designed to lay a foundation for understanding God, Jesus, Bible, church, self, family, others, and the natural world. Each supports learning centers and group activities. Each guide contains 24 units, a full year's worth of material. A companion set of teaching pictures is available for guides for ages two through five.

Available from LifeWay Christian Resources, Customer Service: 1 800-458-2772:

- *WEE Learn Curriculum Guide for Five-Year-Olds*   0-7673-2069-7 $129.95
- *WEE Learn Curriculum Guide for Four-Year-Olds*   0-7673-2068-9 $129.95
- *WEE Learn Curriculum Guide for Three-Year-Olds*   0-7673-2070-0 $129.95
- *WEE Learn Curriculum Guide for Two-Year-Olds*   0-7673-3337-3 $129.95

- *WEE Learn Teaching Pictures for Five-Year-Olds*   0-7673-2060-3 $ 19.95
- *WEE Learn Teaching Pictures for Four-Year-Olds*   0-7673-2059-X $ 19.95
- *WEE Learn Teaching Pictures for Three-Year-Olds*   0-7673-2058-1 $ 19.95
- *WEE Learn Teaching Pictures for Two-Year-Olds*   0-7673-3338-1 $ 22.95

Other Equipment and Supplies:

Contact LifeWay Church Sales (1 800-622-8610; Fax, 615-251-2820) for information on these products or services:
- Changing Stations
- Cribs
- Marker/Bulletin Boards
- Paging Systems
- Partitions/Room Dividers
- Playground Equipment
- Preschool Furniture — Tables, Chairs, Storage, Kitchen/Household Play, Art, Dramatic Play, Activity/Soft play

Other Vendors or Sources of Product Information:

- Battat 1 800-247-6144
- Bemiss-Jason (Paper Supplies) 1 800-544-0093
- Childcraft 1 800-631-5652
- Connor (Puzzles and Blocks) 1 800-544-0093
- Constructive Playthings 1 800-448-4115
- Educational Activities 1 800-645-3739
- The First Years 1 800-533-6708
- Fisher-Price 1 800-432-5437
- Frank Schaffer 1 800-421-5565
   (Including Judy/Instructo and Shining Star)
- Guidecraft (Educational Toys) 1 800-544-6526
- Kaplan (Toys, Supplies Outdoor Equipment) 1 800-334-2014
- Kimbo (Educational Music and Accessories) 1 800-631-2187
- Lakeshore Learning Materials 1 800-421-5354
- Lauri (Educational Toys) 1 800-451-0520
- Melody House (Educational Music, Cassetes, CDs) 1 800-234-9228
- Playskool 1 800-752-9755

NOTE: Call to request a catalog or for information on a specific product. Inclusion in this list recommends the products listed on the resource page and not all resources available from suppliers.

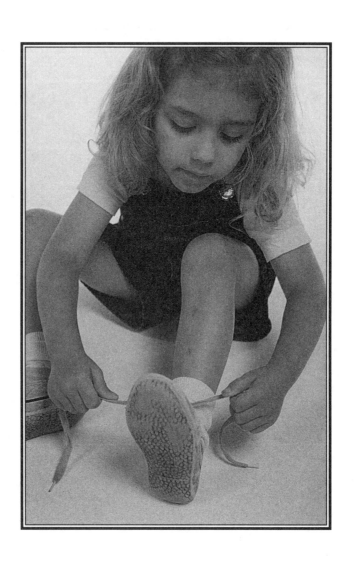

Footnotes

CHapTeR 1:

[1] © Copyright 1986 Shepherd's Fold Music (BMI)/Ariose Music (ASCAP) (both admin. by EMI Christian Music Publishing) and BMG Songs, Inc. All rights reserved. Used by permission.

CHapTeR 2:

None

CHapTeR 3:

[1] "I Am Very Special," Words and Music by Derrell Billingsley, Copyright 1977, Broadman Press, SESAC.

[2] "First Steps: Hey-Look Out, World, Here I Come," *Your Child, Newsweek Special Edition*, Spring/Summer 1997: 14.

[3] "The Senses," *U. S. News and World Report*, 3 Jan. 1997: 56.

[4] "Fertile Minds," *Time*, 3 Feb. 1997: 50.

[5] "Brain Development: The Importance of the First Three Years," *The First Years Last Forever: Leadership Forum in Early Childhood Development*, Internet Article.

[6] "The Language Explosion," *Your Child, Newsweek Special Edition*, Spring/Summer 1997: 17, 20.

[7] "The Senses, *U. S. News and World Report*, 13 Jan. 1997: 55.

[8] Healy, *Your Child's Growing Mind: A Practical Guide to Brain Development and Learning from Birth to Adolescence*, (New York: Doubleday, 1994), 39.

[9] "Your Child's Brain," *Newsweek*, 19 Feb. 1996: 55-62.

[10] "Starting Smart: How Early Experiences Affect Brain Development," *An Ounce of Prevention Fund and ZERO TO THREE* Paper, Provided through an educational grant from Johnson and Johnson Consumer Companies, Inc., 1998.

[11] "Will Piano Lessons Make My Child Smarter?" *Parade Magazine*, 14 June 1998: 13-17.

[12] "Your Child's Brain," *Newsweek*, 19 Feb. 1996: 55-61.

[13] "Teaching Strategies for Fostering Social Competence," Lilian G. Katz and Diane E. McClellan, *Fostering Children's Social Competence: The Teacher's Role*, Washington, D.C. National Association for the Education of Young Children, 1997.

[14] Greenspan and Wieder, *The Child with Special Needs: Encouraging Intellectual and Emotional Growth, Reading*, (Massachusetts: Perseus Books, 1998), 3-4.

[15] "There's No One Exactly Like Me," Words by Trilby Jordan and Music by Betty Ann Ramseth, Copyright 1975, Broadman Press (SESAC).

[16] Howard Gardner, *Multiple Intelligences* (New York: Basic Books, 1993).

CHAPTER 4:

[1] Blackaby and King, *Experiencing God* (Nashville: LifeWay Press, 1990), 20.

CHAPTER 5:

[1] Jewell Wells Nelson, *Cradle Roll=Visitation* (Nashville: Convention Press, 1978), 27.

[2] Louise Ames and Frances Ilg, *Your Four Year Old* (New York: A Delta Book, 1982), 44.

[3] Mabarak Dahir, *Parents Magazine*, July 1998: 54.

[4] Susan Okie, "Babies under 3 Taking Hyperactivity Drugs" *The Charlotte Observer*, 8 June 1998: 3E.

[5] Melinda Mahand and Clara Mae Van Brink, *Love, Laugher & Learning* (Nashville: Convention Press, 1996), 41.

[6] Ibid., Title.

CHAPTER 6:

[1] Louise Ames and Frances Ilg, *Your Three Year Old* (New York: A Delta Book, 1982), 5.

[2] Florence Littauer, *Raising Christians — Not Just Children* (Dallas: Word Publishing, 1988), 34.

[3] Geraldine Carey and Kay Henry, *Teaching in Church Weekday Education* (Nashville: Convention Press, 1988), 16-17.

[4] Miriam Stoppard, *Complete Baby and Child Care* (New York: Dorling Kindersley Publishing, Inc., 1995), 151.

[5] Carey and Henry, *Teaching in Church Weekday Education*, 19.

[6] Ibid., 20.

[7] Louise Ames and Frances Ilg, *Your Three Year Old* (New York: A Delta Book, 1982), 62.

[8] Louise Ames and Frances Ilg, *Your Five Year Old* (New York: A Delta Book, 1982), 9.

[9] Carey and Henry, *Teaching in Church Weekday Education*, 22.

CHAPTER 7:

[1] Glen Schultz, *Kingdom Education* (Nashville: LifeWay Press, 1998), 64-65.

[2] Dawna Markova, *How Your Child Is Smart* (Emeryville, CA: Conari Press, 1992), Title.

[3] Thomas Armstrong, *In Their Own Way*, Live interview, NBC Today, 26 Aug. 1998.

[4] Mimi Brodsky Chenfeld, *Teaching in the Key of Life* (Washington, DC: NAEYC, 1993), 18.

[5] Jane Healy, *Your Child's Growing Mind* (New York: Doubleday, 1987), 28.

[6] David Elkind, *Miseducation: Preschoolers at Risk* (New York: Alfred A. Knopf, 1988), 141.

[7] Dorothy Law Nolte and Rachel Harris, *Children Learn What they Live, Parenting to Inspire Values* (New York: Workman Publishing, 1998), Title.

CHAPTER 8:

[1] Clare Cherry, *Think of Something Quiet* (Carthage, IN: Fearon Teacher Aids, 1981), 11.

[2] Cleatus Moorehead, Amy Marrow, Joan Riddle, Doris Haver Rouse, Barbara Yarbrough, *WEE Learn Curriculum Guide for Five-Year-Olds*, Revised (Nashville: Convention Press, 1995), 15.

[3] Jane Healy, *Your Child's Growing Mind* (New York: Doubleday, 1987), 248.

CHAPTER 9:

None

CHAPTER 10:

[1] Barbara Kantrowitz, "Off to a Good Start," *Newsweek*, Spring/Summer 1997: 9.

[2] Rima Shore, *Rethinking The Brain* (New York: Families and Work Institute, 1997), 18.

[3] Marian Diamond and Jane Hopson, *Magic Trees of the Mind* (New York: Dutton, 1998), 39.

[4] Marc Peyser and Anne Underwood, "Nature or Nurture," *Newsweek*, Spring/Summer 1997: 62.

[5] Diamond and Hopson, *Magic Trees of the Mind*, 39.

[6] Ibid., 38

[7] Shore, *Rethinking the Brain*, 16.

[8] Diamond and Hopson, *Magic Trees of the Mind*, 67.

[9] Ibid., 66.

[10] Colin Rose and Malcolm J. Nicholl, *Accelerated Learning for the 21st Century* (New York: Dell Publishing, 1997), 25.

[11] Carla Hannaford, *Smart Moves* (Arlington, VA: Great Ocean Publishers, 1995), 24.

[12] Shore, *Rethinking the Brain*, x.

[13] Ibid., 21.

[14] Ibid.

[15] Carol Lynn Mithers, "Late Bloomers," *Parenting*, November 1998: 104.

[16] George Constable, *Your Growing Child* (Alexandria, VA: Time-Life Books, 1987), 8.

[17] Mithers, *Parenting*, 104.

[18] Constable, *Your Growing Child*, 9.

[19] Burton L. White, *The First Three Years of Life* (New York: Prentice Hall, 1985), 31.

[20] Ibid., 18.

[21] Ibid., 37.

[22] Ibid., 78.

[23] Karen Miller, *Ages and Stages* (Chelsea, MA: Telshare Publishing Co., 1985), 23.

[24] Ibid., 32.

[25] Ibid., 52.

[26] Ibid., 37.

[27] Ibid., 55.

[28] Jane G. Brooks, *The Process of Parenting* (Mountain View, CA: Mayfield Publishing, 1991), 183.

[29] Laura Walthrer Nathanson, *The Portable Pediatrician for Parents* (New York: HarperCollins, 1994), 257.

[30] David Elkind, *A Sympathetic Understanding of the Child* (Needham Heights, MA: Allyn and Bacon, 1994), 81.

[31] Miller, *Ages and Stages*, 123.

[32] Elkind, *A Sympathetic Understanding of the Child*, 35.

[33] Hannaford, *Smart Moves*, 16.

[34] Ibid., 13.

[35] Ibid., 23.

[36] Rose and Nicholl, *Accelerated Learning for the 21st Century*, 3.

[37] Debra Rosenberg and Larry Reibstein, "Pots, Blocks, and Socks," *Newsweek*, New York, NY: Spring/Summer, 1997: 35.

[38] Jane A. Healy, *Your Child's Growing Mind* (New York: Doubleday, 1994), 34.

[39] Sharon Begley, "How to Build a Baby's Brain," *Newsweek*, Spring/Summer, 1997: 30.

[40] Healy, *Your Child's Growing Mind*, 42.

41 Ibid., 22.

42 Ibid., 21.

43 Dawna Markova, *How Your Child is Smart* (Berkeley, CA: Conari Press, 1992), 24.

44 Ibid., 141.

45 Howard Gardner, *Frames of Mind* (New York: Basic Books, 1993).

46 Howard Gardner, "Reflections on Multiple Intelligances: Myths and Messages," *Phi Delta Kappan* (Nov. 1995): 206.

47 Thomas Armstrong, *7 Kinds of Smart* (New York: Plume, 1993), 1-25.

CHaPteR 11:

1 Lawrence E. Shapiro, *How to Raise a Child with a High EQ* (New York: HarperCollins, 1997), 4.

2 Ibid., x.

3 Carla Hannaford, *Smart Moves* (Arlington, VA: Great Ocean Publishers, 1995), 54.

4 Jane M. Healy, *Your Child's Growing Mind* (New York: Doubleday, 1994), 14.

5 Ibid., 15.

6 Shapiro, *How to Raise a Child with a High EQ*, 13.

7 Ibid., xiii.

8 Shore, *Rethinking the Brain* (New York: Families and Work Institute, 1997), 26.

9 Healy, *Your Child's Growing Mind*, 43,

10 Shore, *Rethinking the Brain*, 29.

11 Ibid.

12 Daniel Goleman, *Emotional Intelligence* (New York: Bantam Book, 1995), xiii

13 Louise Bates Ames and Frances L. Ilg, *Your Three Year Old* (New York: Dell Publishing, 1976), 2.

14 Karen Miller, *Ages and Stages* (Chelsea, MA: Telshare Publishing Company, 1985), 65.

15 John Rosemond, *Parent Power* (Kansas City: Andrews and McMeel Books, 1990), 104.

16 Fitzhugh Dodson, *Your Child* (New York: Simon and Schuster, 1986), 274.

17 Miller, *Ages and Stages*, 105.

18 Ibid., 106.

19 Ibid.

20 Rosemond, *Parent Power*, 118.

21 Joanne Hendrick, *Whole Child* (St. Louis: C. V. Mosby, 1980), 123.

22 Ibid., 69.

23 Madelyn Swift, *Discipline for Life* (Fort Worth: Stairway Educational Programs, 1995), 22.

24 Ibid., 20.

25 Ibid.

26 Ibid., 23.

27 Ibid., 35-47.

28 Ibid., 49-69.

29 Dawna Markova, *How Your Child is Smart* (Berkeley, CA: Conari Press, 1992), 31.

CHaPteR 12:

None

CHaPteR 13:

1 Glen Schultz, *Kingdom Education* (Nashville: LifeWay Press, 1998), 48.

2 C. Sybil Waldrop, *Guiding Your Child Toward God* (Nashville: Broadman Press, 1985), 28.

³ Gary Chapman and Ross Campbell, *The Five Love Languages of Children* (Chicago: Northfield Publishing), 45.

⁴ Colleen L. Reece and Anita Corrine Donihue, *Apples for A Teacher* (Uhrichville, Ohio: Barbour and Company, Inc., 1984), 8.

CHAPTER 14:

¹ Harry K. Wong and Rosemary T. Wong, *How to be an Effective Teacher the First Days of School* (Mountain View, CA: Harry K. Wong Pub. 1998), 55.

² Ibid.

³ Rolf Zettersten. *Train Up a Child* (Dallas: Word Publishing, 1991), vii.

⁴ Thomas Goodman. *The Intentional Minister* (Nashville: Broadman & Holman, 1994), Back cover.

CHAPTER 15:

¹ Paula Jorde Bloom, Marilyn Sheerer and Joan Britz. *Blueprint for Action. Achieving Center-Based Change Through Staff Development* (Mt. Rainier, Maryland, Gyphon House, Inc.,1991), 73.

² Bloom, Sheerer, and Britz, 81.

³ Ibid., 81-82.

⁴ Ibid., 82.

⁵ "When Do I Get a Turn to Play?" *Early Childhood News, The Journal of Professional Development* (Vol. 8, Issue 2), March/April 1996: 35.

⁶ Bloom, Sheerer, and Britz, 75.

⁷ Bloom, P. J., Sheerer, M., & Britz, J. (1991) *Blueprint for Action: Achieving Center-Based Change Through Staff Development*. Lake Forest, IL: New Horizons (pp. 219-224). Adapted from the following original sources: Wonder, J., & Donovan, P. (1984). *Whole Brain Thinking*. New York: W. W. Morrow & Co. Dunn, R., & Dunn, K. (1978). *Teaching Students Through Their Individual Learning Styles*. Reston, VA: Reston Publishing. Used by permission.

⁸ Bloom, Sheerer, and Britz. Used by permission.

⁹ Bloom, Sheerer and Britz, 222.

¹⁰ Helen M. Young, *Children Won't Wait* (Fort Worth, Brownlow Publishing, 1988).

CHAPTER 16:

¹ *ABCs of Safe and Healthy Child Care: A Handbook for Child Care Providers* (Atlanta, GA: Centers for Disease Control and Prevention, 1996).

² *Model Child Care Health Policies*, #716 (Washington, D.C.: NAEYC, 1993). For other NAEYC publications, contact NAEYC, 1509 16th St. N.W., Washington D.C. 20036, 1-800-424-2460.

³ *The ABCs of Safe and Healthy Child Care*, pp. 42-43.

⁴ Ibid., p. 45.

⁵ Ibid.

⁶ Ibid., pp. 45-46.

⁷ Ibid., pp. 87-88.

⁸ Reproducible fact sheets on a number of childhood illnesses and infectious diseases can be copied and given to child care center staff members and parents for further insight, as the need arises. These are found in *The ABCs of Safe and Healthy Child Care*, pp. 67-122.

⁹ *Model Child Care Health Policies*, p. 2. (Also, American Academy of Pediatrics, 141 N. Westpoint Blvd., Elk Grove Village, IL 60007, 1-847-228-5005, www.aap.org; American Public Health

Association, 1015 15th St. N.W., Suite 300, Washington, D.C. 20005, 1-202-789-5600, www.apha.org.).

[10] For product safety guidelines, check CPSC's Internet website at www.cpsc.gov. To report product hazards or receive product alerts and recall notices, use the website address info@cpsc.gov or the CPSC telephone hotline, 1-800-638-2772.

[11] CPSC provides specific crib safety guidelines.

[12] To obtain a choke tester, contact Department Safe Toy, P.O. Box 17, Long Beach, CA 90801.

[13] For a listing of telephone numbers for regional poison control centers, see *The ABCs of Safe and Healthy Child Care*, pp. 130-132.

[14] Abby Kendrick, Roxane Kaufmann, and Katherine Messenger, *Healthy Young Children: A Manual for Programs* (Washington D.C.: NAEYC, 1991), p. 48; and Middle Tennessee Regional Poison Center, 1-615-936-2034.

[15] *Handbook for Public Playground Safety*, Consumer Product Safety Commission, Washington, D.C. 20207, 1-800-638-2772, www.cpsc.gov/cpscpub/prerel/prhtmi/96712.html.

[16] See footnotes 2 and 14 for these resources. In *Model Child Care Health Policies*, see pages 6-7, Appendix Q, and other related pages. In *Healthy Young Children: A Manual for Programs*, see pages 5, 305-309.

[17] For a sample incident report form, see *Model Child Care Health Policies*, Appendix S. Your director also should provide parents with a copy of any incident report filed on a child.

[18] Many dental professionals recommend keeping on hand a first-aid product designed to save a knocked-out tooth. Protective materials and preserving fluid allow a tooth to be replanted 24 hours or more after an accident. Check with local dentists or pharmacists for further information.

[19] For additional guidance in helping young children cope with the aftermath of natural disasters or other crises, consult: Karen Miller, *The Crisis Manual for Early Childhood Teachers: How to Handle the Really Difficult Problems* (Beltsville, MD: Gryphon House, 1996).

[20] *Healthy Young Children: A Manual for Programs*, pp. 191-198.

[21] National Clearinghouse on Child Abuse and Neglect Information, 330 C. St. S.W., Washington D.C. 20447, 1-800-FYI-3366, www.calib.com/nccanch. (This is the information center for the U. S. Department of Health and Human Services Office on Child Abuse and Neglect.)

[22] National Committee to Prevent Child Abuse, Fulfillment Center, 200 State Road, South Deerfield, MA 01373, 1-800-835-2671, www.childabuse.org.

[23] Child Welfare League of America, 440 First St., N.W., Third Floor, Washington, D.C. 20001, 1-202-638-2952, www.cwla.org.

[24] "Safety Tips on a Sensitive Subject: Child Sexual Abuse," p. 14, a brochure in *The Church Mutual Protection Series* published in 1994 by Church Mutual Insurance Company, 3000 Schuster Lane, Merrill, WI 54452, 1-800-542-3465, www.churchmutual.com.

[25] *Healthy Young Children: A Manual for Programs*, p. 195.

[26] National Church Safety Program, Church Law & Tax Report, P.O. Box 1098, Matthews, NC 28106, 1-704-841-8066; Pinkerton Services Group, 6100 Fairview Rd., Suite 900, Charlotte, NC 28210, 1-800-403-4750; The Good Shepherd Program, Nexus Solutions, 418 W. Troutman Parkway, Fort Collins, CO 80526-3681, 1-888-639-8788, www.nexus-solutions.com.

[27] Julie Bloss, *The Church Guide to Employment Law* (Matthews, NC: Christian Ministry Resources, 1993).

[28] *Model Child Care Health Policies*, p. 20.

[29] Commercial tags and security cards may be purchased from NLS Specialties, P.O. Box 1897, Kennesaw, GA 30144, 1-770-422-7867.

---

[30] Richard Hammar, presenter of the Baptist Sunday School Board seminar, "Legal Issues in the Church," held on April 26, 1994, in Nashville, TN.

[31] Samford University's law school provides basic legal information as a service to churches and other nonprofit organizations and publishes a quarterly newsletter, *Law and Church*. Contact the Center for the Study of Law and the Church, Cumberland School of Law, Samford University, Birmingham, Al 35229-7015, 1-800-888-7303.

[32] Kenneth Snyder, "Legal Liability of Daycare and Nursery School Facilities," *Church Administration* (Nashville, TN: Convention Press, March 1993), p. 41.

[33] Negligence generally is understood to mean a breech of duty or failure to exercise reasonable care.

CHAPTER 17:

None

CHAPTER 18:

[1] Tynette W. Hills, *Reaching Potentials: Appropriate Curriculum and Assessment for Young Children, Vol. 1*, Sue Bredekamp and Teresa Rosegrant, Editors, (Washington, D.C.: National Association for the Education of Young Children), 46.

[2] Hills, *Reaching Potentials: Appropriate Curriculum and Assessment for Young Children, Vol. 1*, 46.

[3] Deborah Diffily, "Assessment of Young Children: A Position Statement" (Austin, TX: Texas Association for the Education of Young Children, 1997).

[4] Herbert F. Wright, *Recording and Analyzing Child Behavior* (New York: Harper and Row, 1967), 49-53.

[5] Ann Miles Gordon and Kathryn Williams Browne, *Beginnings and Beyond: Foundations in Early Childhood Education* (Albany, NY: Delmar Publishers, 1985), 145.

[6] D. Michelle Irwin and M. Margaret Bushnell, *Observational Strategies for Child Study*, (New York Holt, Rinehart and Winston, 1980), vii.

[7] Joanne Hendrick, *The Whole Child: Early Education for the Eighties* (St. Louis: C.V. Mosby, 1980), 317

[8] Susan Gold and Carole Abbott, "A Dilemma for Preschool Teachers: When to Refer," *Dimensions*, January 1989, Vol 17, No. 2, 10.

[9] Thomas Armstrong, *7 Kinds of Smart* (New York: Penguin Group, 1993).

CHAPTER 19:

[1] Stanley Coopersmith, *The Antecedents of Self-esteem* (San Francisco: W. B. Freeman, 1967), 34-42.

[2] Dorothy Corkille Briggs, *Your Child's Self-esteem* (Garden City, NJ: Doubleday, 1975), 14.

[3] Coopersmith.

[4] James L. Hymes, Jr., *Teaching the Child Under Six* (Columbus, OH: Charles E. Merrill, 1968), 68.

[5] Don Dinkmeyer and Gary D. McKay, *Raising a Responsible Child: Practical Steps to Successful Family Relationships* (New York: Simon and Schuster, 1973), 11.

[6] E. M. Hetherington et al, "Divorced Fathers," *The Family Coordinator*, 1976: 417-29.

[7] Elizabeth Kubler-Ross, *On Death and Dying* (New York: Macmillan, 1969), 34-121.

[8] Thomas Gordon, P.E.T.: *Parent Effectiveness Training* (New York: Signet, 1975), p. 115-38.

9 Jane Nelsen, *Positive Discipline* (Fair Oaks, CA: Sunrise Press, 1981), 90.

10 Haim Ginott, *Between Parent and Child* (New York: Avon Books, 1969), 45.

11 Ibid., 48.

12 Content for this chapter was excerpted from "Guiding Children" by Geraldine Addison Carey, from Geraldine Addison Carey and Kay Vandevier Henry, *Teaching in Church Weekday Education* (Nashville: Convention Press, 1988), 49-63.

CHAPTER 20:

1 Kennoth O. Gangel and James C. Wilhoit, *The Christian Educator's Handbook on Family Life Education* (Grand Rapids: Baker Books, 1996), 37.

2 D. Glenn Saul and William M. Pinson, Jr., *Building Sermons to Strengthen Families* (Nashville: Convention Press, 1983), 13.

3 Dolores Curran, *Traits of a Healthy Family* (New York: Ballentine Books, 1983), 12.

4 Charles M. Sell, *Family Ministry* (Grand Rapids: Zondervan, 1995) 159.

5 Carol Seefeldt, *Teaching Young Children* (Englewood Cliffs, NJ: Prentice-Hall, Inc., 1980), 122.

6 Marilyn Segal and Abbey Manburg, eds., *All About Childcare* (Fort Launderdale, FL: Nova University, 1981), 122.

7 Diana Garland, *Precious In His Sight* (Birmingham, AL: New Hope, 1993), 63.

8 Ibid., 64.

9 Geraldine Addison Carey and Kay Vandevier Henry, *Teaching in Church Weekday Education* (Nashville: Convention Press, 1988), 84.

10 Segal and Manburg, *All About Childcare*, 123.

11 Seefeldt, *Teaching Young Children*, 171.

12 Richard Shahan, *Good News for Preschoolers & Their Families* (Nashville: Convention Press, 1998), 51

13 Ibid.

CHAPTER 21:

1 Norris Smith, "Conflict Thwarts Church Growth," *Growing Churches*, January, February, March 1992: 48-49.

2 Norris Smith, "Church Conflict Sabotages Personal Growth," *Growing Churches*, April, May, June 1992: 58-59.

3 Norris Smith, speaking on "Relationships," Texas Baptist Church Weekday Education Association State Meeting, Baylor University, Waco, TX: July 1998.

4 C. Sybil Waldrop, *Getting Good at Being You* (Nashville: Broadman Press, 1989), 24, 25.

5 Dorothy Corkille Briggs, *Celebrate Your Self* (New York: Doubleday, 1986), 10.

6 Waldrop, *Getting Good at Being You*, 21.

7 Florence Littauer, *Personality Plus* (Grand Rapids, MI: Fleming H. Revell, 1992).

8 John Trent and Gary Smalley, *Treasure Tree* (Dallas: Word, 1992).

9 Ken Voges, *Adult Disc Survery*, (Houston, TX: In His Grace, Inc. 1997).

10 Mels Carbonell, *Discover Your Giftedness in Christ*, (Fayetteville, GA: Uniquely You, 1998).

11 Ibid., 34-36.

12 Oswald Chambers, *My Utmost for His Highest* (Westwood, NJ: Barbour and Co., 1993), 210.

13 Lilian Katz, "Developmental Stages of Preschool Teachers," *The Elementary School Journal*, Oct. 1972, Vol. 73, Number 1: 50-54.

[14] Judy Williston, "Know and Value Yourself and Your Staff Members," *Early Childhood News*, July, Aug. 1995: 19-22.

[15] J. C. Bradley, "Leadership and Motivation," *Search*, Summer 1974: 39-40.

[16] Henry Ford as quoted by Dale Carnegie in *How to Win Friends and Influence People* (New York: Simon and Schuster, 1981), 43.

[17] Harriet Harral, *Communication Skills* (Birmingham, AL: New Hope, 1994), 45-56.

[18] Dale Carnegie, *How to Win Friends and Influence People* (New York: Simon and Schuster, 1981), 103.

CHAPTER 22:

[1] American Public Health Association and the American Academy of Pediatrics, *Caring for Our Children: National Health and Safety Performance Standards for Out-of-Home Child Care Programs*, Copyright 1992, NA0045 $34.95.

American Public Health Association
1015 Fifteenth Street, N.W.
Washington, D.C. 20005

American Academy of Pediatrics
141 Northwest Point Blvd.
P. O. Box 927
Elk Grove Village, IL 60009

[2] American Public Health Association and the American Academy of Pediatrics, *Caring for Our Children*, 278.

[3] The League of Women Voters is a good source for this information. They generally list committee assignments of state and federal officials in a free information booklet.

CHRISTIAN GROWTH STUDY PLAN

In the **Christian Growth Study Plan (formerly Church Study Course),** this book *TEACHING IN CHRISTIAN WEEKDAY EARLY EDUCATION* is a resource for course credit in the ministry area WEEKDAY EARLY EDUCATION of the Leadership and Development category of diploma plans. To receive credit, read the book, complete the learning activities, show your work to your pastor, a staff member, or church leader, then complete the following information. This page may be duplicated. Send the completed page to:

Christian Growth Study Plan
127 Ninth Avenue, North, MSN 117
Nashville, TN 37234-0117
FAX: (615)251-5067

For information about the Christian Growth Study Plan, refer to the current Christian Growth Study Plan Catalog. Your church office may have a copy. If not, request a free copy from the Christian Growth Study Plan office (615/251-2525).

TEACHING IN CHRISTIAN WEEKDAY EARLY EDUCATION
COURSE NUMBER: LS-0019

PARTICIPANT INFORMATION

Rev. 6-99

Social Security Number (USA Only)

Personal CGSP Number*

Date of Birth (Mo., Day, Yr.)

Name (First, MI, Last)

Home Phone

Address (Street, Route, or P.O. Box)

City, State, or Province

Zip/Postal Code

CHURCH INFORMATION

Church Name

Address (Street, Route, or P.O. Box)

City, State, or Province

Zip/Postal Code

CHANGE REQUEST ONLY

❑Former Name

❑Former Address

City, State, or Province

Zip/Postal Code

❑Former Church

City, State, or Province

Zip/Postal Code

Signature of Pastor, Conference Leader, or Other Church Leader

Date

*New participants are requested but not required to give SS# and date of birth. Existing participants, please give CGSP# when using SS# for the first time. Thereafter, only one ID# is required. *Mail To:* Christian Growth Study Plan, 127 Ninth Ave., North, MSN 117, Nashville, TN 37234-0117. Fax: (615)251-5067

multi age grouping - opportunities to develop language, social, thinking and listening skills

learning centers identified within the space with appropriate materials related to the unit theme & which encourage exploration